MAGNA CARTA

MAGNA CARTA

THROUGH THE AGES

RALPH V. TURNER

PEARSON

Longman

Harlow, England • London • New York • Boston • San Francisco • Toronto
Sydney • Tokyo • Singapore • Hong Kong • Seoul • Taipei • New Delhi
Cape Town • Madrid • Mexico City • Amsterdam • Munich • Paris • Milan

PEARSON EDUCATION LIMITED

Head Office:
Edinburgh Gate
Harlow CM20 2JE
Tel: +44 (0)1279 623623
Fax: +44 (0)1279 431059
Website: www.pearsoned.co.uk

First edition published in Great Britain in 2003

© Pearson Education Limited 2003

The right of Ralph V. Turner to be identified as Author
of this Work has been asserted by him in accordance
with the Copyright, Designs and Patents Act 1988.

ISBN 0 582 43826 8

British Library Cataloguing in Publication Data
A CIP catalogue record for this book can be obtained from the British Library

Library of Congress Cataloging in Publication Data
A CIP catalog record for this book can be obtained from the Library of Congress

10 9 8 7 6 5 4 3 2 1

Set in 10.5/13pt Galliard by Graphicraft Limited, Hong Kong
Printed in Great Britain by Biddles Ltd, Guildford & King's Lynn

The Publishers' policy is to use paper manufactured from sustainable forests.

CONTENTS

PLATES

The plate section can be found at the center of the book.

ACKNOWLEDGMENTS

The author must express his appreciation to the innumerable students who contributed to this book over more than thirty years by taking part in my classes on England's history, law and government, assisting in shaping and sharpening my thinking on Magna Carta and its significance for both Britain and the United States. In addition, friends and colleagues on both sides of the Atlantic contributed to this book with expertise and advice. First, I must express my gratitude to Sir James Holt, dean of Magna Carta studies, without whose scholarship and friendship this book could never have been written. Second, I must thank two other valued friends, former colleagues who took the time to read chapters and to offer their comments, Dr. Eileen Lyon of State University of New York, Fredonia, and Dr. William W. Rogers at Florida State University. Over the years, exchanges of ideas with other scholars, especially Professor David Bates and Dr. Michael Clanchy, contributed greatly to my understanding of the environment that resulted in Magna Carta, as did discussions with my fellow members of the Charles Homer Haskins Society. In quoting short passages from original sources I have taken the liberty of modernizing the spelling and punctuation.

We are grateful to the following for permission to reproduce copyright material:

Taylor & Francis Books Limited of the Thompson Publishing Group (current copyright holder), for permission to reproduce the translation of Magna Carta that appears in the appendix. Originally published in Harry Rothwell *English historical documents*, 3, *1189–1327*, Eyre & Spottiswoode (London, 1975). Plate 1 courtesy of the Conway Library, Courtauld Institute of Art, London; Plates 2, 3, 5 and 7 by permission of the British Library; Plates 6 and 8 courtesy of the Library of Congress Archives; Plates 9 and 10 courtesy of the National Portrait Gallery, London; Plates 11, 12 and 13 © Copyright the British Museum; Plate 14 courtesy of the Bodleian Library, University of Oxford; Plate 15 courtesy of Rare Books Division, The New York Public Library, Astor,

Lenox and Tilden foundations; Plate 16 courtesy of Runnymede Borough Council.

In some instances we have been unable to trace the owners of copyright material, and we would appreciate any information that would enable us to do so.

CHRONOLOGY

25 Aug. 1213	Archbishop Stephen Langton met with discontented barons at St Paul's, London, to propose that they seek confirmation of Henry I's 'charter of liberties'.
Oct. 1213	At a meeting of barons with Nicholas of Tusculum, papal legate, baronial demands were recorded in the 'Unknown Charter of Liberties'.
Oct. 1214	John returned to England from Poitou after the failure of his grand strategy for reconquering his French lands.
Autumn 1214 or early 1215	The 'Unknown Charter of Liberties' was drafted as a series of baronial demands for reform.
6 Jan. 1215	The Epiphany Great Council summoned by John met at London.
4 Mar. 1215	John took the cross of a crusader.
Holy Week 1215	The barons mustered at Stamford, Lincolnshire, to march to Northampton for a meeting with John scheduled for the Sunday following Easter (26 April).
26 Apr. 1215	John failed to meet with the barons at Northampton.
5 May 1215	The barons formally renounced their fealty and named Robert fitz Walter as their general.
9 May 1215	John proposed a board of arbitrators with nominees from each side.
17 May 1215	The city of London opened its gates to the baronial rebels.
29 May 1215	John's proposal for arbitration was refused again.
c. 10 June 1215	Tentative agreement was reached between King John and the rebel barons meeting at Runnymede near Windsor Castle, signified by the king setting his seal to the 'Articles of the Barons'.
15 June 1215	King John set his seal to a draft of Magna Carta, signifying his acceptance of its terms.
19 June 1215	The barons formally made peace with the king, renewing their homage.

19–24 June 1215	Chancery clerks made additional drafts of the Charter to be sent throughout the kingdom.
27 June 1215	An official French translation of the Charter was drawn up to make it accessible to the knights of the counties.
7 July 1215	The pope excommunicated the rebels against the king.
24–25 Aug. 1215	Papal bulls declared the Charter null and void.
Sept. 1215	Civil war between the rebel barons and royalist forces broke out.
May 1216	Prince Louis of France landed in England with his army.
16 Oct. 1216	King John died at Newark.
28 Oct. 1216	Henry III was crowned king of England at Gloucester.
12 Nov. 1216	Magna Carta was reissued on young Henry III's behalf at Bristol.
12 Sept. 1217	Prince Louis and his English supporters came to terms with those ruling England in the young king's name.
6 Nov. 1217	A third version of Magna Carta was confirmed, along with a Charter of Forest Liberties.
11 Feb. 1225	Henry III confirmed Magna Carta and the Forest Charter in their definitive form.

MAGNA CARTA: DISENTANGLING HISTORY FROM MYTH

In the autumn of 1983, one of four surviving original copies of Magna Carta, or the Great Charter, travelled to Tallahassee, capital of Florida, a town little visited by the millions who flock to the state's beaches and theme parks. The copy was in Tallahassee on display as part of a 'Celebration of Freedom' across an ocean from Runnymede Meadow in England where King John had set his seal to it. This charter of liberties, extorted by the English barons from the king in 1215 and confirmed in definitive form by Henry III in 1225, is a crucial document for England's history. Although the British Library's display of the Great Charter describes it as 'a series of detailed concessions on feudal law which often seem at first sight baffling', it has become a symbol of the rule of law, marking one of the earliest attempts to impose the limitations of law on a ruler's sovereign authority. As an indictment of tyrannical rule, it has won a position as the most widely known of all documents surviving from the European Middle Ages. That Magna Carta, repudiated almost at once by its grantor and resulting in civil war, would eventually earn such reverence that its visits to US cities over 750 years later are occasions for celebration is improbable, but true.

The rebel barons who imposed Magna Carta on King John saw it as a practical solution to political problems, not a statement of legal precepts. Yet it sets forth principles of the rule of law that won recognition as fundamental law, part of the common stock of both British and American political thought that has spread throughout the modern world. Its check on royal power is epitomized in two clauses of John's Charter, 39 and 40, 'No free man shall be arrested or imprisoned or disseised or outlawed or exiled or in any way victimised ... except by the lawful judgement of his peers or by the law of the land' and 'To no one will we sell, to no one will we refuse or delay right or justice'.[1] These chapters of the Charter, echoed in modern states' constitutions across the globe, established the basic principle that the rule of law ensures personal liberty. First, the executive power must proceed by recognized legal process, never unlawfully, when taking action against an individual. Second, no one is above the law, however high his or her status, a concept capable of evolving into the principle of equality under the law. Over centuries, the Charter taught these precepts to the English people, shaping their character, fostering pride and confidence in their freedom, prompting their questioning of authority.

As the influential Victorian historian William Stubbs wrote, 'The whole of the constitutional history of England is little more than a commentary on Magna Carta'.[2] Indeed, a myth grew up that imagined the Great Charter to be the cornerstone of the British constitution, a permanent protector of popular liberties against royal tyranny, even though hardly any of its original clauses survive on the statute books. Americans, too, claim the Charter as a bulwark against arbitrary government, the basis for US constitutional guarantees of 'due process of law' and 'equal protection of the law'. Today, Magna Carta possibly enjoys greater prestige in the United States, the land of lawyers, than in the United Kingdom. The US Supreme Court first cited it in an opinion in 1819, and citations increased after post-Civil War constitutional amendments made chapter 39's principle applicable to the former slaves. It is still cited in American political debates, judicial opinions and newspaper opinion pieces. In 1974 at the opening of congressional hearings on the impeachment of President Richard M. Nixon, the chair of the House Judiciary Committee cited its lesson that 'the law must deal fairly with every man', and he noted that 'Seven centuries have now passed since the English barons proclaimed [this] principle by compelling King John at the point of a sword, to accept the great doctrine of Magna Carta'.[3] In 2002, the *New York Times* pointed out in a column commenting on harsh sentences for convicted criminals: 'That the punishment must fit the crime is a principle that has been recognized since Magna Carta'.[4]

In the words of a thirteenth-century lawbook, the barons rebelling against John felt a duty to 'put a bridle, that is the law, on the king'. Resistance to the Angevin (or early Plantagenet) kings' arbitrary rule and excessive demands for men and money for wars in France began in Richard I's last years, 1195–99, and heightened under John Lackland. A rebellion by the barons broke out in John's last years, culminating in his grant of Magna Carta in 1215. Although the Charter failed to prevent civil war, it gained a permanent place in English law with reissues in the name of young Henry III after his father's death in 1216, again in 1217, and in a definitive 1225 version. By the thirteenth and fourteenth centuries, Magna Carta had become a banner under which discontented subjects rallied against their king, and cries for the Charter's reconfirmation formed a fundamental part of programmes for political reform. This dissatisfaction resulted in over forty reconfirmations by the early fifteenth century, proof that the Charter had become the fundamental law of the land.

Under Edward I at the end of the thirteenth century, Magna Carta gained its place as the first of the statutes, and students of the common law learned of it in their readings at the law schools or inns of court. Edward III's parliaments enacted statutes reinterpreting the Charter, most notably a 1354 law that enormously expanded the number of persons protected by chapter 39. Instead of stating that 'no free man' should be denied due process of law, the provision now extended to any man, 'of whatever estate or condition he may be'. Although the Charter no longer held a central place in England's political consciousness under the Yorkists and the Tudors, it was far from forgotten by the end of the Middle Ages, available in some of the earliest books printed in fifteenth-century England. The English landholding classes looked to Magna Carta and the common law as the chief protector of their property, and radical Protestants sought its protection against the Tudors' persecution. The Charter regained a pivotal place in political life early in the seventeenth century when common lawyers, parliamentarians and religious radicals revived it as a key element of England's 'ancient constitution', a focus for complaints against the Stuart monarchs' despotic tendencies.

Over the centuries, pride in England's unique liberty resulted in much myth about Magna Carta, and myth-makers could trace to it both bulwarks of English freedom, the common law and Parliament. During the seventeenth-century conflict between king and Parliament, common lawyers and antiquarians treasured the Great Charter as the fundamental compact or contract between the ruler and his subjects, binding because of its many confirmations in the thirteenth and fourteenth centuries. The chief champion of the doctrine that Magna Carta formed part of an 'ancient constitution' was Sir Edward Coke, a leading opponent of the Stuart kings in the law courts and in Parliament, who urged parliaments to introduce bills calling for its reconfirmation and for new statements of liberties based on it. Coke and other opponents of James I and Charles I construed the Charter's clauses anachronistically and uncritically, convinced that they reaffirmed such rights as trial by jury and freedom from arbitrary arrest or *habeas corpus* belonging to Britons since the earliest settlements. The seventeenth-century reinterpretation carried on a process under way since the fourteenth century of expanding the Charter's special 'liberties' for the privileged classes to general guarantees of 'liberty' for all the king's subjects.

Until the English Civil War, when a handful of religious radicals opposed to the king, the established church and the hierarchical social order preached democratic doctrines arguing for equal rights for all England's inhabitants, the idea of individual liberty was not linked with the concept of democracy. Slowly the connection between liberty and democracy became widespread, and some political thinkers recognized that Magna Carta's promise of the people's liberty under the law depended on popular participation in law-making. Accompanying the growth of democratic ideas was the eighteenth-century Enlightenment's belief that rule of law means equality under the law, elimination of unequal treatment based on ancestry, property, religion or other distinctions. This shift in political thought resulted largely from late-seventeenth-century philosophical speculations that looked to reason and natural law, not history, as the basis for human rights. Eighteenth-century rationalists, particularly French thinkers, had little taste for the Middle Ages, and Magna Carta did not play an important part in their theorizing. None the less, its guarantee of fundamental rights for English free men provided historical precedent to reinforce Enlightenment notions of natural rights that inspired democratic revolutions in Britain's North American colonies in 1776 and in France in 1789. Both American colonists protesting 'no taxation without representation' and British radicals seeking reform of a corrupt and unrepresentative Parliament found the Great Charter useful.

During the deposition of King James II and the assertion of Parliament's supremacy in 1688–89, many viewed the Glorious Revolution as a repetition of the events of 1215, re-enacting the baronial rebellion against King John. The settlement following the accession of James II's daughter Mary and her husband, William of Orange, included a Declaration of Rights, enacted by Parliament as a new Magna Carta. With the triumph of Parliament and the Hanoverian kings' retreat from active supervision of government in the early eighteenth century, the Great Charter lost its special place as England's 'fundamental law' standing above statute law, and Parliament was expected to defend the people's liberties. With the monarch limited to a ceremonial role as head of state, with Parliament – supposedly speaking for the people – the superior branch of government and with executive power vested in cabinet ministers who were members of Parliament themselves, no higher law stood above parliamentary statutes. Yet Magna Carta continued to hold significance for eighteenth-century common lawyers, who learned their law from Sir William Blackstone's *Commentaries*, in which he acknowledged the Charter's central place in the kingdom's tradition of government under law.

By the late eighteenth century, Parliament was hardly representative of the people; and some radical politicians, alarmed at its unrepresentative nature and unlimited power, sought sanction for reform in Magna Carta. Others such as the Utilitarian philosophers supplied purely pragmatic arguments for parliamentary reform. In the course of the nineteenth century, a series of reform bills would cement the new link between the liberty promised in Magna Carta and democracy, each new bill enlarging the electorate. Yet Utilitarian empiricism strengthened parliamentary sovereignty by disregarding fundamental law enshrined in history, and lawyers and legislators felt free to discard the Great Charter as they modernized English law. By the end of the nineteenth century, Parliament had repealed almost all the Charter's provisions.

Magna Carta came to the new world through the common law, brought to the thirteen North American colonies by the English settlers who held themselves to be the king's free subjects. They saw the seventeenth-century struggle against the Stuart kings as part of their own history, and they accepted the Great Charter as part of the ancient constitution, providing them with the same protections that their cousins in the mother-country enjoyed. Magna Carta in its seventeenth-century incarnation coloured the colonists' schemes for provincial governments, and charters of most of the thirteen American colonies contain clauses echoing its provisions. In the eighteenth century and long after, American students trained to become lawyers by studying Sir Edward Coke's lawbooks that taught them that the Charter was 'fundamental law', standing above the king and parliamentary statutes. After the United States won their independence, the federal Constitution became the new nation's fundamental law. Among the first ten amendments to the Constitution, collectively known as the Bill of Rights, was an article promising that no person shall be 'deprived of life, liberty, or property without due process of law', a paraphrase of the Charter's most important clause. As a modern author remarks, the 'semi-religious veneration' accorded to Magna Carta today is chiefly owed to 'the thousands of Englishmen who had flooded across the Atlantic to colonize the New World'.[5] The American Bar Association made concrete this reverence when it erected a memorial on Runnymede Meadow in 1957 commemorating the Charter (see Plate 16).

Later in other parts of the British Empire, parliamentary acts such as the British North America Act (1876) or the Government of India Acts (1919, 1935) authorized patterns for government in effect granting former colonies written constitutions. Most British colonies, once they became independent countries incorporated within the Commonwealth, followed the American example of adding bills of rights to their written constitutions. Of course, these principles of limited government took deepest root in North America, Australia and New Zealand, territories with large numbers of settlers from the British Isles. Although members of the bench and bar in former African and Asian colonies who were trained in the Anglo-American legal tradition tried to keep alive Magna Carta's principle of limited government and the rule of law, high hopes of transplanting such ideas faded in countries where military coups and extra-legal dictatorships quickly became the norm. Only in India have the Great Charter's principles flourished outside Commonwealth countries settled by large populations of British descent. Few former colonies had the experiences that would have instilled in both office-holders and those whom they govern the 'sense of law-abidingness' essential for representative democracies; indeed, it took centuries for Magna Carta to foster such a legal sensibility among the British and North Americans.

Magna Carta's message of the supremacy of law and condemnation of governments' arbitrary power is now accepted, in principle if not in practice, by the world community. At the United Nations General Assembly in 1948, the Universal Declaration of Human Rights was adopted. This document defines as fundamental rights for all the world's inhabitants the right to life, liberty and security of person that the Great Charter promised to English free men in 1215. After the collapse of communism in 1989–91, Anglo-American legal associations worked with citizens of former Soviet bloc countries to encourage the reception of Magna Carta's precepts in Eastern Europe. The Charter's principles have travelled far from Runnymede in almost eight centuries.

Each generation has reinterpreted Magna Carta in light of intellectual currents of its own time, as histories written in different epochs show. In the nineteenth century, seemingly opposed intellectual movements exercised powerful effects on historical understanding. Romantic writers and artists admired primitive folk, and they accepted an organic view of the past that led them to visualize modern institutions growing plant-like from medieval roots, evolving unique qualities. The idea of evolution appealed to romantics though borrowed from biology, and it encouraged 'the idea of progress', a notion that history manifests the slow but steady advance of peoples toward higher levels of civilization. Both evolutionary doctrine and romanticism accorded with nationalism and nation-building, motivating historians to stress the uniqueness – and even the superiority – of their own country's history, traditions and institutions. Most nineteenth-century historians were nationalists, eager to arouse readers' pride in their own nation's past.

Like other peoples in the nationalistic nineteenth century, the English looked for larger meaning in their past, and historians found an organizing principle for their works in the kingdom's progress toward liberty. This bolstered the 'Whig interpretation', a triumphalist view that praised Magna Carta as a uniquely English document, a symbol of the kingdom's exceptional political system. For the Whigs, the 1688–89 Glorious Revolution was the least violent and most beneficent of political upheavals, paving the way for a steady march toward nineteenth-century parliamentary democracy, religious toleration and bourgeois values. The Whig historians' outlook imposed present-mindedness on historians, restricting interest in the past to events that had contributed to modern achievements. The Whig practice of writing history with an eye on the present tended to impede an understanding of the past on its own terms, and it infected writers with a propensity for passing moral judgements on actors in historical events. In the 1870s, William Stubbs's *Constitutional History of England* summed up Whig historical assumptions for generations of students in the Victorian era and beyond. It was natural for Stubbs, living at a time when great reform bills were transforming Great Britain into a parliamentary democracy, to make the evolution of Parliament a central theme of medieval English history. For him, Magna Carta represented a major step in the process by which the various communities constituting the English kingdom reached political maturity and began to take their places in governance. He wrote: 'The Great Charter is then the act of the united nation, the church, the barons, and the commons, for the first time thoroughly at one'.[6]

By Stubbs's time, history was passing from a pastime of learned amateurs to a profession practised by specialists seeking to make it a more scientific discipline. Their supposedly detached and objective approach led them to reject Stubbs's Whiggish outlook, and by the beginning of the twentieth century historians were questioning the Charter's significance as a bastion of liberty. Nearly all academic historians at the end of the twentieth century rejected the Whig notion that study of the past offers proof of progress toward a better world; not even the Marxist vision of the triumph of the working class was any longer popular with them. Today few scholars share the Victorians' confidence that English history represents purposeful progress toward representative democracy at home and acquisition of an empire abroad. Indeed, they are unlikely to take much interest in the impact of the past on the present. Instead, they seek to understand the Middle Ages on the period's own terms by adopting the methods of anthropologists, sociologists or folklorists. Among those who continue to study rulers and governments, many take a tough-minded view, depicting medieval England's monarchs as less beneficent and more predatory, exploiting rather than protecting the people. They see changes occurring through competition between social classes or special interests pursuing power, not through leaders inspired by great ideas; and they identify such tangible matters as royal finances, court factions or patronage as the chief factors causing political change.

The story of Magna Carta and its fate does not entirely vindicate such a hard-headed view of the past, and mildly Whiggish views of English history leading slowly and haltingly toward representative democracy contain a kernel of truth. Many struggles surrounding the Charter had aspects of conflicts between power blocs or special interests, exploiting the kingdom for selfish purposes opposed to the majority's best interest. Yet a political community emerged in the course of the thirteenth century in spite of mixed motives, as baronage or aristocracy, rural knights and urban merchants became conscious of themselves as groups capable of defining their own interests and defending themselves against a tyrannical government. Magna Carta appeared to the various groups comprising medieval English society as a powerful weapon for protecting their privileges, and they repeatedly took it up in the later Middle Ages. The Charter's original purpose of forcing royal government to take into account the concerns of the baronial class proved capable of growth. Eventually, those protected by its liberties extended from free men, a small portion of a largely servile population in 1215, to the entire English population, and collective liberties for corporate groups evolved into liberty for individuals.

The Great Charter's capacity for growth, as long after 1215 as the seventeenth century and as far away as eighteenth-century North America, makes it a unique political document, a standard for judging a state's treatment of its citizens today. Although many traditional British institutions seem to be in decay at the beginning of the twenty-first century, Magna Carta survives in spirit, if not in the statute books. Over the centuries, it has fostered, first among the English, and later among North Americans and British settlers in the Antipodes, a tradition of opposing government's threats to individual liberties that peoples throughout the world now seek to imitate in their struggles against tyranny.

Notes

1. The translation of the 1215 Magna Carta cited throughout is Rothwell (1975), 316–24; the volume also contains translations of later versions of the Charter.
2. Stubbs (1874–78), as excerpted in Cantor (1966), 116.
3. Cited by Wood (1988), 232.
4. *New York Times*, editorial page, 5 November 2002.
5. Hindley (1990), 192.
6. Stubbs (1874–78), as excerpted in Cantor (1966), 116.

chapter 1

ENGLAND UNDER THE ANGEVIN KINGS: HENRY II AND HIS SONS, RICHARD I AND JOHN

Two dates in English history that school children once memorized are 1066 and 1215. Of course, the latter date is King John's grant of Magna Carta to his barons, and the former marks William the Conqueror's invasion of England, culminating in the death of the last Anglo-Saxon king at the battle of Hastings. Not merely a change in ruling dynasties, the Norman Conquest was an upheaval that altered drastically the nature of English government, social structure and landholding patterns, giving rise to the kingdom that John ruled from 1199 to 1216. Post-Conquest England retained a base of Old English laws and governmental institutions, particularly in local government, but surmounting its Anglo-Saxon base was a Norman or French superstructure to expedite the invaders' exploitation of their new lands and subject people.

It is often said that the Norman conquerors of England introduced 'feudalism', a confusing term for historians and their readers alike, for definitions of feudalism have fluctuated over the years with changes in fashions in historical interpretation. Indeed, some authorities today deny that it ever existed. Essentially, the term refers to the network of ties linking medieval lords to their vassals or knights, mounted warriors, and to the peasants who worked their lands. Ties of mutual obligations bound together lords and their knights, symbolized by homage and the oath of fealty. This pattern of dependent relationships is traditionally believed to have taken shape in western Europe with the so-called 'feudal transformation' of the eleventh century, when regional princes who had usurped the authority of the later Carolingian rulers could no longer enforce law and order. Castellans, minor nobles with their own castles, recruited bands of knights to seize control of the countryside surrounding their fortified centres.

Once the castellans succeeded in defying the old public officials' authority, anything resembling a state collapsed, and public services performed today by public authorities apparently fell into private hands. With effective power reduced to the range of knights riding out from a castle, government lost its present-day meaning. It was localized in the hands of amateurs, keeping no written records. Safety for the head of a family depended on cementing ties of vassalage to a strong lord; no longer did allegiance to an impersonal state or to a faraway emperor or king afford security. A consequence of everyone's seeking protection from lords was a hierarchically structured society, a great chain of ties of dependency. In the Middle Ages, no one questioned this social structure of unequal ranks, rising from non-free peasants to the landed aristocracy and the royal family. Today debate rages among historians about the consequences of this failure of the state. Some deny such a complete collapse of public authority, others find the network of lordship ties and mutual obligations fostering a spirit of community that provided social stability, while some still describe chaotic conditions of fighting among the warrior class and lords' merciless exploitation of agricultural labourers.

This pattern of weak government was far from universal, for princes in different regions preserved differing degrees of Roman or Carolingian traditions of public authority. In Normandy, the duke lost less power than some other French dukes or counts, retaining much of his position as a public official responsible for the general welfare. William the Conqueror succeeded in subduing the Norman nobles and forcing them to fulfil their obligations owed as his vassals. Neither did the general pattern of feudalism prevail in England before the Normans landed there. English resistance to the Danish threat in the ninth and tenth centuries had not produced a collapse of central authority, but resulted rather in Alfred the Great's unification of the country. The eleventh-century Anglo-Saxon kingdom preserved such typically Carolingian characteristics as direct ties of lordship linking the monarch to the free landholders and the royal household exercising effective control over the chief local officials, the sheriffs.

The government that William the Conqueror and his sons devised for their new kingdom across the Channel was powerful, constructed with native Anglo-Saxon materials mixed with features imported from Normandy. When Henry II took the English throne in 1154, he built on this foundation to erect a superstructure of 'administrative kingship', staffed by literate professionals functioning apart from the royal household. With such a structure, he and his sons Richard Lionheart and John Lackland would wield almost autocratic powers threatening their great nobles' privileges and oppressing them as well as lesser subjects with heavy financial burdens. Such accumulated grievances would culminate in an uprising against King John, triggered by his military defeat in 1214.

The king

The fundamental fact of political life in twelfth- and thirteenth-century England was that government was in the hands of a monarch, crowned in a religious ceremony that set him above all his subjects and conferred on him an aura of sanctity derived from his anointing in imitation of Old Testament kings. The coronation ceremony stressed both the king's God-given authority over his subjects and his responsibility as a Christian to protect his subjects and the Church. This view of kingship, tracing back to the fifth century, stressed the monarch's responsibility to God for his subjects' care as if he were their parent or guardian. Although the eleventh-century reform movement of the Church had blunted the king's sacred character, its effect on English kings' traditional authority over the spiritual sphere was minimal. Not even the long and bitter conflict between Henry II and his archbishop of Canterbury, Thomas Becket, resulted in major loss of royal control over the Church.

Some English royal clerks continued to support royal supremacy throughout the twelfth century, promoting near-absolutist ideas of kingship lingering from the late Roman Empire. These clerics recognized the king's responsibility for his subjects' general welfare and concluded that he could override the law in emergencies, for example by imposing extraordinary levies on his subjects. The late-twelfth-century *Dialogue of the Exchequer*, authored by a longtime royal financial official, states that God entrusts the king with 'the general care of his subjects'; it admitted that rulers sometimes act arbitrarily, but denied that their subjects had a right 'to question or condemn their actions'.[1] Although some royal servants promoted theories stressing the king's duties toward his subjects, most entered his household because they saw opportunities for enriching themselves and their families through graft, influence peddling or outright theft. Despite survival of Roman concepts of the state as a provider of public services, twelfth-century rulers took little responsibility for the public welfare; kings did little more than defend their possessions and conquer new ones, protect their subjects from foreign threats, and maintain a modicum of law and order to safeguard their wealthier subjects' property. Even though created by coronation ceremonies emphasizing the public responsibilities of kingship, a medieval monarch rarely distinguished his kingdom from his private property, and he viewed it as a family legacy to be passed down intact to his heirs, or enlarged if possible.

The diverse sources of medieval ideas about kingship, a mixed bag of classical and Christian doctrines mingled with Germanic tribal traditions, sent confusing messages about the nature of royal power. The late-twelfth-century lawbook *Glanvill* illustrates this confusion. On one hand, its author cites the Roman law maxim, 'What pleases the prince has the force of law'; yet on the other hand, he asserts that England's laws were made 'on the advice of the magnates'.[2] The English coronation ceremony emphasized the divine source of royal power, but included oaths that subjected the king to obligations, notably his duty to protect his people and give them justice. The notion of the king as the guardian of his subjects implied that any rights or liberties that they enjoyed were due to grants by him. Early on, monastic houses, knowing the value of written records, sought royal charters confirming royal grants of their properties and privileges. This desire for charters specifying royal responsibilities spread to the baronage, and Henry I (1100–35) issued a charter on his coronation, renouncing his predecessor's unjust rule and promising good government.

Henry I's coronation charter and collections of old English laws circulated by the early thirteenth century to nourish notions of the ruler's subjection to law, and some contemporary writers condemned the Angevin kings as tyrants who ruled by their own will, not in accordance with the law. Although the doctrine of the law's supremacy acknowledged that a king could do wrong, his subjects had no machinery for righting a tyrannical ruler's wrongs against them or for forcing him to submit to the law. The lawbook *Bracton*, authored by a royal judge active in the 1220s and 1230s, pointed to a solution, proposing that the baronage act to curb a law-breaking monarch. A frequently cited passage declared that the king has a superior, namely God, but also the law and the earls and barons who constituted his great council. The author had lived through both the baronial rebellion against King John (1215–16) and the first crisis of Henry III's personal rule (1232–34), two early attempts to restrain the king with the bridle of the law.

Contributing to English notions of kingship were ties of mutual rights and responsibilities between aristocratic lords and their knightly vassals, key aspects of a feudal society. England's feudal institutions were unique in Europe because the work of the Anglo-Saxon kings in preserving and strengthening royal governance survived. The Anglo-Norman kings (1066–1154), as well as their successors, the early Plantagenet or Angevin kings, preserved their native English predecessors' authority as public officials. Late Roman and Frankish traditions of state power also inspired post-Conquest rulers to construct mechanisms for exercising effective power. Once Henry II attained the English crown, he moved quickly to curb the power of earls and barons who had taken advantage of the confusion during the disputed reign of his predecessor, Stephen of Blois (1135–54). They had defied royal agents in the counties, recruited armed bands, constructed private castles, and consolidated control over their lands. Henry besieged unauthorized baronial castles and constructed new royal castles, a work continued by his sons that brought half of the kingdom's castles under the king's control before the end of the twelfth century. These royal fortifications stood as solid reminders of a shift in power away from the barons and toward the monarch.

Under Henry II (1154–89), a process of converting the magnates' personal ties of loyalty to the king into tenurial relationships proceeded, and they were forced to admit that they held their estates from the king in return for services, chiefly supplying quotas of knights for his army. The barons' landholding position as the king's tenants-in-chief overtook their traditional role as his vassals, bound by personal loyalty. In effect, the post-Conquest kings 'territorialized' obligations owed by their baronage and loaded ever heavier military and fiscal burdens on them as conditions by which they held their baronies. Paradoxically, it was the public authority of the Norman monarchs and their Angevin successors that garnered the resources that they required to enforce these personal obligations on their baronage.

In the eleventh and twelfth centuries, England was the sole European kingdom where public tribunals capable of handing down conclusive and impartial decisions survived and where the king exercised effective power to carry out public courts' judgements. None the less, great landholders even in England, by virtue of their standing in local communities, exercised considerable responsibility for justice and for other services that public agencies provide in modern times. Anglo-Norman aristocrats maintained their own tribunals that settled the disputes of their knights and other dependants. Longstanding custom that survived the post-Carolingian collapse of public authority insisted that judgements in such private courts be a collective finding by the lord with his vassals or knights. The aim was to settle property disputes with amicable agreements, negotiated by panels of spokesmen for the community. Such a pattern of collective judgement, common in earlier primitive societies, prevailed in many judicial processes before the twelfth-century revival of Roman law. The jury, a feature of Henry II's legal innovations, preserved this concept of collective judgement.

Creation of machinery to strengthen central authority began with Henry I, if not earlier, and his reign marks the beginnings of 'administrative kingship',[3] as such specialized offices as the exchequer, staffed with literate and numerate servants auditing his financial accounts, separated from the king's household and his direct supervision. When Henry II and his sons Richard I (1189–99) and John (1199–1216) were absent fighting in France, the justiciar acted as both head of the administration and as regent, a post formerly held by the queen or another close relative. Authority was divided, with the justiciar at Westminster overseeing royal finances, justice, and local agents in the counties, while royal servants travelling with the king's household abroad dealt with matters of war and diplomacy. By Henry II's reign, growth of agencies binding the shires to the royal court – chancery clerks issuing royal writs and charters, the exchequer auditing sheriffs' accounts, and itinerant justices taking royal justice to the people – constituted a revolution in government.

Henry's legal innovations transformed England's law from customary norms into a legal system, a common law for the kingdom. They threatened magnates' traditional control over their vassals or tenants, for knights and other free landholders could purchase royal writs transferring their lawsuits from their lords' courts to the king's court. The shire courts became temporary royal tribunals when justices from the king's court arrived on their circuits about the counties. Wider access to royal justice began to undermine freeholders' dependent relationship with their lords and to change their relationship into a reciprocal one of landlords' and tenants' rights. At the same time that the common law's protection of free men's property was weakening lords' domination of their tenants, it was also strengthening the direct ruler–subject relationship. Strong governmental structures enabled the Angevin kings to rule in an authoritarian, if not absolutist manner even when absent for long periods, thereby setting twelfth-century England apart from France, where the monarch was too weak to control his outlying provinces.

England's precocious professionalization or bureaucratization of government under the three Angevin kings was driven less by principles of good government than by their need for enormous sums of money for almost continuous warfare on the continent. War was a medieval monarch's vocation, his route to fame, and the Angevin rulers spent English treasure on protecting the frontiers of their Norman duchy, their county of Anjou, and the inheritance of Henry II's queen, Eleanor of Aquitaine, in southwestern France. All these Angevin-held lands lay within the kingdom of France, and the French monarch was technically their lord. The Capetian kings were reasserting royal authority over these territories, posing a growing threat to Henry and his sons. The first French monarch powerful enough to challenge them was Philip II or Philip Augustus (1180–1223), and he seized every opportunity to undermine their position within their continental possessions.

Henry II and his sons viewed their English kingdom as a vast treasure trove to supply funds for conflicts in France. They needed ever more resources to pay mercenaries defending the Norman and Angevin borders against the Capetians and crushing rebellious nobles in the queen's provinces of Poitou and Gascony. By the end of the twelfth century, the French ruler's resources equalled those of Richard Lionheart, and Philip Augustus eventually overtook John in wealth, enabling him to deal John decisive defeats. Contributing to increased costs of warfare in the twelfth century was a shift away from mounted knights in heavy armour, supplied by the barons, and toward reliance on mercenaries, paid infantry companies and specialists in siege engines.

The medieval English kings had three types of revenues from which to raise funds for their wars. First was income derived from their position as public officials, a legacy lingering from the Roman political tradition that yielded less than in pre-Conquest times. General taxes collected regularly by Anglo-Saxon kings were allowed to lapse after Henry II's early years, but he and his sons still profited from a royal monopoly over mints and coinage and from royal responsibility for justice. The king did not provide courts for his subjects merely out of a sense of duty, for royal justice was a product to be sold. The profits were substantial, including confiscated goods of condemned felons and numerous fines from convicted criminals, as well as fees charged for the new common law procedures in civil cases. A second source of royal revenue was the king's private income from his own estates, peopled by peasants owing him labour services and periodic payments. The king, like lesser lords, had the privilege of assessing arbitrary payments known as tallages on the villagers of his lands whenever he felt necessary, and this source of revenue became more and more profitable because some villages sited on the royal domain grew into prosperous towns, royal boroughs. The borough inhabitants soon became wealthy enough to bargain with the king for a lump sum to pay as tallage and to negotiate a collective annual rent for their royal grant of rights of self-government.

The third category was the king's feudal income centred on his lordship over the earls and barons, for they owed him financial obligations as well as loyalty and military service. Henry II and his sons exploited vigorously these financial resources, triggering increasing resistance from the baronage. As the character of warfare changed, Henry, Richard Lionheart and John preferred to forgo their vassals' military service in favour of collecting scutage or shield-money, payments that could be used to hire mercenary soldiers. Over time, scutage came to be levied so often that it resembled a tax on the nobility; King John levied eleven scutages in sixteen years. The king's feudal position as lord over England's great landholders gave him other financial advantages. Custom sanctioned a lord's demand of extraordinary levies from his knights in emergencies, the so-called gracious aids demanded on the knighting of the lord's eldest son, on the marriage of his eldest daughter, and on his ransoming if captured in battle. Like other lords, the king could collect an aid from his barons in other emergencies, but only after taking counsel with them. Perhaps because of this requirement, John never sought a gracious aid from his great men; instead, he exploited the 'feudal incidents', occasional financial opportunities for a lord to exploit a tenant's lands. These included relief, a fee that a vassal's heir paid to his lord for his acceptance of the heir's succession to his father's land. Both Richard and John demanded exorbitant sums from baronial heirs, especially when an heir's legal claim was shaky; and as a result, many young nobles were driven deeply into debt. Another of the feudal incidents was the lord's wardship of minors and control of their marriage, rights that arose when a baronial tenant died leaving an underage heir. The lord then took custody of minor children and the widow, keeping the late tenant's estates in his hands and taking all profits until the heir came of age. In cases of noble widows' custody, the king had the right to arrange their marriages, sometimes selling them off to the highest bidder. Closely related to wardship of noble children was the royal right to custody of vacant bishoprics and abbacies. Royal exploitation of vacant ecclesiastical lands triggered complaints from religious reformers and clerical writers.

Competition with Philip Augustus of France forced Richard Lionheart and his brother John Lackland to weigh down the baronage with ever more burdensome feudal payments and services, collected by zealous royal servants. As the nature of their rule increasingly became military, they seemed to draw little distinction between their subjects and their enemies; they demanded hostages from friends as well as from foes, and all in the kingdom, even great aristocrats, lived in fear of the royal wrath. The Angevin monarchs engaged in a gigantic shakedown of great landholders to extort excessive amounts of money, arbitrarily seizing barons' land without judgement if they failed to make payments or perform services. Those offending the king might find themselves also falling into 'the king's mercy', subject to crushing fines. For such victims of the king's ill-will, their only recourse was to purchase restoration to his goodwill by offering him a handsome gift of horses, falcons or cash – in effect, a bribe. Even with these extortionate steps, the aristocracy alone could not meet the need for additional revenues, and experiments with general taxation began, for example the taxing of the whole kingdom for Richard's ransom.

Not surprisingly, many among the nobility felt threatened by the Angevin kings' arbitrary acts that were weakening them financially; and because they treasured their traditional domination over the countryside, they also resented the interposition of royal judges between themselves and their dependants subject to their private courts. Although some barons became courtiers, currying favour with the king, many more stayed in the country rarely attending his court. When Henry I, his grandson Henry II and their successors hired specialists, often lowborn or foreign-born, with the literacy and numeracy needed for government's effective functioning, the country baronage grew resentful. Furthermore, the kings' new servants saw advantage in expanding royal authority, for it increased the favours flowing to themselves and their families. Kings saw such obscure knights and clerks' dependence on royal favour as making them more reliable than great nobles capable of mounting armed resistance with their castles and bands of knights. With the royal household's increasing importance, politics in Angevin England became court politics, as scions of aristocratic families competed for patronage with newcomers to court. In one historian's words, 'The royal patronage machine was the single most important instrument for making or breaking individual fortunes in the medieval period'.[4]

This shift from eleventh-century informal, part-time government by household servants to full-time officials dedicated to enhancing royal power and wealth had an impact on political thought. As the English kings' subjects dealt with the twelfth-century bureaucracy and its complex rules and regulations, their new awareness of government's impersonal and public aspects provoked a reaction. Once the strong governance of Henry II and his sons turned to intimidation and violence to collect funds and compel services, it aroused the fear and hatred of their subjects. Old assumptions that the kingdom was a single political community revived to strengthen the solidarity of the English as a unique people with their own customs and laws. Thinking people saw that the interests of the king and the kingdom were not always identical; indeed, the best interest of the people or their noble spokesmen – the community of the realm – could conflict with the king's personal wishes. A crucial stage in this definition of the political community with its own concerns opposed to the king's personal interest arrived with Magna Carta. Debate over the Charter and periodic demands for its reissue inspired debates on instruments for limiting royal power, imposing public accountability on royal officials, and finding a voice by which the political community could speak in opposition to the king's will.

The aristocracy or baronage

The English kingdom's great landholders possessing castles and commanding large numbers of knightly tenants formed the first body that visualized itself as a distinct order or political community with its own interests differing from the king's agenda. Although the twelfth-century aristocracy had no formal legal standing, descendants of William the Conqueror's companions quickly came to view themselves as a hereditary caste. Second and third generation Anglo-Norman barons adopted surnames derived from their ancestral lands in Normandy, and they began to see themselves as a power bloc or community. They expected royal patronage simply because of their superior status and distinguished ancestry, not as a reward for services rendered to the king. Yet the aristocracy was never a completely closed class in medieval England, but was a fluid group of dynasties often lasting no more than three or four generations, constantly replaced by newcomers who were awarded extinct titles through royal favour or who married heiresses. Indeed, England's nobility would have no legal definition before the fourteenth century, when individual summonses to Parliament became heritable, creating a hereditary peerage. At the end of the twelfth century, they already felt themselves entitled to an official place among the king's counsellors, and they resented the professional royal servants and mercenary military captains who were usurping their proper places at his side.

A synonym for the medieval English nobility is the term 'baronage', tenants-in-chief of the king holding substantial lands from him in return for services. Because barons held widely varying amounts of land and resources including at least one castle, it is difficult to define them by wealth or territory. Although barons varied widely in wealth and power, from the most powerful with over a hundred knights holding land of them to a few with only two or three, a rough average is around thirty knights and an annual income of £200. Applying this standard, about 165 men ranked as barons at the end of the twelfth century, including those holding portions of baronies that had been partitioned among female heirs. Among the aristocracy, the highest rank was 'earl' (Latin *comes*), and earls were often the king's kinsmen, although the title was largely honorific after Henry II's accession. Their number ranged from about a half dozen during the Anglo-Norman era to fourteen or fifteen on John's accession in 1199. Some barons without the title of earl equalled them in landholdings and wealth, however; for example, one of the leaders of the baronial opposition to King John, Robert fitz Walter of Essex, had over a hundred knightly tenures.

Ranking alongside earls and barons in status and joining them in attending great councils were the bishops and abbots. Despite the Church's definition of the clergy as separate from and superior to all laity, the higher clergy had dual status as both spiritual leaders and lay lords, holding lands from the king and owing him quotas of knight service. Some came from baronial families, although many had won their ecclesiastical posts through royal favour after years of service to the king in administrative posts; and some frequented the king's court after their elevation, continuing to serve as officials in the royal administration. All prelates shared with the lay barons a preoccupation with protecting property, the landed endowment of their churches. In addition, the higher clergy firmly believed that the monarch should respect the English Church's liberties, especially its right to select bishops without royal interference.

In the years following the Norman Conquest, the new monarch and his aristocracy were united by a common interest in protecting the kingdom from foreign threats, keeping a subject population under control, and preserving and expanding their possessions. English barons maintained armed bands, knights who were their vassals bound to them by homage and fealty. In return for his knight's loyalty and service in combat, a baron was expected to protect the knight, give him justice, and provide for his sustenance, either by keeping him in his household or by settling him on land with the labour of unfree peasants living on it. Since the Anglo-Norman barons were bound to the king by individual ties of homage and fealty, as well as by shared interests, they had little sense of themselves as a corporate body or estate with concerns that conflicted with the king's goals. They shared in common a concern for their collection of estates that they regarded in some sense as their own principality, headed by an elaborate baronial household and a court that played an important part in peace-keeping and dispute settlement for their tenants. Indeed, along the Welsh frontier and in the north of England, the authority of great men's private courts rivalled that of the public courts of shire and hundred.

Although king and baronage were bound together by common concerns and an ideal of co-operation, a certain tension always marked their relations. On one hand, William I and his sons William II and Henry I relied on their nobles' castles and knights to crush rebellions and to defend their territories, both in England and in Normandy. On the other hand, nobles' military strength tempted them to challenge their ruler with rebellion when his demands pressed on them too hard; and their capacity for violence could obstruct his enforcement of royal authority over the entire kingdom. The post-Conquest magnates had an appetite for territories along the Welsh borders and in Ireland, and throughout the twelfth century they carved out large liberties or franchises in those regions and in the far north of England beyond the reach of sheriffs or itinerant justices. A number of powerful barons were cross-Channel landholders with estates in both England and Normandy, and they shared with their king-duke a determination to defend the Norman duchy from the aggression of the French monarch. By the end of the twelfth century, however, most English barons no longer had enough land across the Channel to care about Normandy's fate.

The monarch saw his task as preventing his great men from forming factions capable of overwhelming him with armed force. The seriousness of a baronial threat would determine his response; he could subdue them by instilling fear, threatening force, and confiscating their lands. Another option was keeping them contented by luring them to his court and showering them with flattery and patronage. If the king paid attention to judicious distribution of patronage to his nobles, he could recruit a 'court party' of loyal supporters; yet he had to avoid a number of pitfalls. When rewarding faithful nobles, he had to take care not to arouse the jealousy of others and to guard against creating over-mighty magnates, greedy for more patronage and capable of contesting royal power. Also he needed to avoid neglecting the country nobles who remained in the counties and resented their colleagues at court, nursing grievances on account of the patronage flowing to courtier nobles through proximity to the king. They especially envied baseborn or alien courtiers rising above their proper station, usurping the right to advise the king and reaping the rewards of his favour. Fostering new men's rapid rise in fortune was sure to arouse resentment among old aristocratic families. Nonetheless, as early as William II (1089–1100), kings were choosing as their counsellors and officials former low-ranking servants, military retainers or clerics of undistinguished ancestry.

Some great men always accompanied the king on his travels about the kingdom or fought at his side on campaign in France, counselling him on matters of state, and adding to their families' power and prestige; a well-known example is William Marshal, earl of Pembroke, companion of three Angevin kings. Other barons remained on their lands, seldom attending the royal court; and for these country nobles, protecting their lineage and securing heirs' smooth succession to their property took precedence over service to the king at court or on military campaigns. They saw their own power diminishing as courtiers in the royal household won favours in the form of disputed inheritances, custody of estates in the king's hand, marriages to wealthy heiresses or widows, and remission of debts and tax obligations. Country barons' growing national consciousness complicated the patronage picture under King John. They were losing any interest in Normandy, their ancestral homeland, and becoming entirely English, and they resented the king's increasing demands for money and military service overseas to defend the duchy. By the last quarter of the twelfth century, it was no longer possible to distinguish between the king's subjects of French ancestry and those descended from the native English. When alien mercenaries who had fled Normandy with John in 1204 became royal favourites, the native baronage disdained the newcomers as unworthy companions for the king, and they were scandalized by his appointment of them to offices in England.

Noble rebellions were not infrequent in twelfth- and thirteenth-century England, and they fall into three categories. First were isolated outbursts by individual barons defying the king, provoked by real or imagined personal grievances, often resulting from failure to secure royal patronage. In the Norman and Angevin periods, a single magnate's quarrel with the king was more likely to end in mutual accommodation than in harsh punishment. The mildness of the punishments that the Anglo-Norman and Angevin monarchs meted out to rebellious nobles contrasts strongly with the bloody executions of defeated rebels earlier in the Anglo-Saxon kingdoms and in the later medieval and Tudor periods. The Angevin kings hesitated to dispossess their nobles permanently, for opinion supported a free man's hereditary right to his patrimony. Custom sanctioned an individual vassal's renunciation of his homage to a lord who treated him cruelly or unjustly, but it did not approve compacts or conspiracies by bands of vassals.

A second category of rebellion includes larger-scale movements among the baronage seeking to replace the king with a rival claimant, frequently a disgruntled member of the royal family, although the warring barons rarely presented an enduring or unified front. Characteristic is the revolt by Henry II's sons in 1173–74, and the earlier 1139–53 civil war between King Stephen and Henry II's mother, the Empress Matilda, was an extended version of this category of rebellion. Since the conflict of Stephen's reign ended in a negotiated settlement, opponents of Matilda and her son suffered little for their support of Stephen. Later, Henry proved to be forgiving toward the defeated rebels who had joined his sons' great revolt in 1173–74, few of whom lost their property, much less life or limb.

A third category encompasses the large-scale baronial rebellions with agendas of limiting royal power first appearing in the thirteenth century, against King John in 1215–16, and later against his son Henry III from 1258 to 1265, and continuing in the fourteenth century. By the first decade of the thirteenth century, the baronage was beginning to think of itself as a corporate body with collective rights and responsibilities, spokesmen for the 'community of the realm'. In their collective action against King John, they bound themselves together by oath as a band, united not simply by private complaints but by principled opposition to his rule based on their version of the proper lord–vassal relationship. It was clear to them that the twelfth-century revolution in government had imperilled their privileged position within the kingdom. An indication is the Angevin kings' abandonment of aristocratic assemblies that the Anglo-Norman monarchs had summoned on great festivals of the ecclesiastical calendar. Although great councils resurfaced temporarily during the crisis of Richard Lionheart's absence on crusade and in captivity, 1190–94, John reverted to his father's practice and seldom sought his magnates' counsel. Yet the great men – not only earls and barons, but also bishops and abbots – saw themselves as the king's rightful advisers and assumed that because of their superior rank they spoke not only for themselves, but also for all the kingdom's inhabitants. Tendencies toward royal centralization also threatened aristocrats' autonomy within their territories, weakening their control over their tenants. They were feeling financial pressures from the English monarch's efficient exchequer that loaded them down with arbitrarily assessed payments and saddled them with staggering debts. Some nobles, hoping to swell their fortunes, made over-optimistic bids for profitable custodies or other privileges, and these crown debtors became dependent on the king's exchequer for defer-ment or remission of their debts. Also resented was the king's control over baronial inheritances and custody of minor heirs, arranging their marriages, and sometimes threatening the survival of noble lineages.

The new corps of professional royal servants in England not only challenged the magnates' social and economic superiority, but also proposed theoretical justifications of royal absolutism. Opinions on the nature of government diverged once the barons devised their own notion of the proper nature of royal government. They condemned innovations under Henry II and his sons as departures from ancient custom, and they looked back with nostalgia to an idealized picture of Anglo-Norman England, where they imagined the king ruling with the counsel of his tenants-in-chief and safeguarding baronial courts' integrity. By King John's reign, two political concepts were taking root among the baronage. They sought to replace arbitrary rule by the king's will with governance in accordance with the good old law, and they demanded a role for themselves in adjudicating conflicts between the monarch and his magnates at frequent great councils. In short, they wanted King John to rule 'by judgement' and 'by counsel'.

The knights or gentry and burgesses or townspeople

Throughout the Middle Ages, the English population below baronial rank had at best a minor share in the periodic political crises ignited by royal oppression. Aside from the baronage, the only group with enough political consciousness by the early thirteenth century to comprehend that its own interests could conflict with those of the monarch, and sometimes with baronial interests as well, was the knights. Defined chiefly by their military livelihood in the late eleventh and early twelfth centuries, the knights, numbering a little less than 5,000 in King John's time, were evolving into a rural gentry busy with county affairs, attending shire courts and sitting on juries, practised in the royal courts and versed in the common law. Many knights suffered from the Angevin kings' financial policies, and some shared their lords' concerns about royal misgovernment.

Medieval England was primarily an agricultural land without heavily populated urban centres. London, by far the largest city, had only some 20,000 inhabitants by 1100, and most English towns had fewer than 1,500 inhabitants. Townspeople, the bourgeoisie or burgesses, always had an uncertain position in an agrarian medieval society because their commercial activity set them apart from the majority dwelling on the land as farmers. The abnormal situation of merchants in a largely rural society led them to seek rights of town self-government, yet at the same time they favoured a strong ruler as protection for their trading ventures. While they were not drawn into royal government on a scale equal to the knights, they too gained legal and political experience, for nearly all commercial centres had some measure of self-government. Leaders of the mercantile community dominated their towns' governments, and their service as mayors and aldermen or councillors gave them class-consciousness and self-confidence comparable to that gained by knights in the shire courts. Also contributing to town dwellers' solidarity and local pride was membership in guilds, originally drinking societies or religious confraternities that quickly took on economic functions. In broadening Magna Carta in 1215 to remedy grievances of the knights and townspeople, negotiators for the rebel cause were responding to these two groups' growing importance in England's society.

The mass of English population, the peasants, did not figure in the political sphere before the end of the Middle Ages, unless their limited participation in decision-making in their villages is counted. In medieval Europe, liberty or freedom was not an abstract concept, and the twelfth-century English population possessed degrees of liberties or freedoms depending on the payments and services they owed to their lords, for liberty was tied to lordship. Before the Norman Conquest, unsettled conditions had forced England's peasants to make bargains with local lords to secure protection, and they steadily lost status as the formerly free sank into semi-free or unfree categories. Following Henry II's legal reforms, the common law tended to reinforce the unfree peasants' relegation to the bottom of society. Since they held land from their lords in return for 'servile' dues and labour services, their holdings were without the protection that the royal courts accorded to free men's tenures. Upper classes unanimously held the peasantry in contempt, and in the twelfth and thirteenth centuries everyone simply assumed that the peasants' betters – at first the baronage and later knights and burgesses as well – could represent to the ruler the whole kingdom's best interest without taking account of the needs of those at the bottom of society who fed the upper classes.

The knights of England did not constitute a class categorized by wealth or social standing before about 1180. Until then, they were defined by their function as warriors for hire with a reputation similar to that of 'hired guns' in America's pioneer West, and their violence seemed symptomatic of the breakdown of law and order associated with the eleventh-century feudal transformation. Many knights at the beginning of the twelfth century, although free and sometimes bound by blood to noble families, held relatively low social or economic status, and their military service could consist of castle guard or fighting in a lightly armed cavalry force, not exclusively combat in heavy armour. Early-twelfth-century knights' holdings were sometimes little larger than peasant plots, and many knights were landless, serving in armed retinues for a stipend, although their ambition was to acquire a landed estate from their lord. Later a knight's holding was large enough to support him, his family and his warhorse, and living on it were peasants to cultivate its fields, freeing him for military pursuits. A typical thirteenth-century knight possessed an estate averaging 600 acres with an annual income of £10 to £20, although many held two, three or more estates, and a few held so much land that they rivalled barons in income.

Once these fighting men became possessors of land tilled by peasants, personal ties of loyalty to lords tended to weaken; a process of 'territorialization' set in, and knights' services and payments seemed to be obligations due from the land rather than personal commitments to their lords. Knights came to consider their holdings as their own hereditary possessions, expecting eldest sons to succeed to them on the land, and they wanted full proprietary rights, freedom to grant away pieces of land to younger sons, to daughters as marriage portions or to monastic houses as gifts. Naturally, their lords resisted this trend, seeking to retain control over lands they had granted to their knights and to insist on performance of services and payments that symbolized their proprietary right. Yet Henry II's legal reforms gave knightly tenants and lesser freeholders weapons in the form of common law procedures that enabled them to sue their lords in the royal courts, limiting barons' control over their tenants' holdings. As the knights became preoccupied with their new role as landholders, their warrior skills tended to wither, and their military service became less useful to their lords or to the king. Throughout the twelfth century, lords retained some soldiers with whom they had no tenurial connection, for such bands of landless armed retainers made better fighters. Such knights without ties of land to their lord differed little from the noble retinues associated with so-called bastard feudalism of the fourteenth and fifteenth centuries. Numbers of them would remain landless, for barons had less and less surplus lands for compensating them, although some colonized new lands in Wales or Ireland in search of reward for their retainers.

Throughout western Europe, the status of knights tended to rise in the twelfth century, as the two distinct groups – nobles and knights – fused. As aristocrats, encouraged by ecclesiastical writers, accepted the knightly or chivalric code of conduct, their adherence to the ethos of the mounted warrior fostered a new definition of aristocracy or nobility. It was no longer honourable ancestry, old wealth and public service that distinguished nobles, but imitation of the warrior's model of behaviour that defined the word 'nobility'. Knighthood and nobility blended in people's minds, as qualities of courage and courtesy identified knight and noble heir alike as members of a single superior caste, standing above peasants and townspeople. By the early decades of the thirteenth century, aristocrats had adopted the Latin term *miles*, soldier or knight, for themselves. The imitation moved in the other direction as well, for prosperous knights took on aristocratic trappings, using seals, painting heraldic devices on their shields, and building stone houses. Ties of kinship reinforced this merger, for many knights were kinsmen of barons, descended from their younger sons or bastard offspring.

Paradoxically, this growing emphasis on martial tradition appeared just as English knights' actual military function was declining, and by the beginning of the thirteenth century their military function no longer defined them. Knights' social or economic status as landed proprietors with holdings smaller than those of barons but greater than ordinary freeholders' plots came to designate them as precursors of the late medieval 'gentry'. The legal term 'knights of the county' was applied to a class that was increasingly significant as semi-professionals in local government, once Henry II's legal innovations made collective testimony by juries the preferred means of settling disputes in the royal courts. Soon knights had a powerful role in county government, dominating such local offices as sheriff, coroner, escheator, and collector of taxes.

Their presence before the royal justices not only as litigants and witnesses, but as jurors and sureties for their neighbours, taught them the common law; and their attendance at courts of all kinds, their lords' private courts and courts of shire and hundred, gave them expertise in traditional law and custom. In addition, knights were acquiring a modicum of literacy in Latin that impressed on them the importance of written documents as support for claims to property or other rights.

Knights first showed signs of political consciousness during John's reign, and they had a semblance of a political programme in their desire that local government be in the hands of local men. The men of some shires joined together to petition the king to replace sheriffs recruited from the royal household with local residents. In 1212 and 1213, with his troubles mounting, John summoned representatives of the knights of the counties for talks about the state of the kingdom. Yet he failed to win them to his cause, for they resented the arbitrary and exploitative methods of Angevin government; many had experienced for themselves harsh treatment by the king's agents, or at least his failure to make royal justice more easily available. Half-hearted attempts to draw the knights into political life revived early in Henry III's time, when grants of general taxes to the king in 1225 and 1232 supposedly were approved by them and other free men as well as by the barons and bishops. Such gestures signify that lesser ranks of society were coming to be considered members of the political community, though secondary to the baronage.

Social classes in medieval England were never immutable castes, and barriers between barons, knights or gentry, lesser 'law-worthy men', and urban elites or burgesses, were not impenetrable. At the bottom rungs of the knightly class, unfortunate sons of the gentry, inheriting little or no land, slid down the social ladder from knighthood to the level of village free men; if luckier, they competed for posts as estate stewards or settled in towns to embark on commercial careers. Some 'law-worthy men' of less than knightly rank were little different in their landed property holdings from the richest peasants, although they joined the knights in sitting on juries and commissions by the late twelfth century, and they occasionally climbed to the lower rungs of the gentry or migrated to towns, where some prospered in trade. Although tradesmen had an uncertain status in a largely agrarian society, urban elites and the knights of the counties developed ties, for they served alongside each other on government commissions, did business together, even married into one another's families. Ambitious knights invested in urban rental property, and prosperous businessmen bought land in the country. Despite shared experiences, however, the two groups never merged into a single 'middling' class. Knights continued to consider themselves a superior order, their chivalric tradition reinforcing their rank in the social hierarchy above townspeople.

Within English towns, society was structured hierarchically in classes that stretched from day labourers at the bottom to small-scale shopkeepers with a top category of rich families in wholesale trade, who dominated their town's most powerful guilds and governing bodies. Londoners in this highest class called themselves the barons of the city. Yet all members of an urban community shared a sense of solidarity, and the peculiar conditions of a commercial economy set them apart from rural folk. The special needs of townspeople, especially freedom of movement, release from labour services, and courts capable of dealing with commercial disputes, impelled them to seek rights of self-government for their communities. Business activity required literacy, and townspeople saw the value of written contracts and other documents; like religious foundations, town governments were eager to purchase charters from the king that set down in writing their liberties.

Some urban centres had begun to bargain with their lords for a degree of autonomy before 1066, and in the twelfth century towns were winning varying measures of self-government, depending on the bargains that they could strike with the lord of the land on which they stood. Although English towns never achieved the degree of autonomy won by the communal movements of some continental cities, citizens of English boroughs, especially of London, proved to be strong advocates of liberties documented in charters. Although the Angevin kings were unenthusiastic about urban autonomy, a number of English towns located on the royal domain secured status as royal boroughs, enjoying liberties set forth in royal charters. Their growing wealth enabled them to negotiate for liberties in exchange for grants of money or military service by their militias. Cambridge paid Henry II over £200 for the right to pay the king a fixed sum annually and to be free of the sheriff's intervention. Among the liberties accorded boroughs was the right to 'burgage tenure': that is, property-holding that could be freely bought and sold and was not burdened with the dues and services of conditional landholdings in the countryside.

Since London, along with nearby Westminster, was the centre of royal government, 'the metropolis and queen of the whole country', Londoners proved especially eager and aggressive in seeking rights of self-government for their city.[5] Monarchs eventually gave in to them because control of the city and its wealth was essential for royal control of the kingdom. Early in Henry I's reign, Londoners purchased the right to elect their own sheriff. Royal financial accounts as early as 1130 record leading London merchants providing spices, wine, fine cloth, and other luxury goods to the royal court. The merchants supplying luxury goods to the royal household mingled with courtiers and noble visitors to the royal court, and the scale of their business gave them boldness. Some, such as the Cornhill family, started as suppliers to the royal household, invested in country lands, married into the knightly class and climbed to baronial status.

London's citizens participated in a civic militia, and they played a crucial part in disputed successions and civil wars. Winning the support of England's chief city would be crucial for any claimant of the crown. Londoners were quick to accept the claim of Stephen of Blois to the crown in 1135, and they supported him in the civil war that threatened his hold on the kingdom. Stephen's weak rule enabled them to imitate the communal movement sweeping continental towns, banding together in a sworn association to secure rights of self-government, and the embattled king obligingly recognized their commune. Once Henry II secured the throne, he issued a charter for London that confirmed most of its privileges, but restored features of a charter granted by Henry I that the Londoners considered oppressive. During Richard Lionheart's absence on crusade in the early 1190s, London played an important part in the rivalry between the absent king's viceroy and John Lackland, the king's brother, taking advantage of the confusion to win John's support for a revived commune. Londoners organized a communal government headed by a mayor presiding over twenty-four aldermen elected from the city's wards, and after Richard's return to England in 1194, he tacitly recognized this commune.

When John Lackland succeeded Richard, he granted London a charter that failed to acknowledge the commune, but he allowed the city to choose its own sheriffs in exchange for £2,000. In May 1215, as the king's troubles were mounting, he confirmed to the 'barons of the city of London' their ancient liberties and the right to elect their mayor annually. Nonetheless, the Londoners went over to the rebel barons' side, and they secured a clause in Magna Carta protecting their rights. Among the twenty-five barons charged with enforcement of the Charter in 1215 was the mayor of London. The citizens of London remained rebels throughout the civil war that followed the events at Runnymede, but soon after John's death they made peace with the royalists fighting in the name of the boy Henry III, and their reward was another confirmation of their liberties. Londoners, and also citizens of other cities, would take part in the struggles for confirmation of Magna Carta that continued long after King John's time into the reigns of his son and more distant successors.

Notes

1. Johnson (1950), 3, 101.
2. Hall (1965), Prologue.
3. Phrase of Baldwin and Hollister (1978).
4. Bartlett (2000), 32.
5. Quotations, Harding (1993), 144; Bartlett (2000), 342.

chapter 2

THE REIGN OF KING JOHN, 1199–1216

King John's designation as 'Bad King John' sums up his historical reputation, even among some professional historians today. He had the bad luck to succeed as England's king his brother Richard Lionheart, whose courage on the Third Crusade had earned him admiration, inspiring contemporaries to hail him as the perfect exemplar of the chivalric king. John's lack of chivalric virtues and shortcomings as a warrior combined with his suspicious personality to earn him a poor reputation, even in his own day, that contrasted with his predecessor's and thwarted him in winning the respect of his baronage. Yet it seems possible that the Lionheart's positive reputation merely postponed a reaction against the authoritarian nature of Angevin rule, for John Lackland's extortionate policies differed only in degree from those of his brother or his father.

Whether John was bad simply in comparison to his brother Richard or bad by any definition, he was a failure in confronting four great crises that marked his reign. The first crisis facing him was defence of his French possessions from the Capetian threat, and his loss of the Norman duchy in 1204 was a blow to his standing with his English subjects as a leader. John then failed at the greatest task he set for himself, a campaign to reconquer his lands lost to Philip Augustus of France, for the battle of Bouvines in 1214 ended in complete disaster after a decade of furious activity preparing a great expedition. A second crisis confronted him in his middle years, 1205 to 1213, a quarrel with Pope Innocent III over naming a new archbishop of Canterbury; this conflict also ended in the king's failure, total surrender to the papacy. Casting a shadow over John's entire reign was a third crisis, an unending struggle to find funds for campaigns in France that forced him to load his subjects with heavier and heavier financial burdens. The Barnwell annalist, the most balanced of the contemporary chroniclers of John's reign, calls him 'a robber of his own people'.[1] Anger at John's insatiable thirst for money brought on a final crisis, his alienation of the English baronage in his last years. The result was his grant of Magna Carta and a stalemated civil war against his barons that was still raging on the king's death in October 1216 and continued for another year.

'Bad King John'?

Most historians have followed the lead of writers in John's own time who first characterized him as a bad king, seizing on his unpleasant personality to paint a portrait not in tragic tones, but in mocking or contemptuous ones. Contemporary chroniclers who first sketched King John's character were subject to prejudices or preconceptions that distorted their perceptions. They were churchmen, following criteria established by earlier clerical writers for evaluating medieval kings to paint a conventional portrait of the 'good' king. Medieval chroniclers praised monarchs who provided protection for the Church and its property and who proved submissive to papal authority. They made little distinction between a monarch's public role and his private morality, expecting him to be an exemplar of conventional piety, and monastic writers' verdict on a ruler was 'essentially a moral judgment upon an individual sinner'.[2] Because Victorian scholars adopted a similar moralistic approach centuries later, it continues to influence estimates of John today.

King John lacked official historians to gloss over his failures, for unlike in France, where the Capetian monarchs sponsored historians producing royalist propaganda, royal patronage did not support the writing of history in medieval England. In contrast, English chroniclers, preoccupied with preserving their monastic houses' privileges, were unsympathetic to royal government, suspicious of change threatening social stability. The chroniclers most influential in creating John Lackland's poor historical reputation are the two thirteenth-century writers at St Albans' Abbey, Roger of Wendover and Matthew Paris. Unlike some twelfth-century historians who had praised Henry II's governance, these two shared their old and rich monastery's conservative outlook and adopted an anti-royalist bias, acting as apologists for the baronage. Roger of Wendover was writing during Henry III's minority, when a 'myth' of John's wickedness already was taking shape in clerical circles, and he added shading and colour to this sinister portrait. Wendover handed on his pro-baronial bias to Matthew Paris, his successor as historian at St Albans after 1235. In borrowing from Wendover, Matthew Paris only changed his portrait of Bad King John to darken it more deeply, since he viewed Henry III's conflict with his barons as a continuation of his father's earlier quarrel.

Chief among King John's faults among contemporaries in a chivalric age were his failures on the battlefield. Although warfare was a central concern for John throughout his reign, he appeared, in contrast to his crusader brother, incompetent in combat, failing to defend Normandy, unsuccessful in regaining the duchy, and dying during a stalemated civil war. His reputed lack of courage comes chiefly from comments by chroniclers with little interest in warfare or comprehension of its nature. Some modern historians have looked beyond chroniclers' amusing anecdotes about John's military incapacity, to evaluate him as no coward and a competent enough military planner. They recognize that victory in medieval warfare went to cautious commanders who avoided pitched battles in favour of besieging the enemy's castles and plundering their resources, not to chivalric heroes in rash pursuit of glory.

After John's withdrawal from Normandy in 1203, he became a resident ruler in England, unlike his absentee predecessors, and he was very much a hands-on monarch. Many twentieth-century historians, writing in an age of bureaucracy, painted an admiring picture of John governing with enthusiasm and expertise, although others insisted that praise for him as an administrator primarily derived from abundant documentation surviving from his reign. This tendency to accent John's attention to administration is anachronistic, applying standards of the twentieth century rather than the thirteenth. Whether or not John exemplifies 'administrative kingship', a phrase coined by two American authorities in the 1970s, his personal involvement did not improve his contemporaries' impression of him. Since his father and brother had ruled largely from across the Channel, 'evil counsellors' took blame for their oppressive rule, whereas John's subjects heaped such blame on him personally. A factor in his concentration of more and more decision-making in his own hands was his overly suspicious temperament. An example is his suspension in 1209 of the royal court at Westminster that heard 'common pleas', mostly private litigation over property, to centre all justice in a tribunal that formed part of his household.

Not all reports of King John's wickedness can be attributed to idle monks' over-active imaginations. Clearly, he did not possess the likeable qualities of his two predecessors that had won them popularity in spite of their arbitrary acts and financial extortions. Although subjects of Henry II and Richard I had suffered from royal anger or ill-will, those two rulers could display on occasion chivalric courtesy and magnanimity missing in John Lackland. His disagreeable, even fearsome personality, including a streak of pettiness or spitefulness, impelled him toward tyrannical acts; and there can be no doubt of his cruelty, even if embellished in chroniclers' tales. He thirsted for revenge and revelled in humbling his rivals, an especially damaging defect in a ruler who turned his spite against powerful and popular men. Since John could not win his barons' affection, he sought to rule them through fear and demanded that they surrender their sons as hostages. Yet they were hesitant to turn their sons over to him after rumours spread of his political murders, most notably the disappearance of his nephew, Arthur of Brittany. The killing of one's close kin, even a dangerous political rival, outraged medieval aristocrats with their strong sense of family solidarity.

In the view of many of John's subjects, his despotism differed little from his father's or brother's predatory rule. Twelfth- and thirteenth-century writers defined tyranny as rule 'by the king's will', and they contrasted the Angevins' arbitrary rule with mythical accounts of earlier monarchs governing and giving judgements through counsel with their magnates. Henry II and Richard I had introduced a new vocabulary of power into royal documents, adding to their titles the term 'by grace of God' and adopting the plural of majesty. King John's own statements indicate that he held a notion of royal power that placed the monarch above the law, in contradiction to mainstream medieval political theories stressing the monarch's subjection to the law. Even John sometimes tried to place his arbitrary acts within the context of law and custom. In his view, the law of the exchequer that enforced his financial demands constituted part of the law of the land, although the barons saw it as little more than enforcement of the king's will. How to force a tyrannical monarch to obey the law proved an unanswerable question for medieval political thinkers, and their only suggestion was to await God's judgement. At the core of the barons' demand for a charter of liberties was the problem of finding a means of subjecting King John to the law, defining and limiting his lawful authority.

Crises of John's reign: military defeat at the hands of Philip Augustus

Along with the English crown, John Lackland inherited his brother's conflict with Philip Augustus of France, who had taken as his chief task driving the English king from French territory. The split between the Angevins' English kingdom and their continental possessions seems to have started with Philip Augustus's accession in 1180, and his innovations in government before departing on the Third Crusade strengthened the French monarchy and cancelled the English kings' fiscal advantage, tipping the balance in the Capetians' favour by the beginning of the thirteenth century. Philip's return to France from the Holy Land in 1191 initiated more than a decade of conflict, broken only by sporadic unstable truces.

For the last five years of the Lionheart's life, he was fighting his Capetian lord in France, mainly in Normandy, in a struggle that required enormous resources, and Richard's exploitation of England for funds reached unprecedented levels by the time of his death in 1199.

Richard's death without an heir of his body created new tensions between the French and English royal houses. Despite Philip's earlier alliance with John Lackland while Richard was on crusade and in captivity in Germany (1190–94), John's accession to the English throne did not dent the Capetian effort to drive the Plantagenets from their French possessions. Uncertainty over the succession in the French territories, with Norman magnates opting for John and the nobles of Anjou, Maine, and Touraine proclaiming his nephew Arthur of Brittany as their lord, gave Philip Augustus an opening for mischief-making. He could revive his family's policy of pitting one member of the Plantagenet family against another by supporting young Arthur's claims. When conflict resumed by 1202, it turned in the French monarch's favour, whether due to John Lackland's many personal failings or to larger shifts in politics, economics, and society that had their beginning before his accession. John's failure to hold the Norman duchy and his loss of other portions of his Angevin patrimony to Philip Augustus defined his entire reign. After Normandy was lost in 1204, John directed his energies toward organizing a giant campaign for its recovery, and the collapse of his campaign in 1214 almost totally tarnished his reputation.

Richard Lionheart had raised and spent money on a scale like no previous English monarch. He financed his crusading venture by selling favours and offices recklessly; then his capture during his return from the Holy Land required a ransom of £100,000, necessitating staggering levies on his subjects; and once Richard was ransomed in early 1194, warfare against Philip Augustus required still more resources. Richard made his heaviest demands on his English subjects, since his island kingdom was the richest of all his possessions. In another rich province, Normandy, the Lionheart also expanded his revenues despite the ravages its inhabitants were suffering from the war on their soil; Richard was raising almost £25,000 sterling annually in the duchy by 1198, a figure equal to his English income. By the time of John's flagging defence of Normandy in 1202 and 1203, it was drained, yielding less than half its 1198 income, and the formerly wealthy duchy was dependent on sums shipped across the Channel from England. The English king also had to contend with Capetian threats to his mother Eleanor's duchy of Aquitaine, and its defence depended on cash from England and Normandy. Such great military costs led some scholars to conclude that the impossibility of matching the Capetians' growing revenues would have prevented any English ruler, no matter how capable, from defending the Angevin 'empire' during the first decade of the thirteenth century.

A key problem for the Angevin kings in governing their far-flung possessions was the differing degrees of authority over their island-kingdom and over their continental possessions. In England, they were sovereign lords bearing a royal title, and with an efficient exchequer to collect money; elsewhere, their territories' administrative efficiency ranged from almost equal to England's in Normandy to almost non-existent in Aquitaine. Their greatest handicap, however, was their vassalage within their cross-Channel lands to a superior lord, the French monarch. Philip Augustus viewed his English vassals' position of 'super-prince' within his kingdom of France as a threat to Capetian supremacy. Philip aimed to use his theoretical rights as lord over Normandy, Anjou and Aquitaine as a practical weapon for subverting his English rivals' authority, a pretext for armed intervention in their lands in western France, yet Richard Lionheart and later John Lackland stubbornly refused to see the danger in their fealty to him. They seemed unable to counter the Capetians' prestige, achieved by cloaking themselves in the near-sacred status of their Carolingian precursors, and Capetian lordship eventually would spell disaster for the empire assembled by Henry II.

Philip won tacit recognition of his claim to superiority over Richard and John when both paid him relief on their succession to their French possessions. Then in 1191 at the beginning of the Third Crusade, Richard acknowledged that he was Philip Augustus's liege man and that his French territories were fiefs held of Philip. John, in a treaty of 1200, formally acknowledged that his vassalage meant subjection to the French royal court's jurisdiction. Soon Philip Augustus's right to summon the English king to Paris to judge him gained acceptance among John's French subjects, and the royal court became an alternative power to which they could appeal. Such a plea by one of John's Poitevin vassals in 1201 brought his condemnation in Philip's court as a disobedient vassal, setting in motion the disasters that ended in the English king's loss of Normandy, his Loire valley patrimony, and much of Poitou.

King John had created an opportunity for Philip Augustus to exercise his lordship in August 1200 with his marriage to Isabelle, heir to the county of Angoulême. This impetuous act without regard for his bride's prior betrothal to Hugh IX, lord of Lusignan in lower Poitou, angered and humiliated the powerful Lusignan family and also outraged other important Poitevin nobles. On the surface, John's marriage appeared an astute strategic move, for it gave him control of the Angoumois, a territory on the main road from Poitou to Gascony that would have kept key castles from falling under the Lusignans' domination. Despite

John's theft of young Isabelle, he made no effort to placate Hugh's wounded pride, and his contemptuous treatment spurred Hugh's clan to revolt. By autumn 1201, Hugh de Lusignan had taken his complaint to Philip's court; and the next spring, the French royal court condemned John for failing to appear in Paris to answer his Poitevin vassal's charges. John's condemnation brought on another round of the long Capetian–Plantagenet conflict, with Philip taking advantage of the crisis to revive Arthur of Brittany's claim to Henry II's heritage. The French king put the fifteen-year-old Arthur at the head of an invading force headed for Poitou in the summer of 1202, while he led an invasion of Normandy. The revived conflict would result in the murder of Arthur at his uncle's order, defections by major Angevin and Poitevin magnates, and John's loss of his Loire valley lands.

The Capetian advance into Normandy proved unstoppable, and John fled his duchy for England at the end of 1203. Since Richard's last years, the combination of ruthless taxation and repeated French invasions had exhausted the Normans, alienating them from their duke, and their indifference turned to outright hostility by 1203, causing defections of Norman nobles to the Capetians. The Normans, especially the clergy, began to look favourably on the prospect of peaceful rule under Philip Augustus, who presented himself as a protector of ecclesiastical liberties and a model of good lordship. By May 1204, Philip had almost completely overrun the duchy, and Rouen surrendered without a fight in late June. John's failure to defend Normandy damaged his military reputation beyond repair and led historians to label him a hopeless incompetent, a striking contrast with his brother Richard, hailed as the ideal medieval general.

King John refused to accept his loss of Normandy as permanent, and he set his sights on raising whatever sums of money from England were needed to purchase allies, professional soldiers and supplies for a mammoth military operation against Philip Augustus. Preparing for an attack on Normandy in the summer of 1205, he assembled an invasion fleet and a large fighting force on the south coast of England, but resistance from some English barons to overseas military service forced him to abandon his planned expedition. In 1206, John succeeded in mounting a campaign to defend Aquitaine, and he planned expeditions to his southern French lands in 1212 and again in 1213, but his barons' resistance again forced him to abandon them. The connection between John's unquenchable thirst for money for military goals on the continent and the disenchantment of his English barons is clear. His search for funds made his subjects see him as an oppressor, a tyrannical ruler, and they had less and less interest in the fate of his lands in France.

Early in 1214, John was ready for a continental campaign planned on a grand scale and probably too ambitious, given the limitations of medieval communications and intelligence. He had constructed a pattern of alliances with princes in the Low Countries and the Rhineland for an invasion of France from the northeast to be combined with his own attack from Poitou in the southwest. John's plan was to force Philip Augustus to divide his forces between his southern and northeastern frontiers, but French forces stopped the English king in Poitou before his German and Low Country allies were ready for their assault. The Capetian heir, Prince Louis, blocked John's northward march at La Roche-aux-Moines on 2 July 1214, and he retreated to the port city of La Rochelle. It was another three weeks before John's northern allies marched into French territory, and this delay gave Philip Augustus time to mobilize his forces without fearing an attack from the rear by John. The armies of the French monarch and John's allies met at Bouvines in that rarity in medieval warfare, a pitched battle. Philip, confident of victory, risked all on the outcome of a single battle, and he won his gamble. The battle of Bouvines was a decisive victory for the Capetian monarch and a fatal blow to John's scheme of reconquest, showing his English subjects that all his frantic extortion of treasure had been futile. When the defeated king returned to his island kingdom in autumn 1214 with his reputation in tatters, a revolt by discontented barons was almost certain. John's insistence on levying a scutage to pay for his thwarted plan ensured the certainty of a baronial rising, for it heralded levies of funds for another attempt to recover Normandy.

Crisis over the succession to the archbishopric of Canterbury

John had the bad luck to be England's king during the pontificate of Innocent III, one of the most ambitious and aggressive of the medieval popes, a pontiff who meant to enforce all his rights and responsibilities as God's viceregent on earth. Innocent challenged the monarch's traditional authority over the English Church in a long and bitter conflict over the succession to the archbishopric of Canterbury following Archbishop Hubert Walter's death in 1205. The quarrel with the pope that followed, 1207 to 1213, coloured chroniclers' accounts of King John, filling them with accusations of his impiety and personal immorality.

Such a conflict could arise because the boundary between the English king's role in the spiritual domain and the Church's power in the secular sphere remained undefined, even after the quarrel between John's father and Thomas Becket. Because bishops were also barons, holding large estates of the king and owing him quotas of knights as well as serving as royal officials and counsellors, English monarchs tried to keep control over episcopal elections. They regularly secured the election of royal clerks as reward for faithful service, and they expected their former courtiers to continue to further royal interests as prelates. An example is Hubert Walter, who had acted as Richard Lionheart's justiciar and later as John's chancellor while heading the English Church. Although many English ecclesiastics accepted a royal role in governing the Church, the murder of Thomas Becket had embittered a number of clerical intellectuals and soured them toward the Angevin dynasty.

Details of the election of Hubert Walter's successor are complicated, involving three separate elections and numerous irregularities that allowed the various parties involved in the process to appeal to the pope. John had resented the restraining influence of his over-mighty servant, and he looked forward to selecting his own archbishop of Canterbury. He wished to position his own man in the powerful post, someone in whom he had complete confidence; and he assumed that, like previous English monarchs, he could control the selection of a new archbishop, although custom dictated formal election by the monks who constituted the cathedral chapter. The Canterbury monks first elected one of their own number, then under royal pressure they held a second election, and when it resulted in the election of the king's candidate some of the monks appealed to Rome. John's furious response to the Canterbury monks' double dealing in refusing to obey him and ratify his choice for Canterbury is not surprising. Innocent III annulled the two previous elections and proposed that the monks present in Rome for the appeal hold a third one. In 1206, he pushed forward his own candidate, Stephen Langton, a cardinal at the papal court who was English by birth, but had made his career in the schools of Paris. Not surprisingly, the monks followed the pope's lead and elected Langton as archbishop of Canterbury. The pope's thrusting his own choice on the king was deliberately provocative, certain to bring on a confrontation, and when John withheld royal assent, the pontiff consecrated Langton at Rome in June 1207 without the king's acquiescence.

John was furious at being frustrated in securing his own candidate's election, and he protested on two grounds. First, he declared that Stephen Langton was unacceptable to him as an English subject who had passed his career in Paris, capital of his chief enemy. Langton's connections in Paris, where he belonged to a circle of pro-Capetian scholars, were bound to arouse John's suspicions. Second, the king complained of a violation of traditional royal rights, for English kings had made episcopal appointments since pre-Conquest times. Innocent brushed aside John's misgivings, for he held royal objections to be irrelevant once Langton was duly elected and consecrated. Langton's own thoughts on the matter are not known, but he was either imperceptive or presumptuous to believe that he could function effectively as primate of England in the face of determined royal opposition.

The king took reprisals against the Canterbury monks who had defied him, expelling them from their house and sending them fleeing into exile; also he barred Langton from entering England, seizing his archiepiscopal estates. Innocent offered to negotiate with John, commissioning three English bishops to conduct the negotiations, but authorizing them to proclaim an interdict over the kingdom if the king remained adamant against Langton. The purpose of an interdict was to pressure a prince indirectly through his subjects, for denying the people the comfort of the Church's sacraments was expected to inspire them to compel their ruler to submit. When the commissioners proclaimed an interdict in March 1208, the king was enraged, regarding the interdict as a papal declaration of war, and he lost little time before retaliating. He confiscated all the English Church's property, increasing his revenues by about £11,000 each year that the interdict was in force. This flow of funds from church lands into the royal treasury may have curbed John's interest in coming to terms, since it improved his financial position without burdening his lay subjects with new taxes.

Even though papal proclamation of the interdict initiated psychological warfare, it did not preclude periodic negotiations throughout the crisis. King John held out a possibility of accepting Langton, if he had guarantees that the election should not set a precedent for selecting future prelates. In any case, he saw an advantage in stretching out negotiations as a means of preventing Innocent III from imposing further sanctions. In autumn 1209, the pope, suspicious that John was stalling, increased his pressure by excommunicating the king. Because of the Church's overuse of the ban of excommunication as a political weapon, it was less feared by the faithful, and John showed no anxiety about his soul. The greatest problem that John's excommunication caused him was the departure of some clerical officials from his service, and the flight of most English bishops from the kingdom.

Negotiations continued intermittently, and by autumn 1212 John's increasingly precarious position gave him new incentives for coming to terms with the pontiff. That summer, widespread discontent among the English baronage became evident when two prominent barons fled from the kingdom after word of their conspiracy against the king leaked. Also a diplomatic revolution strengthened Innocent III's position, for he settled a long quarrel with Philip Augustus of France, and John faced the danger of a papal alliance with the Capetian king. The next steps available to the pontiff for pressuring the excommunicate English king were to release his vassals from their oaths of fealty to him, declare him deposed, and preach a crusade against him. It seems likely that the pope was preparing to declare the deposition by February 1213, and John feared that his French adversary would volunteer to implement a papal decree by leading a crusade against England. John knew that he must forestall an alliance of the pontiff and Philip against him, and he saw that the easiest way of accomplishing this was by buying off Pope Innocent and accepting the papal demands that he had earlier refused.

Negotiations resumed in the spring of 1213, when a papal agent arrived in England with the pope's peace proposals; and the English king quickly agreed, even surpassing papal demands. John offered to 'freely yield to God, and His holy apostles Peter and Paul, and to the Holy Roman Church . . . the whole kingdom of England and the whole kingdom of Ireland', surrendering his two realms and receiving them from Innocent III as fiefs of the papacy.[3] John hypocritically stated that he wished to humble himself as Christ had humbled himself for all people by placing himself and his two domains under papal lordship. To make concrete his subservience to the papacy, John bound himself and his successors to annual payments of £666 as tribute, and he also promised to make restitution to the English Church for damages suffered from the confiscation of its property.

A contemporary chronicler wrote of the English king's submission to papal lordship: 'From the moment [John] put himself under apostolic protection and made his kingdom part of St. Peter's Patrimony, there was no prince in the Roman world who would dare attack him or invade his lands to the damage of the Apostolic See'.[4] Innocent III's seeming triumph meant little to the papacy in terms of material power, but the ideological victory of John's formal acceptance of papal sovereignty satisfied the pontiff. The king had succeeded in suddenly transforming a stubborn enemy into a indulgent friend and a potent protector, averting papal blessing for Philip Augustus's projected 1213 invasion of England. He calculated correctly that his submission would flatter Innocent enormously, earn him the pope's gratitude, and induce the pope to set aside doubts about John's character. During the king's last three years, his new friend gave consistent support against the French king, against Stephen Langton and against rebellious barons, whom John could threaten with the penalties of a more potent spiritual lord standing above him. In the early thirteenth century, it was no disgrace for a monarch to be a papal vassal, and only a minority in England thought John's capitulation degrading. Unfortunately for the king, among the small number who disapproved were the anti-papal and anti-Plantagenet chroniclers of St Albans' Abbey, who influenced many later historians.

A papal legate landed in England in May 1213, and Stephen Langton followed in early July. Friction soon flared between the two ecclesiastics, for in negotiating the details of the settlement, it became clear that Langton trusted King John far less than did the pope and his legate. Innocent III was eager to bring the conflict to a conclusion, as was John, who was busy preparing his long planned expedition to France; but discussions over compensation for the Church's damages dragged on, delaying the lifting of the interdict and the king's excommunication. One of the conditions that Langton insisted on before restoring John to full communion in July 1213 was a reaffirmation of his coronation oath to protect the Church and to rule in accordance with the good old law. This condition would have unforeseen consequences, for it stirred interest in early English law among the king's extremist clerical enemies that influenced his baronial opponents.

After John's return in defeat from France in autumn 1214, he shored up support among the English clergy, granting the English Church a charter guaranteeing cathedral churches and monastic houses the right to elect freely their bishops and abbots, a promise that would be repeated in chapter 1 of Magna Carta. The king was confident that he could find ways to ensure election of his own candidates to bishoprics, and his efforts further inflamed friction with the archbishop of Canterbury. Whenever Langton opposed the king's candidates for vacant bishoprics, John could appeal to the pope; and with Innocent's support, he largely succeeded in securing his nominees' election. This betrayal of his promises angered some clerical intellectuals, strong advocates of the Church's supremacy; and in their animosity against the king, they made common cause with barons hostile to John. Foremost among such disaffected clerics was Archbishop Stephen Langton, ready to teach John's subjects that the king must be under God and divine law.

Continuing financial crisis

Throughout King John's reign, his financial exigency constituted a continual crisis that complicated his conflicts with Philip Augustus of France, with the Church and with his barons. Costs of warfare had crept upward steadily throughout the last half of the twelfth century, and the financial burden of fighting to defend Plantagenet lands in France had become heavier following Richard Lionheart's return from German captivity in 1194. Almost continuous conflicts demanded mercenary soldiers willing to remain in the field for long periods, and advances in military science required construction of more elaborate fortifications and the hiring of siege engineers and crossbowmen. Less often noticed was the cost of the impressive standard of living that John maintained for himself and his household, for he took great pleasure in the splendour of royalty. Records from his reign list expenses for costly banquets and silver tableware, ornate jewellery, fur-trimmed robes, and renovation and redecoration of royal residences and hunting lodges.

Recent studies of Angevin royal finances point to a dramatic divergence between Henry II's demands for money and the heavier demands of Richard I and John. Expenditures rose rapidly in the Lionheart's last years, and a comparison of English royal revenues before and after his return from the crusade confirms his growing thirst for money. Before 1194, annual royal revenues averaged slightly less than £12,000; but in Richard's final five years, revenues doubled, averaging around £25,000. In the first years following Richard's death, John's annual revenue was no more than his late brother's. Although Normandy was no longer supplying funds for its own defence by 1202–3, John made little attempt to boost his income until too late to help in repulsing the French. Adding to his financial urgency, multiplying expenses for soldiers and military supplies, was rapid inflation in England that caused an unprecedented surge in prices between 1200 and 1206 and rose at a slower rate in following years. It is unlikely that John's money-raising offset the rate of inflation before 1208, when his ruthlessness began to pay off, and he accumulated enormous stocks of cash for his projected military expedition to retake Normandy. In John's middle years, his income rose to £83,000 or possibly as much as £145,000 by 1211, if large sums diverted directly to his chamber, his household treasury, without accounting at the exchequer, are included.

A key to grasping John's financial crisis is a comparison of his resources with those of his rival, Philip Augustus. Although medieval financial records are notoriously spotty and no French royal accounts earlier than 1202–3 survive, research on the limited materials suggests that the balance of wealth was tipping toward Philip. In the time of Philip's father, Louis VII, the English king had held the advantage of superior wealth, but by the turn of the century Philip was gaining an edge in resources, able to finance larger and longer wars. Capetian government had grown more efficient in the 1190s, and acquisition of additional territories for the royal domain increased Philip's income at the same time as Richard Lionheart was giving away the royal family's lands. Studies comparing English and French kings' revenues indicate that their income was almost equal by 1202–3, with John's intake totalling from 82 to 95 per cent of his Capetian rival's. Because of gaps in the financial records, some scholars can argue that Philip Augustus's expanding resources made John's loss of Normandy inevitable, while others conclude that John had adequate revenues and that his expulsion from the duchy was entirely due to his flawed leadership. By the time of John's 1214 campaign to recover his French lands, his single-minded pursuit of money gave him assets at least equal to those of Philip, if not greater. Such parity could only be temporary, however, for John could not keep up for long such a level of fund-raising, as the outbreak of rebellion in 1215 shows.

Because of inflation increasing the price of John's already costly wars, plus perhaps his own extravagance, his government's inadequate sources of revenue created a fiscal crisis. A key source of funds was the royal demesne, the royal family's own estates, but they were under the sheriffs' often inefficient and corrupt administration. Even worse was a steady decrease under Richard of the extent of the landed endowment recovered by Henry II; Richard undid much of his father's work, granting away so much land that John was left with far less. Without a steady, dependable flow of funds in the face of rapidly rising expenses, John had to rule as a predator, turning to every possible expedient to squeeze money out of his subjects, particularly the barons who were the richest of them.

By John's middle years, his ruthless programme for revenue-raising was evident to all, and his gouging of his subjects did not stop during the interdict, when confiscated clerical property supplemented his income. Exchequer rolls record ever more payments being offered for the king's goodwill or release from his ill-will. He even exploited his common law courts, extracting higher fees and fines from litigants and soliciting gifts for special procedures that reached a peak from 1210 to 1212. The usual price for writs, postponements of pleas, or other procedural matters was less than a pound, although larger fees were demanded of those able to pay, perhaps as much as £100. It is little wonder that some litigants voiced complaints against the sale of justice or that a chapter of Magna Carta would give heed to their outcry.

King John's harshness in exploiting the fiscal aspects of his barons' ties of vassalage to him, previously secondary to their military service, convinced many that his money-raising measures were unwarranted innovations departing from established standards of good lordship. As a result of John's thirst for money, the barons saw his relationship with them as less and less about personal loyalty, and more and more about financial obligations. His levies of scutage, supposedly payments substituting for military service, became so frequent – eleven in sixteen years – that they seemed tantamount to regular taxation, and each was assessed at a higher rate. In reaction, barons argued that custom obligated them to fight overseas only in territories held by the Anglo-Norman kings before 1154, not in Henry II's Angevin patrimony or in Aquitaine.

Most lucrative were John's rights as lord to the 'feudal incidents', payment of relief and rights of wardship and marriage of his vassals' minor heirs. The Angevin kings regarded relief for a barony, collected from an heir on his succession to his father's estates, as a negotiable figure, although the barons argued that custom limited it to £100. John often extracted much larger sums from heirs to baronies, especially if their claim was dubious, deriving from distant relatives; by 1210 the figures could reach higher than £6,000. Another privilege of royal lordship was wardship, which gave the king the right to take a deceased royal vassal's underage heir into his household and occupy the boy's landed inheritance until he came of age. Like other lords, John controlled the marriages of his deceased tenants' daughters, and he exploited this perquisite to the full, sometimes marrying them to favoured courtiers or soldiers or even selling them off to the highest bidder. Noble widows also fell into the king's custody, giving him the right to arrange their remarriages, and John exploited this right, either selling widows off to suitors seeking a great estate through marriage or pressuring them for large payments for the privilege of remaining unmarried. In 1212, a noble lady with two northern lordships, already widowed and remarried three times, offered the king £3,330 to escape marrying a fourth time.

As a result of King John's exploitation of the feudal incidents, many noble youths entered adulthood mired in debt, and purchasers of custodies, marriages or other favours also became crown debtors. John strengthened the law of the exchequer for more efficient pursuit of his debtors, disciplining delinquents by taking their lands into the king's hand, even imprisoning them. Many barons assumed, mistakenly, that their high status would protect them from paying their full debt, for John tightened or loosened pressure for repayment as he saw fit. Those enjoying the king's favour were not pressured to pay outstanding debts and were pardoned occasionally, while those suffering from his ill-will lived in fear of demands for payment that would bring loss of lands or imprisonment. An alternative for crown debtors was to repay the king by borrowing cash at high interest rates from Jewish money-lenders, although this did not improve their situation. In practical terms, they remained the king's debtors, since England's Jews were royal wards and a special exchequer enforced repayment of their loans. The Jews were an important financial resource for the king, tolerated in the kingdom only because their money-lending profited him and because their precarious position made their own treasure accessible to him. In crises, he could always shake them down for large sums of cash.

King John needed a new source of income, a general levy on all classes that would tap the kingdom's resources effectively. In most of western Europe, general taxation had vanished with the collapse of the Carolingian Empire, and one of the last, an Anglo-Saxon land tax, had disappeared by the mid-twelfth century. The Church's concern for funding crusades revived interest in general taxation, and in 1188 Henry II's preparations for a projected expedition to Palestine included the so-called Saladin tithe, a percentage of the value of the goods of those not embarking on the crusade. When huge sums of money had to be raised to pay Richard Lionheart's ransom in 1193, his agents in England demanded a quarter of the kingdom's moveable wealth. The levy for Richard's ransom resembled both a 'gracious aid', a baronial obligation, and a tallage falling on the peasant farmers of the king's own lands and the inhabitants of royal boroughs, though broader in application. John followed this precedent of general taxation with another percentage tax on personal property, a seventh in 1203. In 1207, he demanded a thirteenth, the first time that such a tax was imposed without the excuse of an emergency; none the less, it was an extraordinary levy, and he took care to secure 'the common counsel and assent of our council'.[5] John's thirteenth was very profitable, raising £60,000, but aroused such spirited opposition that he thought it inadvisable to repeat this novel form of taxation.

King John's barons and many lesser-ranking subjects convinced them-selves that his regular royal resources were sufficient and that he should be able to 'live of his own', that is, to manage on his traditional sources of income. Just as the English were tiring of constant demands for cash, John sought still more funds in the years 1204 to 1214 to fill a huge war chest for his campaign to recover his lost lands in France. The English barons were losing interest in their ruler's overseas possessions, however, and they could see no benefit for themselves in his ambitious military plans. When John returned from France in the autumn of 1214, not only had he suffered defeat, but he had emptied his treasury. His insolvency in the months before Magna Carta weakened his hand in handling the rebel barons, and his poverty partially explains his indecision in dealing with militant barons' demands in the spring of 1215.

John's barons and their discontents

Mutual mistrust characterized King John's relations with his barons, and his inability to win their loyalty contributed to his loss of Normandy and his lack of success in recovering his lost French lands. While John's suspicious nature and personal vendettas against individual barons added to his problems, the very nature of Angevin government made predictable a rebellion early in the thirteenth century. Late in the previous century, Henry II's reforms had tipped the balance of power in England from the barons toward the royal government, and the pervasiveness of Angevin rule – its expansion of royal jurisdiction and insatiable financial demands – made accusations of predatory kingship almost inevitable. The tyrannical Angevin structure challenged the magnates' traditional dominance over their tenants and undermined their authority in the counties. It is not surprising that a monastic annalist summarized the baronial opposition to John as a struggle for 'the laws and good customs of the realm which had been perverted by the obstinacy of the king and by the greed of wrongheaded foreigners'.[6]

King John's failure to enlist the devotion of his baronage contributed to his other failures, for it was still a formidable force, though weakened by Angevin innovations. Barons with their armed men and castles were capable of challenging royal control of the countryside with military force, and any monarch needed to keep them contented if his realm was to remain peaceful. Although many barons had grievances against the king, only a minority, most with personal grievances, was goaded into taking up arms against John in the winter of 1214–15. At least two claimed that their wives or daughters had been objects of his lust, and others had relatives who had been victims of his cruelty. Lustfulness was a complaint that monastic writers commonly levelled against unpopular princes, but the accusation against John was more serious because it was claimed that his victims were noble ladies. A more plausible explanation for the barons' rebellion is resentment of John's endless demands for military service and funds to finance wars for his overseas possessions.

Early-thirteenth-century English barons and knights had more interest in improving and enlarging their estates than in performing military service owed to the king as a condition of holding their lands. Baronial reluctance to perform service overseas had increased, since few English barons any longer held cross-Channel lands that would have motivated them to join John in defending Normandy. The baronage showed even less enthusiasm for projected expeditions to Poitou, and the king had to abandon Poitevin campaigns planned for 1205, 1212 and 1213. When he summoned his feudal levy to gather at Portsmouth in July 1213, a number of northern barons refused to cross the sea with him. Since John was convinced that custom sanctioned summoning his men to serve overseas, he saw their refusal as tantamount to rebellion and proposed military action against them. The king prepared to march northwards with a mercenary force to punish the recalcitrant barons, but the newly arrived archbishop of Canterbury, Stephen Langton, insisted that he proceed against them only after judgement in the royal court and threatened to excommunicate John's soldiers. When the Poitevin expedition finally embarked early in 1214, however, the barons' chivalric ethos outweighed their dissatisfaction, and most set sail, with only a handful of northern barons refusing to serve or to send their knights. Enfeebled as John was in October when he returned to England, he still insisted on collecting a scutage from barons who had not participated in his failed expedition. His demand aroused wide protest, especially in the north and East Anglia, regions that later became rebel centres.

Undoubtedly the major factor in John's troubles with his barons was his insistence on increasing their contributions to royal revenues and their resistance to any change in their traditional obligations. John abandoned the general levy on moveable goods after 1207, finding it easier to manipulate his perquisites of lordship, insisting on rigorous enforcement of the services and financial obligations by which the barons held their estates. By 1208 and 1209, John's aggressive use of the feudal incidents was surpassing his predecessors' practice, and because he was directly involved in the details of fund-raising, many barons blamed him for entangling them in debt. As the leading living authority on King John and Magna Carta characterizes the 1215 baronial opposition, 'It was a rebellion of the king's debtors'.[7]

Most of the northern barons who would join the rebellion were deeply in debt to the king or to the Jews, although it was not only northerners who fell into debt. Barons became crown debtors because of John's demands for high reliefs, which they regarded as fixed by custom, or by costly legal challenges to their claims to land that they felt was rightfully theirs. Rival claimants to disputed successions to baronies sought to outbid each other with large sums to purchase royal support for their claim. Speculative ventures caused some to fall into the exchequer's clutches, luring them to compete with royal servants in extravagant offerings for custodies, rights to marriages, and other means of enlarging their estates that they thought would prove profitable. King John was a master at entangling subjects who had lost his favour in financial difficulties and then using their indebtedness to impose political discipline. To fall into the king's debt risked arousing the full force of the king's anger, possibly seizure of lands, or even imprisonment, unlawful acts from the victim's point of view, although well within the law of the exchequer in John's eyes. For some unlucky crown debtors, their only hope was to regain the king's goodwill with a substantial cash offering.

The most shocking instance of John's harrying a royal debtor is his cruel treatment of his former favourite, William de Braose. John maintained that the outlawing of William was 'according to the law and custom of England' because of his violent resistance against seizure of his lands after he was unable to make good on an offering of over £13,000. William de Braose died in exile in Paris in 1211; his wife and eldest son suffered imprisonment and death by starvation on John's order; and his grandsons were still imprisoned several years after the king's death. The hounding of Braose and his family to exile and death was an example to the barons that the king would apply rigorously his law of the exchequer to the greatest crown debtors, even magnates who had previously basked in royal favour. It taught John's greatest subjects that his notion of legal procedure bore little resemblance to their own perception of proceeding by lawful judgement.

Numerous baronial complaints against King John concerned his refusal to abide by custom in their disputes with him, and the rolls of cases from his reign record frequent payments to speed, smooth or otherwise alter the course of justice. The royal court opened and closed to litigants at his will, and John could revoke barons' cases for personal hearing before him. Despite an appearance of venality, the king's common law courts attracted more and more suits by ordinary free men, often involving small plots of land, that were settled by juries, providing a standard of justice that the people found acceptable. It is one of the paradoxes of John's reign that the common law courts were achieving a high standard of justice at the same time that the barons' cries against their failure to secure justice from the king were rising in volume.

This paradox is explained by the two levels of justice that existed in Angevin England. The common law courts at Westminster and itinerant justices in the shires operated at one level, settling common pleas or disputes between individuals – knights, their lords and lesser freeholders – that normally went forward without royal intervention. For the barons, royal justice operated at another level, complicated by the king's lordship; they were his tenants, holding their lands of him and owing him services and payments, yet he was their sovereign, the source of all justice. In their quarrels with the king, they lacked the legal safeguards that the common law provided to their own tenants in suits against them; they could not purchase a writ summoning a jury to determine whether the king had taken their property 'unjustly and without judgment'. Without access either to the common law's juries or to baronial courts' collective judgement of knights to adjudicate their disputes with the king, they experienced arbitrary application of the royal will through the law of the exchequer.

The barons were faced with a dilemma, for the king's active role as lord in proceedings concerning their lands caused them great insecurity about their possessions. Royal interference was almost certain in successions to baronies that did not pass directly from father to son. Worse for the barons, the exchequer was John's preferred instrument for frustrating his enemies and favouring his friends. Those who had offended the king found themselves coerced into offering exorbitant sums for properties and privileges that they considered rightfully theirs; otherwise, he might encourage his favourites to challenge their right to property with lawsuits. Not surprisingly, barons subjected to such suits felt that the king was trampling on their legitimate rights of inheritance, and among those who found him using the law's uncertainty to persecute them were some who would be rebel leaders in 1215.

While John's suspicions and vendettas poisoned his personal relations with his great men, they also felt their privileged position endangered by the increasing complexity of royal government by the end of the twelfth century. Under the Angevins, more and more professional royal servants, ambitious 'new men', often knights or clerks of obscure origin, became the king's intimate counsellors with influence rivalling that of the great officers of state. John's courtiers held exalted views of royal power that owed more to old traditions of sacral kingship or Roman law than to English custom, making them punctilious in applying his harsh policies. The aristocrats felt their traditional chivalric values threatened by a bureaucratic monarchy staffed with these new men, calculating and rational, more concerned with material gain than with chivalric virtues. Courtiers competed with barons for royal patronage, using their contacts and influence in the royal household to enrich themselves and their families and to climb up the social scale. Upstart members of the royal entourage pushed their way into the baronage with rewards from the king in the form of grants of extinct titles or marriages to heiresses.

No monarch could afford to alienate his great men by ignoring their views in favour of alien or lowborn newcomers' advice. From the time of Henry II, the concentration of courtiers around the king encouraged fears that 'household' or 'secret' government was denying his traditional counsellors, the magnates, their proper places at his side. While John claimed to take counsel with his great men, he consulted them only infrequently in formal assemblies, preferring to consult with professional officials of his household, as well as a handful of barons who happened to be present at his court. In fact, no sharp line separated matters decided by the king with his intimate counsellors from those requiring ratification by his magnates assembled in a great council. Yet the barons' notion of the mutual obligations of lords and vassals taught them that the king must take counsel with them about great matters, particularly new financial burdens. John's preference for foreigners and mercenary soldiers as his intimate counsellors heightened baronial suspicions; they most resented mercenaries from Poitou and Touraine, and a chapter of Magna Carta (50) would name such men and call for their removal from office.

Another result of Angevin enlargement and professionalization of royal government was a cleavage dividing the baronage similar to the seventeenth-century division of the gentry into 'court' and 'country' factions. Some barons always attended the king's court, and a few became successful courtiers, winning friendships and enjoying royal patronage. The 'country' barons were suspicious of courtiers, with little taste for the court and royal servants. Northern barons were especially likely to remain in the countryside, preoccupied with their estates and family interests. They saw such local officers as sheriffs undermining their long dominant position in the community, threatening their traditional autonomy, and they resented the royal favourites holding such posts. Competition with courtiers by country barons in search of estates for their sons and rewards for their military retainers was bound to be unequal. Country-dwelling barons seeking royal bounty would leave the court disappointed, and among the rebels in 1215 were a number whose ambitions were frustrated by competition with John's favourites.

Also threatening barons' local power were Henry II's judicial innovations that supplanted the traditional pattern of baronial courts settling tenants' disputes. Private courts were losing influence throughout the century as ties of homage and fealty between lords and their men evolved into tenurial relationships, but Henry's legal reforms hastened their decline, allowing tenants easy transfers of their suits into the common law courts. Increasingly, knights of the counties had direct contacts with the central administration, bringing suits in the royal courts, serving on commissions and juries, holding new local offices, and the barons were losing their old role as intermediaries between their men and the royal government. Yet some connections still bound knights closely to the baronage. Both groups shared a common culture, holding in common chivalric values; but the strongest bonds were those of family, for many members of the knightly class were kinsmen of barons.

Not all the knights' contacts with royal government were positive, for they could encounter the same harshness from John's officials that their baronial lords endured. About a quarter of the knights in England held some land directly of the king, and as his tenants-in-chief they experienced for themselves the exploitation of his direct lordship. Despite weakened bonds of personal lordship, barons and their knights came together in shared antipathy toward John's arbitrary and exploitative governance. Some would follow their lords in taking up arms against the king, and others joined the rebellion even though their lords remained loyal to John.

English barons responded to the political and social changes of the twelfth century by reasserting their special position in the kingdom. They were versed in the custom of the realm, by which they meant the good old law of Edward the Confessor and Henry I, not the Angevin kings' innovations, and they considered themselves its defenders. Traditional lord–vassal relationships taught them fundamental notions of good governance. They learned from their experience as lords that a free man had privileges denied to the unfree, at the least protection from extralegal punishment, and they knew that no free man should be dispossessed of land or goods except by a lawful judgement in his lord's court in which his fellow free tenants participated. While some precepts of Roman and canon law influenced them, their ideal of good government was largely an idealized version of an eleventh-century great baron's court, with the king surrounded by high officials chosen from among his great men, governing by their counsel and sharing with them the duty of giving judgement. Although the Angevin kings' expansion of royal authority had threatened the barons' power, that power was not broken, and the barons could hope to achieve their ideal through armed revolt.

Notes

1. Stubbs (1872–73), 2: 232; also known as the Barnwell Annals.
2. Galbraith (1945), 120.
3. Warren (1978), 208.
4. Cheney (1979), 339, citing Walter of Coventry.
5. Stubbs (1913), 278.
6. Gransden (1974), 335, quoting the Stanley Chronicle.
7. Holt (1961), 34.

chapter 3

THE MAKING AND UNMAKING
OF MAGNA CARTA,
1215–16

King John's crises culminated in the baronial uprising of 1215–16 that resulted in Magna Carta. Unlike earlier English revolts, the great rebellion of John's last years was a broad-based movement, not aimed at mere amendment of personal grievances but at redressing general charges of misgovernment. In Stephen's reign, individual barons had taken advantage of the king's weakness to coerce royal charters granting them privileges, but in 1215 a large corps of barons co-operated to force John to grant a general charter of liberties including safeguards for ordinary free men. Baronial dissatisfaction was not due to John's unpopularity alone, for twelfth-century centralization of government set in motion a broad backlash that would have caused trouble for a monarch with a more winning personality. Unlike seventeenth-century foes of Stuart absolutism who looked back to immemorial custom, the barons turned to the laws of the king's great-grandfather, Henry I, whose reign they imagined as a society marked by good lordship. In their view, the Angevins' extension of royal government into all corners of the kingdom and over all classes constituted unlawful innovations, challenging baronial control over the countryside. According to a contemporary chronicler, the 1215 rebellion aimed at abolition of the evil customs 'which both the father and brother of the king had raised up to the detriment of the Church and kingdom, together with the abuses which [King John] had added'.[1]

By the early thirteenth century, animosity provoked by the Angevin kings' authoritarian government was promoting a sense of community among the baronage. Although a handful of barons with personal grievances had begun to plot against John earlier, a large-scale rising only took shape after John's return in defeat from Poitou in autumn 1214. By then, those opposing John were thinking of the baronage as a corporate body with collective rights and responsibilities. They would form a *conjuratio*, a band bound together by oath in pursuit of a common goal based on principle, not solely to avenge personal grievances. The

1215–16 rebellion, with a sworn band of leaders and a reform programme, points toward the revolt in John's son Henry III's middle years and to similar reform movements in the later Middle Ages.

Confrontations culminating in rebellion

King John's personal slights and financial extortions against individual barons set off rumblings of wider discontent as early as 1208 and 1209. By then, he had reason to feel insecure about frontier territories, where nobles holding great liberties had potential for successful opposition. One source of worry for the king was the strength of the marcher barons of South Wales, whose substantial landholdings in Ireland made him uneasy. Another was the almost autonomous position of the barons in the north of England. They resented John's efforts at bringing their landholdings under closer royal control; moreover, several had suffered injustices or financial exactions at his hands. A letter of Philip Augustus in 1209 to one of the northern lords suggests that they were conspiring with the French monarch. Evidently, John had some inkling of a conspiracy that summer that included the king of the Scots, William the Lion, and fears for control of northern England likely had a role in his decision to launch a campaign against William. John's advance with a large army toward northern frontier in August 1209 inspired the Scottish monarch to seek peace, however, and the show of force likely led potential conspirators to conclude that the time was not yet ripe for action.

The next conflict between barons and the king came in the summer of 1212, when a handful of barons hatched a conspiracy to murder him during a military expedition to Wales. John had heard rumours of a baronial plot to kill him before launching his Welsh campaign, and the news forced him to disband in mid-August the large army summoned for an invasion of North Wales. His demand for hostages from barons suspected of being parties to the plot caused Robert fitz Walter, a leading East Anglian baron, to flee to the French court and Eustace de Vesci, a Northumberland lord, to take refuge in Scotland. John moved quickly to seize their castles, and he outlawed them and their followers, some of whom were prominent clerics. In Paris, Robert fitz Walter met English clerics who had fled there during the papal interdict, and he depicted himself as a devoted son of the Church suffering for refusal to serve an excommunicate king. As a result of ingratiating himself with clerical dissidents, Robert was included in the 1213 settlement ending the Canterbury succession crisis and returned to England with Stephen Langton and exiled clerics who had become John's ideological adversaries.

This 1212 plot led to a crucial loss of political initiative for King John, and it factored in his decision to settle his long quarrel with the pope the next year. Settlement of the Canterbury succession crisis gave his baronial critics clerical allies in formulating a reform programme based on restoration of good old custom. Rumours of plots continued, pushing the king into contradictory policies of conciliation and repression. Early in 1213 and in 1214, he moved to moderate his previous harsh political and financial policies, naming commissioners to investigate wrong-doing by royal officials in Yorkshire and Lincolnshire and replacing some sheriffs in northern shires. Also John attempted to conciliate some of those alienated by his heavy financial demands, negotiating new schedules for their debt payments. In November 1213, he made vague promises to the northern barons 'to restore their ancient liberties'.[2] At the same time, however, John worked to bring the barons under closer control, demanding custody of their castles, surrender of hostages for their good behaviour and charters of fealty binding them to him. Such repressive steps and the king's continuation of fierce money-raising efforts for his projected campaign on the continent counteracted any conciliatory gestures and raised new fears among the baronage.

By 1213 and 1214 John's tenants in the north of England were protesting against military service in Poitou, insisting that their overseas service was limited to the old Anglo-Norman lands across the Channel. John was never hesitant about disciplining his men for default of service, and he prepared to march northward on a punitive expedition to punish barons who had rejected their 1213 summons. He was prevented only by the last-minute persuasion of his great men, among them the new archbishop of Canterbury, Stephen Langton, who had started seeking influence among the baronage almost as soon as he arrived in England. When John's Poitevin expedition finally got under way early in 1214, however, only a few northern barons refused to follow the king across the sea.

Although many barons and knights had grievances against King John, only a minority would move actively toward rebellion during the autumn and winter of 1214–15. Opposition was concentrated in three regions: the north of England, the west, and East Anglia. Most extreme in hostility were northern barons, united in their hatred of the king because of private complaints. A group of eighteen who held lands as far south as Lincolnshire felt that John had wrongfully withheld from them lands, castles, or other privileges that rightfully belonged to them; or if granted, the price he had required was too high, locking them in deep debt to the exchequer or to the Jews. They appeared to contemporaries to form the core of baronial opposition; indeed, chroniclers continued to label the rebels 'Northerners' even after it became evident that the movement extended beyond that region. Centred in Essex and East Anglia were twelve powerful rebel barons who included one of the earliest defectors, Robert fitz Walter. Much of the rebel leadership came from this eastern region, with East Anglians named as almost half the members of the committee of twenty-five that would be charged with enforcing Magna Carta. A less well defined group of ten or so barons scattered in western shires also rebelled. In the spring of 1215, no more than forty-five significant landholders can be counted among the rebels, only thirty-nine of them with definite baronial rank; by autumn 1216 when John died, the number of rebel barons had risen to ninety-seven. It seems unlikely, then, that a majority of the English baronage defected to the baronial cause, although many may have passively sympathized with the rebels without taking up arms. Some royalist barons were less than enthusiastic followers of John; they deplored his arbitrary and ruthless rule and yearned for some means of restraining him, yet rejected taking up arms against their anointed and crowned monarch. Such lukewarm royalists were capable of looking beyond class or personal interest to seek wider public good and to preserve positive aspects of the Angevin revolution in government.

Although many knights joined in the baronial movement opposing the king, it was not because of ties of fealty binding them tightly to their lords; indeed, many held lands of several different lords, weakening personal loyalties. Earlier baronial rebellions had centred on personal grievances of a few magnates, whose knights readily followed them into battle; by the early thirteenth century, however, knights were no longer so eager for combat. They were losing their predominantly military character and changing into a rural landlord class resembling the later gentry. Benefiting from Henry II's expansion of royal justice that liberated them from the baronial courts' jurisdiction, knights no longer considered their estates precarious holdings dependent on performing services for their lords. As a result, the rebel barons had to rely largely on landless retainers for their fighting force. Some knights doubtless shared the outlook of their lords, for many traced their ancestry to baronial families, binding them with ties of kinship as well as lordship. They took up arms against John, following their lords or their kin; others had personal experience of John's tyranny and joined the rebel ranks even when their lords remained loyal to the king.

The knightly class had grievances against John that, unlike specific personal complaints of barons, could not be redressed through private arrangements with the king. These knightly complaints would force the negotiators framing Magna Carta to think in terms of generalized remedies and would make an impact on the Charter's nature, incorporating general political principles applying to all free men. John sought to exploit the widening gap between baronial and knightly interests in order to enlist knightly support. In the summer of 1212 and again in autumn 1213, he summoned representatives of the knights to meetings; at the first, sheriffs summoned six from each shire to hear his wishes, and at the second, four from each shire were sent 'to speak with us concerning the affairs of our realm'.[3] Although these meetings may have marked the first kingdom-wide assembly of spokesmen for the knights of the shires, John hardly deserves credit for being a founder of the House of Commons.

The leaders of the baronial rebels fail to inspire confidence as defenders of English liberties against an oppressive Angevin political system; few can be credited with statesmen's responsibility or dedication to the public welfare that would have prepared them for formulating a coherent reform programme. Members of the group of twenty-five executors of Magna Carta would fail to distinguish themselves with deep loyalty to the principle of the rule of law during Henry III's minority. Prominent rebels would have no place among the statesmen surrounding the boy-king, in contrast to royalist barons working to restore England to peace and order following John's death in the midst of civil war. Leading rebel leaders such as Robert fitz Walter or Eustace de Vesci, who had been implicated in plots against John as early as the summer of 1212, had no broad political vision. Fitz Walter had little experience in government, and his earlier attempts to enforce claims against others, rejecting legal processes in favour of force and violence, give little hint of respect for law and custom. Robert's obstinacy in the weeks after the settlement of June 1215 also casts doubt on his statesmanship. An extremist standing in the way of implementation of Magna Carta, his refusal to return London to the king as agreed at Runnymede would contribute to renewal of fighting by the end of summer.

The propensity toward violence among the rebel leadership long led some historians to condemn the entire English baronage as feudal reactionaries, illiterate louts lacking any sense of public responsibility and pursuing only selfish goals, and they suggest that learned clerics supplied ideological support. Many writers assign credit for the demand for a charter of liberties to Archbishop Stephen Langton, convinced that the barons were incapable of such an idea. They follow Roger of Wendover's chronicle, source of numerous misconceptions about John's reign, which credits Langton with suggesting the laws of Henry I as the model for a political reform programme as early as August 1213. The chronicler reports rumours of the archbishop's discussion of the laws of Henry I at

St Paul's Cathedral, London. According to Wendover, Langton met secretly with a group of barons, showing them Henry I's coronation charter and espousing it as a means for reclaiming their ancient liberties. It is certain that the new primate sought influence among the barons, instructing them about their lawful rights, and John soon suspected that he was too hostile to act as a neutral mediator. Although Langton shared the barons' hatred for King John, stories of such early conversations with the barons are doubtful, since other evidence dates his discussions of Henry I's charter more than a year later.

While the rebel leaders nursed personal grievances against the king, convinced that he had cheated them of inherited lands, castles, or other privileges, other barons' capacity to look beyond themselves to the public good invalidates blanket condemnations of the entire baronage. Some rebels recognized a need to appeal to uncommitted barons who were alarmed by John's arbitrary rule, yet placed high value on loyalty to their sworn monarch. Due to Angevin governmental innovations, both barons and knights had gained experience in the shires serving in lesser governmental posts, and had thereby participated in what has been called 'self-government by the king's command'. Both political concepts that trickled down to the barons from clerical ideologues and their own experience in the common law courts as jurors and as litigants gave them a healthy respect for the principle of 'due process of law'. Furthermore, many among the baronage, whether rebels or royalists, could extrapolate from their own experiences as lords over men a conviction that the king ought to govern 'by judgement' and 'by counsel'. Both barons' and knights' experience in the private courts of great men taught them that there was little difference between 'judgement' and 'counsel', for traditions of dispute settlement stretching back to the barbarian kingdoms favoured discussion and face-saving compromise. In their lords' tribunals, they saw disputes settled through informal negotiation as often as through formal legal proceedings. It was not a large step for them, then, to move from demanding that John govern 'by judgement' to an insistence that he also govern 'by counsel'.

Many barons and knights had at least limited levels of literacy by the early thirteenth century, enabling them to read Latin charters or Anglo-Norman romances. Literacy gave them access to such key documents as the Laws of Edward the Confessor or the coronation charters of the Anglo-Norman monarchs, some of which were available in French translations by 1215. Not only Stephen Langton but other clerical intellectuals opposing King John, such as the canons of St Paul's, London, were happy to point out precedents found in these half-forgotten documents. The Canterbury succession conflict had strengthened hostile feelings against the Angevin dynasty lingering from Henry II's long quarrel with Becket, and some ecclesiastics, eager to subject the king to divine law, promoted the barons' goal of curbing royal power. Copies of Henry I's coronation charter convinced disaffected barons that a similar royal charter could supply them with a mechanism for tempering King John's tyranny. Resuscitating the good old law supposedly predating Henry II was useful propaganda for both barons and ecclesiastics, presenting a contrast with the Angevins' wicked innovations.

In the early thirteenth century, charters of liberties or privileges were familiar, for it was not uncommon for communities to purchase them from their lords. London had won a large measure of self-government from the king in the twelfth century and had formed communes in such times of weak royal power as Stephen's reign and Richard's absence on crusade. Following London's lead, other English towns and a few shires secured collective grants of liberties that gave them rights to select their own officials. John had demanded £2,000 from the citizens of London for confirmation of their privileges in 1200, and in early May 1215 in the hope of forestalling an alliance with the barons, he issued a new charter of liberties. He failed to win over the Londoners, however, and shortly after they received their new charter, they would betray him and open the city to the rebels. Not long before the rebellion, the knights and free tenants of two northern baronies were granted charters of liberties by their lords; the charter granted by one of them, the earl of Chester, contained features found later in Magna Carta. The barons had ample precedents for their call for a charter of liberties to curb King John; Magna Carta's novelty was its general grant of liberties to all free men of the kingdom, not to a specific community.

Nothing came of complaints of tyrannical royal governance before John's 1214 expedition to France, but once he returned from Poitou in October following his grand strategy's collapse, his low standing emboldened his baronial opponents. Not long after the king's return to England proposals for reform were circulating as early as November, when, according to Roger of Wendover, hostile barons gathered at Bury St Edmunds Abbey. The chronicler reports that before leaving Bury, they pledged themselves to press for reforms, grounding their proposals on Henry I's coronation charter, and they begged the king to confirm his coronation oath and his predecessors' charters. Whatever the truth of the Bury meeting, baronial dissatisfaction was now unmistakable, and John could not avoid summoning a great council to meet in London on the feast of the Epiphany, 6 January 1215. By the time of the London council, disaffected barons had formed a sworn association or *conjuratio*, binding themselves together to seek redress. A group of them arrived fully armed, but the king put off responding to the baronial demands, accusing them of disrespectful manners and threats of force. John's opponents alleged that he not only refused to recognize 'their ancient and customary liberties', but sought to force them to promise in writing 'never again to demand such liberties from him or his successors'.[4] He postponed discussions to another council that he summoned to meet in Northampton just after Easter.

The king's indecision in facing the threat of rebellion after the Epiphany council in London resembles his lethargic response to Philip Augustus's attack on Normandy in 1202. John began preparations for war, sending to Poitou for soldiers and strengthening royal castle garrisons; however, he soon reversed his plans and sent word that the troops would not be needed. While his policy in early 1215 appears ineffectual and inconsistent, he saw that delaying tactics served him better than direct confrontation. The king sought to appear reasonable and moderate in order to keep wavering barons from going over to the rebel side, and he worked to win over potential defectors with concessions. He had already secured the approval of many English churchmen with his charter granting free episcopal elections. He tried to calm the country by keeping within the letter of the law, rejecting first resort to force.

Above all, John wanted to do nothing that would jeopardize the papacy's powerful protection, and he presented his conduct as cautious and conciliatory in letters to Innocent III, characterizing the barons as totally intransigent. To shore up Innocent's sympathy, John sent a royal clerk to Rome in February 1215, and this envoy had greater success at the papal curia than either the barons' inexperienced spokesmen or Stephen Langton. The pontiff suspected the archbishop of supporting John's opponents, for Langton refused to act on the king's request that he excommunicate the rebels, and his standing with the pope was steadily declining. Early in March John took up the crusader's cross, a diplomatic coup that pleased the pope and won him the Church's special protection. One of Innocent's dreams was to sponsor a successful crusade, and he regarded a baronial rebellion in England as an obstacle to fulfilment of his ambition.

Devising a charter of liberties

King John and the baronial party were engaging in negotiations almost continuously throughout the time between the London council in January 1215 and the great council scheduled for the Sunday after Easter. In March, the king offered significant concessions, promising to abolish his own and his brother's evil customs and to submit his father's customs to the judgement of his men. The barons rejected this proposal, and another meeting the next month produced no agreement. In Holy Week, the barons mustered at Stamford in Lincolnshire, to march south for the Easter council at Northampton accompanied by armed men. Open conflict came, however, when the barons arrived at Northampton, prepared to present a list of non-negotiable demands. They had taken advantage of the months since the London council in January to frame a programme that strengthened their political position. When the king failed to appear, they had to send their demands to him at his castle of Wallingford nearby.

John had no intention of making concessions that would threaten what he held to be the traditional rights of the crown. He expected papal missives from Rome supporting his monarchical prerogatives, and three papal letters arrived at the end of April, too late to prevent an open break between king and barons. One, addressed to the barons, advised them to abandon their conspiracies and coercion, and instead to petition the king respectfully for redress of their grievances; a second was addressed to the archbishop of Canterbury and the English episcopate, chastising them for failing to mediate and accusing them of siding with the barons; and a third letter, addressed to John, has not survived.

The rebels formally renounced their fealty to John on 5 May, and they chose as their commander John's longtime foe, Robert fitz Walter, who took a grandiose title, 'Marshal of the Host of God and Holy Church'. King John continued to make proposals for a settlement, proposing on 9 May a panel of eight arbitrators, four to be named by him and four by the barons, with the pope presiding. Complicated schemes for arbitration were often adopted to resolve princes' disputes peacefully in the thirteenth century, and Innocent was eager to play the role of peace-maker in his new vassal-state. The king made his offer not so much out of a genuine desire for reconciliation as a wish to strengthen his moral position in the eyes of the pope and uncommitted barons. Throughout the spring of 1215, one of his principal aims was to preserve papal support by placing his actions in an impeccable legal and moral context, and he promised that he would not take action against the rebels 'except by the law of our realm or by judgement of their peers in our court'.[5] Once the dissidents had withdrawn their homage, arbitration no longer interested them, for they knew better than to expect impartiality from either the king's court or the papal court at Rome.

When armed rebellion began in early May with the barons' failed attack on Northampton Castle, John had outmanoeuvred them with his delays and proffered concessions and had made them appear to reject legal process and to resort to force. Yet he had missed his opportunity to crush the rebels quickly. Once the Londoners went over to the rebel side and opened the city to them in mid-May, the military situation tipped in the barons' favour; their possession of London was a major blow to the royalist cause and an inducement for John to come to terms. Also this early rebel success shoved wavering barons into their arms, leaving the king almost without allies. Soon Stephen Langton and some leading royalist barons were urging him to reach an accommodation with the rebels.

By late May, John acknowledged his predicament and, deciding to seek a settlement at least to buy time, asked Archbishop Langton to arrange a truce. As Sir James Holt, the leading twentieth-century authority on the Great Charter, observes: 'Throughout, even when he sealed Magna Carta, John had not the slightest intention of giving in or permanently abandoning the powers which the Angevin kings had come to enjoy'.[6] The king was confident that ancient custom was on his side, for he saw himself defending longstanding monarchical prerogatives, and in his view the rebel barons were the revolutionaries, attempting to place unprecedented limitations on royal power. John assumed that England's new sovereign, Innocent III, would condemn and invalidate any concessions seriously weakening monarchical authority, imposing spiritual penalties on the insurgents. The pope had no patience with armed rebellions, especially those impeding his proposed crusade, and he insisted that the barons seek redress by petitioning the king humbly, or by petitioning him directly. In early July 1215, the pope excommunicated 'all such disturbers of the king and kingdom of England together with their accomplices and supporters', unaware of the settlement already reached in June by the king and the rebels.[7]

Final negotiations to settle the baronial quarrel with King John got under way at the latest by 10 June at Runnymede Meadow, lying between Windsor Castle and the rebel barons' camp at Staines. Two documents survive that apparently served as the basis for discussions between the two parties. First is the so-called 'Unknown Charter of Liberties', a document of uncertain date surviving only in a copy found in the French archives at Paris and most likely dating from autumn 1214 or early 1215, although some clauses suggest a 1213 date. It is not in fact a charter, but a series of baronial proposals in the form of notes added to a copy of Henry I's charter. When this Unknown Charter first became accessible to scholars in 1893, its radical demands tended to undermine positive portrayals of the rebel barons painted by Whig historians, and it gave support to revisionist scholars at the beginning of the twentieth century who depicted Magna Carta as a product of selfish and reactionary aristocrats. Its main points are similar to those incorporated into Magna

Carta in 1215, but the part that it played in negotiations is unclear, for its more extreme proposals do not appear in the Great Charter. Its proposals for strict protections for lands of royal wards and rolling back the royal forests to their pre-Henry II boundaries are missing from the Charter. Another noteworthy omission is the Unknown Charter's limitation on barons' overseas military service to Normandy and Brittany only, a provision that suggests a date before John's 1214 expedition to Poitou.

The second document is the 'Articles of the Barons', also undated, although apparently from a late stage in the discussions. Bearing the heading 'These are the articles that the barons ask for and the lord king grants', it outlines in forty-nine articles a preliminary agreement between rebel and royal agents.[8] A product of weeks of negotiations, its text was copied by a clerk of the royal chancery before a meeting with John, and the king likely set his seal to it as a sign that he accepted its provisions on 10 June. The Articles' definite demands marked the barons' abandonment of a vague desire for 'good lordship' and an attempt to limit the king with specific restrictions, set down in writing that would place him under the law. Apparently Stephen Langton acted as mediator between the contending parties, since the original copy of the Articles turned up in the archiepiscopal archives at Lambeth Palace. In the mid-seventeenth century, Archbishop William Laud allowed the bishop of Rochester to have the document, and it later passed to the historian of the Glorious Revolution, Gilbert Burnet, who mistakenly assumed that it was the original copy of the Great Charter. Still later it belonged to the earl of Stanhope, who presented it to the nation in 1769, and it is displayed today at the British Library (Additional MS 4938) (see Plate 2). Although the royal seal became detached from the document long ago, it survived and is displayed alongside the Articles (see Plate 3).

Actual shaping of the agreement was largely the work of moderates among both the rebel and royalist parties. Open-minded royalist bishops and barons, capable of admitting King John's shortcomings and counselling moderation, worked alongside experienced administrators to draft both the Articles and the Great Charter of Liberties. The names in the preamble of Magna Carta acknowledging those who had counselled the king include the archbishop of Canterbury, Stephen Langton; seven other bishops, including two of the king's most trusted servants, Henry, archbishop of Dublin, and Peter des Roches, bishop of Winchester; four loyal earls, headed by William Marshal, earl of Pembroke, who had quarrelled with John but remained loyal to the Angevin line, and the king's half-brother, William Longsword, earl of Salisbury; and several royal officials, among them Hubert de Burgh, who would play a powerful role in protecting young Henry III. Also listed is the papal legate, but no names from the ranks of active rebels appear.

It is not an overstatement to describe Magna Carta as little more than 'the Articles of the Barons carefully worked over by highly intelligent men with a thorough knowledge of the English government'.[9] Clearly, it formed a basis for discussions on a few disputed points and for formal drafting of the Charter. Thirteen of the Articles' provisions reappear in the final version with little change, and a number of others with more detailed language for greater legal precision. The two documents show that the barons wished to force John to treat them as the royal courts required them to treat their own free tenants. A text of Magna Carta dated at Windsor on 15 June 1215, surviving today at the Huntington Library in California, is apparently a draft prepared by chancery clerks for final agreement with the barons at Runnymede. One point left for resolution was the barons' insistence that the king disavow any appeal to the pope 'whereby any of the things here agreed might be revoked or diminished'.[10] John resisted, no doubt already planning to petition his new lord; instead, he promised in Magna Carta (chapter 61) that he would not seek annulment of the agreement 'from anyone', in place of 'from the lord pope'. Although working in haste, the royal clerks produced a final draft with precise language that points to their competence as Latinists and their learning in the common law.

The official text of Magna Carta is dated 15 June 1215, and there is little reason for questioning that date. Doubtless, the barons would have wanted a document drafted quickly for sealing by the king as a token of his acceptance of its terms. Since the beginning of the twentieth century, however, historians have rejected the document's dating and have proposed other dates for its final drafting and sealing; as a 1961 biography of King John phrases it, the 15 June date for the charter is 'simply a nominal date'.[11] Some scholars conclude that final agreement on terms was not reached until 19 June, the day that the rebel barons made a 'firm peace' with the king, exchanging with him the kiss of peace and renewing their homage. To buttress this chronology, scholars argue that it was essential that the barons' return to the king's peace precede John's grant of the Charter; otherwise, it would have appeared too obviously exacted by force, making its validity dubious. In any case, some time between 19 and 24 June chancery clerks copied and sealed other copies of an official draft, likely sealed on 15 June, to be sent throughout the kingdom to sheriffs and bishops. The king named a committee of high-ranking clerics, headed by Archbishop Stephen Langton and the papal legate, to send out letters accompanying these copies, testifying to its authenticity. No single master copy of the Great

Charter was ever copied by royal clerks on to the official roll of royal charters.

Magna Carta is above all a charter of liberties, presumably the king's spontaneous grant, and it was accepted as such by both the baronage and royal officials. The people's knowledge of their new liberties was essential if they were to take advantage of the Charter's promises, and steps were taken to publicize it. Once King John sealed the document, royal letters went out to all sheriffs, foresters, and other local officials, ordering that it 'should be publicly read throughout your whole bailiwick and firmly held'.[12] Doubtless, a high level of interest in this guarantee of the people's liberties demanded that it be read in the vernacular, not in Latin. Indeed, a text of Magna Carta survives in French, and a letter accompanying it, dated 27 June 1215, makes clear that it was an official text translated to ensure that knights of the counties understood it. Although scholars have paid little attention to this text since its discovery in a Norman leper hospital in the seventeenth century, its survival establishes the Charter as the first major official document issued in a vernacular version since the Norman Conquest of England.

Four of the Latin copies sent to the shires still survive, two in the British Library, one at Lincoln Cathedral, and another in the library of Salisbury Cathedral. These copies consist of single sheets of long-lasting parchment that vary slightly in size from twenty to seventeen inches long and between thirteen and seventeen inches wide. The four survivors are very much working documents, without decorated initial letters in colours or other ornamentation. It is not surprising that the texts of all four surviving copies differ slightly in spelling and show some transpositions of words, since they were written in haste by different hands, and the copyists likely found it difficult to work from a much-revised master text. One annalist reports that a copy of the Charter was 'deposited in every see in a safe place',[13] and the two surviving cathedral copies were doubtless placed there by sheriffs for safekeeping.

In the seventeenth century, the two copies now in the British Library came into the possession of Sir Robert Cotton, an avid collector of medieval manuscripts and a founder of the Society of Antiquaries. His manuscript collection drew scholars, common lawyers, and members of Parliament to his house to pore over them in search of material for polemics against Charles I's absolutist rule. Long after Cotton's death, legislation enacted under William and Mary placed his library in the hands of trustees to preserve it for the nation, and the Cottonian manuscripts passed to the British Museum on its founding in 1753, joining two other private collections as the basis of the present-day British Library. One of the two copies (Cotton Charter XIII. 31a) had been sent in 1215 to the Cinq Ports, a group of towns on the southeast coast whose maritime significance gave them special status. It was discovered among Dover Castle's documents and acquired by Cotton from the lieutenant of the castle in 1630. Unfortunately, this copy, along with a number of Cotton's other manuscripts, suffered damage in a fire in 1731. It was still legible two years later, when an engraving was made that Sir William Blackstone reproduced in his 1759 edition of Magna Carta, although botched attempts at restoration later rendered it illegible. Cotton's second copy, displayed at the British Library today (Cotton MS. Augustus II. 106), is still completely legible (see Plate 5). A colourful legend has it that he rescued this copy from a London tailor's shop in 1629 before it could be cut up for collar backing, but nothing beyond the name of its owner, a barrister Humphrey Wyems, is known of its fate before coming into Cotton's possession.

The other two surviving copies of Magna Carta at Lincoln and Salisbury Cathedrals narrowly escaped loss. The Lincoln copy seems to have lain forgotten for centuries, but it regained attention early in the nineteenth century. The Record Commissioners, a body created to preserve and publish key documents of British history, chose it in 1810 as the basis for its edition of Magna Carta printed in the first volume of the *Statutes of the Realm*. In the twentieth century, the Lincoln Charter travelled overseas often. It made frequent trips to the United States, first in 1939 for the New York World's Fair, and remained in America for the duration of the Second World War. It was displayed at the Library of Congress until the US entered the war in December 1941, when it was removed with other Library treasures to Fort Knox, Kentucky, for safekeeping alongside the nation's gold reserves (see Plate 6). The Salisbury Cathedral copy disappeared some time after 1700 and remained missing until 1814. Some scholars doubt that it is an authentic 1215 original, for it contains more clerical errors than the other three copies, and its handwriting does not match as closely the royal chancery style. None the less, the current scholarly consensus is for accepting it as one of the official 1215 Charters. A fifth copy, housed at Tewkesbury Abbey, still existed in the seventeenth century, but has not surfaced since then.

The content of the 1215 Charter

The terms that John accepted at Runnymede are set forth in the document that would become known as Magna Carta or the Great Charter drafted and dated 15 June 1215 by clerks of his chancery, and sealed with the king's seal. It takes the form of the king's solemn grant of concessions to 'all the free men of our kingdom, for ourselves and our heirs for ever'.[14] Its language gives no suggestion that John did not make this grant freely, for the Church and popular opinion regarded promises exacted under duress as invalid. Although this version of the charter of liberties remained in effect for only a few weeks, it was reissued in revised versions following John's death in 1216 and 1217, and finally in a definitive version in 1225 issued by young Henry III. The 1225 version of the Great Charter was copied as the first of England's statutes on to the earliest statute roll during Edward I's reign at the end of the thirteenth century, and periodic confirmations throughout the thirteenth and fourteenth centuries preserved it as potent protection against royal tyranny.

Obviously, much myth has grown up about this document over the centuries, as successive ages sought new meanings in Magna Carta, and these fluctuations in meaning must be cleared away in order to understand its significance for the English people in 1215. Since the rise of a 'scientific' approach to historical study in the late nineteenth century, two extremes have characterized discussions of the Charter's significance. One school follows the traditional Whig interpretation, praising the rebel barons as visionaries. In the Whig view, they formulated a document of permanent importance, capable of maturing into a powerful guardian of the English people's liberties and pointing the way to the 1689 Bill of Rights, parliamentary supremacy and nineteenth-century political democracy. By the end of the nineteenth century, an opposing camp of revisionists sought to isolate the Charter in its medieval context, rejecting traditional interpretations. Applying a rigorous scientific approach, this school inspired the Charter's 'debunking'. These historians depicted it as a 'feudal' document, reflecting what they judged to be the rebel barons' yearning for the kind of weak monarchy that had permitted their grandfathers to exploit the countryside for their own enrichment. Revisionists condemned the baronage for raising the Charter as a roadblock to construction of a powerful state with effective central government. Even in the mid-twentieth century, some academics' admiration for Angevin administrative efficiency caused them to condemn the rebels for equating 'modernization' with tyranny.

Doubtless, the rebel barons' aims in pressing for Magna Carta were neither visionary nor reactionary, and today's historians have arrived at a more balanced estimate. Most can admit the predatory side of Angevin governance and can acknowledge that the rebels were not entirely backward-looking. They understand the adjective 'feudal' not simply as a synonym for 'antiquated' or 'reactionary', but as referring to the ties between medieval lords and their vassals or knights and their mutual obligations, symbolized by homage and fealty. Yet they concede that feudal law and custom never fully replaced earlier legal traditions. Because they know that both longstanding legal practices and current intellectual trends influenced the barons and their clerical advisers, as well as the king and his counsellors, they can come closer to comprehending the thinking underlying Magna Carta. Certainly individual rebels sought remedies in Magna Carta for their concrete complaints against King John's lordship over them, yet idealistic images of lordship and vassalage inspired them to incorporate into the Charter a reform programme that cannot be dismissed as a narrow 'feudal' document. The text resulting from negotiations at Runnymede was not simply a shopping list of particular grievances without widely applicable principles, but a broad reform programme.

Although the Charter must be recognized as a product of its own time and circumstances, some barons rebelling against King John were capable of political vision, inspired by the implicit contract between lords and vassals and expanded by contacts with churchmen and their antiquarian interests in old English laws and early royal grants of liberties. Since laity and clergy alike recognized the difference between tyrannical and lawful governance, the barons and their ecclesiastical allies, as well as knights and the urban mercantile class, shared a set of assumptions about the nature and purpose of government. Their model for England's governance was the 'good old law' of their grandfathers' time as it appeared to them embellished by myth, an imagined picture of the Conqueror and his sons' rule. Chivalric literature enticed them into imagining the king's court as a magnification of a noble court with the monarch's great tenants-in-chief gathered round giving judgement and counselling him on great matters. Discussions among baronial leaders, Stephen Langton and royal administrators resulted in a document with two basic principles embedded in its clauses: that royal government must function both through judicial processes and with the counsel of the great men of the kingdom. Because of rebel barons' ties to other groups, however, their list of grievances expanded into a reform programme benefiting ranks below the baronage, and Magna Carta would take into account complaints of knights, burgesses, and even lesser landholders. The barons appreciated the place that the common law courts had come to occupy, and they did not reject the extension of royal jurisdiction to their knights; rather they sought to perfect common law procedures. By defining John's relationship with his subjects in a written document, they moved England from customary law based on social norms toward a true legal system.

Magna Carta as drafted in June 1215 consists of sixty-three chapters, although today's numbering of the chapters only dates from the eighteenth century, introduced by Blackstone. It appears to be a practical, detailed document without abstract assumptions, aimed at remedying specific problems, chiefly concessions to specific groups within the kingdom or in certain instances to all the king's free subjects. Yet the Great Charter's provisions clearly reflect widely accepted twelfth-century political doctrines, and they set forth some lasting political principles. Its chapters range over a wide number of points, not always arranged in topical order, but they can be grouped into six topical categories. The first chapter stands apart from all others, confirming the freedom of the English Church; it is chiefly a confirmation of John's promise of free episcopal and abbatial elections made in his 1214 charter, adding nothing new. Since it appears in neither the Unknown Charter of Liberties nor the Articles of the Barons, perhaps its inspiration is Henry I's coronation charter; in any case, its premier position is witness to churchmen's influence on the document's drafting. Chapter 42 of the Charter, appearing also in the Articles of the Barons, was particularly important to the Church, for it granted all the king's subjects the right to leave and return to England freely except in time of war. Previously, English monarchs had restricted the clergy's right to travel to Rome as a means of limiting the papacy's control over English ecclesiastics.

Next come fifteen chapters dealing with King John's lordship over his barons, defining the services and payments due to him as a condition by which they held their lands. The Angevin kings had shamelessly exploited the financial privileges of their lordship, and these chapters attempted to define the barons' customary payments, such as aids and scutages, in order to limit increasing financial demands. Chapters 12 and 14 restricted the 'gracious aids' that John could demand to the three occasions on which lords traditionally collected them and specified that the king could levy no scutages or additional aids without seeking 'the common counsel of the kingdom'. Other chapters dealt with the relief paid by heirs of the king's tenants-in-chief; they set figures of £100 on relief for baronies and 100 shillings (£5) for knights' fees (chapter 2) and banned demands for relief from youths whose estates had been in the king's hands while they were his wards (3). Several clauses sought to remedy abuses of the royal right to wardship and to control marriage of barons' heirs and widows, such as excessive exploitation of wards' property while it was in the hands of the king's agents (chapters 4 and 5), forcing heirs to marry beneath their social rank (6) or compelling widowed noble ladies to remarry (8).

A third group of chapters dealt with administrative matters; for example, ten treat finances. One chapter banned sheriffs' payment of increments, that is, supplements added to the farm of the shire, their traditional fixed payment to the exchequer (25), while others defined proper methods for collecting debts owed to the crown or to Jews (chapters 9–11). The king had enforced collection of debts of Jewish moneylenders to ensure that they made profits for him to pillage from them periodically, and two chapters eased the terms for widows and heirs of men who died with such debts unpaid. The final phrase of chapter 11 made it applicable to debts owed to non-Jews, acknowledging that Christians also were engaging in lending money at interest. Three chapters (44, 47, 48) dealt with the royal forests, a constant cause of complaint, for wide swathes of territory and the animals roaming there were subject to arbitrary forest law administered by a host of royal officials. These chapters called for removal of all lands annexed by John to the royal forests and investigations into the 'evil customs' enforced by royal foresters.

A number of the administrative chapters centred on effective functioning of the common law courts. Only one chapter reflects baronial resentment at the expansion of royal justice at the expense of their private courts; chapter 34 declared that the writ *praecipe* should not be used in a way 'whereby a free man may lose his court'. This writ had enabled tenants to bring disputes over their landholdings directly before the royal justices, bypassing their lords' courts. Although chapter 34 aimed at simplifying the procedure by which a lord could reclaim such property disputes for hearing in his own court, it had little lasting effect on the common law courts' jurisdiction. In fact, most of the chapters treating judicial matters concede the popularity of the common law courts and indicate baronial concern for ensuring the people's ready access to them. One chapter sought to make the king's courts accessible to all free men by requiring more frequent visits to the shires by itinerant justices than were manageable (18), calling for the most popular common law procedures, the possessory assizes, to be heard four times a year in all counties. It also reflects the increasing prominence of the knights of the county by mandating that the itinerant justices taking the assizes associate with them four knights chosen by the county court. Another chapter required that common pleas should not be heard at the court following the king, but at some fixed place (17); this clause represents a criticism of John's suspension of the Bench at Westminster after 1209 and his concentration of all justice in a tribunal travelling about the kingdom with the royal household.

Three chapters concerned criminal proceedings. Chapter 24 barred sheriffs, constables, coroners or other local royal officers from hearing pleas of the crown, reserving serious criminal cases for the royal justices. Chapter 36 made freely available writs 'of life and limb', popular because they allowed the defendant to escape going to the ordeal by allowing a special jury, the jury of attaint. The writ authorized an accused person to challenge his accuser for bringing charges maliciously, and if the jurors confirmed that the charge was false, he was set free. Another chapter concerning criminal proceedings (54) limited women's rights to initiate prosecutions for homicide. It restated the custom that a woman could initiate such proceedings only when her husband was the victim, yet in practice, justices proved willing to allow women to bring charges against the murderers of other relatives.

Five chapters in the Charter granting concessions to England's towns comprise a fourth category. Reflecting London's prominent part in rebel success is chapter 13 confirming to the city 'all its ancient liberties and free customs', and it conferred similar rights on all other cities, boroughs, towns and ports. Chapter 41 promised all merchants, except those from lands at war with the king, free movement in and out of the kingdom without being subjected to evil tolls, and chapter 42 extended this right of free entry and exit to all English subjects. Chapter 33 called for removal of fish weirs from major rivers, an advantage for maritime trade, since such barriers hampered ships' passage from the sea to ports upriver. Chapter 35 simplified the sale of goods by setting up a single standard for weights and measures of wine, ale, grain and cloth throughout the kingdom.

A fifth group of chapters created machinery for enforcing the Charter to guarantee that the king carried out his promises. One of these named alien soldiers who had followed John to England after the loss of Normandy and required their removal from office (50), and another required withdrawal of all foreign mercenaries from the kingdom (51). The most important of these chapters (61) called for the barons to choose a committee of twenty-five to ensure John's observance of the Charter, to reprimand him for violations of its terms and to threaten renewed warfare if he refused to correct his fault. If the king failed to rectify an infraction promptly after a warning by a subcommittee of four barons, then the twenty-five 'together with the community of the whole land shall distrain and distress us [the king] in every way they can, namely, by seizing castles, lands, possessions, and in such other ways as they can'. This clause does not list the names of members of the committee of twenty-five barons, most likely because the rebels had not yet chosen them by 15 June. Chapter 61 actually authorized this baronial committee to make war on the monarch, although it was thinly disguised in the legal language of 'distraint and distress', or seizure of a litigant's property to enforce a court's finding. Not surprisingly, King John and his adherents saw this security clause as an unacceptable limitation on monarchical power requiring him to rule through the baronial committee, and co-operation between the king and the baronial committee would prove impossible. Chapter 61 concluded with John's promise not to seek release from his commitments from anyone, a clause added because the rebel barons hoped to avert his petitioning his new ally, Pope Innocent III, for an annulment of the agreement. The last chapter (63) declared that both the king and the barons had sworn an oath to observe 'in good faith and without evil disposition' all promises in the earlier chapters.

A sixth category consists of chapters that set forth principles of lasting political importance with implications for the future, for their cumulative effect was to compel the king to rule in accord with the law. While some attribute the underlying assumptions of Magna Carta to clerical influences, it is plausible to derive them also from the barons' idealized notion of lords' relationships with their men. Out of the barons' so-called 'feudal' outlook arose ideas that could be expanded from their narrow perspective, moving the kingdom toward concepts of government that still shape today's views on relations between government and the governed. Four basic assumptions that appear in the Great Charter have their origin in the barons' vision of good lordship, and their understanding of the personal bonds of lordship and vassalage informed their concept of governance by counsel and by judgement. The Charter's transfer of these ideas to the larger ruler–subject relationship continues to have significance for Anglo-American political thought.

First, Magna Carta sought to place under the protection of the law all 'free men', at that time a term defining those of knightly rank plus some smaller landholders who held their land 'freely', in return for honourable services, not for labour in their lord's fields. 'Knight', originally a military term and later a social one, was not a juridical term conferring legal status. The most important distinction in twelfth-century English law was between the free and the unfree; knights and lesser freeholders were classified together without much distinction, but differentiated from unfree peasants or serfs. The free man in medieval England had special privileges denied the unfree, including the right to bear arms and freedom from capricious work assignments and humiliating corporal punishments by his lord; and with Henry II's legal innovations, he acquired the royal courts' protection against arbitrary seizure of his property. While the Charter shared similarities with charters of liberties granted by contemporary continental princes, its promises were more generous, not restricted to knights, but covering free men of less than knightly rank.

The free man's privileges are recognized in chapter 39 of the 1215 Charter: 'No free man shall be taken or imprisoned or dispossessed or outlawed or exiled or in any way ruined, nor will we [the king] go or send against him, except by the lawful judgements of his peers or by the law of the land'. Although the hierarchical structure of thirteenth-century English society precluded the principle of equality under the law, the Charter's employment of such a broad term as free man ensured that increasing numbers in England would enjoy its protection as they won free status. Chapter 60 required all lords in the kingdom to make available to those subject to their authority the same customs and liberties that the king was granting to his own men. This clause continues a tendency of the Angevin kings to curb their magnates' freedom to dictate to their free tenants with impunity and to claim royal responsibility for all free men, strengthening the direct ruler–subject relationship and weakening local ties of lordship.

Stacks of learned papers and books have sought to clarify the meaning of the final phrase of chapter 39 in its original Latin: *legale judicium parium vel per legem terre*. Questions arise about the pair of terms 'lawful judgements of peers' and 'law of the land' because the word *vel* can be translated as 'and', but also as 'or'. Are the phrases equivalent terms, merely synonyms, or do they denote two different procedures? Most likely, an adequate solution is to translate *vel* as 'and/or', a common usage in legal documents today. In the early thirteenth century, neither phrase had a precise legal definition, and different people applied them in different senses. Judgement by peers meant neither the common law inquest by twelve neighbours nor a modern jury trial, but a proceeding before a panel consisting of social equals, as in the baronial courts where a lord's knights met together to settle disputes with each other or with him. Barons wanted to be tried by their fellow magnates, not by professional royal servants of obscure origin in the common law courts or at the exchequer. Similarly, the phrase 'law of the land' had no specialized meaning in 1215, but over the centuries has proven exceedingly flexible. For many of John's contemporaries, the term meant the ancient custom of the realm enshrined in popular memory as the laws of Edward the Confessor; the royal justices, however, understood it as the shire courts' traditional proceedings that they contrasted with newer common law processes by writ and jury. King John paid lip-service to the 'law of the land' or 'custom of the realm', scattering his writs with such phrases, seeking to place his arbitrary acts within the letter of the law; for example, he equated his exchequer's peremptory procedures for collecting crown debts with the law of the land. Most likely, the barons understood by the term 'law of the land' both longstanding custom of shire and hundred courts and processes in the common law courts introduced by Henry II. Barons' tenants could use common law procedures against their lords to sue them in the royal courts, but the barons were denied them in quarrels against their own lord, the king.

Despite ambiguity about the specific meaning of certain words, everyone could grasp the general tenor of chapter 39. It guaranteed free men what the barons termed government by judgement and what constitutional lawyers today call 'due process of law'. It protected them from extra-legal or illegal arrest, seizure of property, or pursuit with armed force by the king or royal officials. John was constrained to proceed against his subjects by the common law courts' system of writs and juries or by customary processes of the shire and hundred courts that still included trial by combat, the ordeal, or compurgation, the practice of neighbours' collectively swearing to the good character of the accused. In short, the chapter bound the king to follow the law in his dealings with his free subjects.

Immediately following this clause is chapter 40, redressing baronial complaints against the king's abuses of the royal courts for financial and political purposes: 'To no one will we sell, to no one will we deny or delay right or justice'. Another chapter also promised a higher standard of justice, committing the king to choose as judges, sheriffs, and other officers only 'such as know the law of the kingdom and mean to observe it well' (45). Several additional chapters aimed at putting the principle of due process into effect, providing remedies to victims of arbitrary actions by John and his predecessors. Chapter 52 promised immediate restitution to anyone dispossessed or deprived 'without lawful judgement of his peers' of lands, castles, private jurisdiction or other rights. Chapter 57 made a similar commitment to John's Welsh subjects, promising them full justice in accordance with the law of Wales. Other chapters limited the king's right of *prise* or purveyance, outlawing a wartime practice by which royal officers arbitrarily requisitioned food supplies, horses, carts, and other goods for the king's household (28, 30, 31). Two chapters afforded protection against arbitrary fines imposed by the courts; they were to be proportionate to the seriousness of the offence (20, 21, 22). Barons' fines were to be set only by their peers, although no method for arriving at a proper figure was specified. Lesser men's fines were to be determined by the testimony of upstanding neighbours, and they were to be left with sufficient means for making a living. In the only instance of Magna Carta's grant of a guarantee to the unfree, the overwhelming majority of the population, chapter 20 protected them from heavy fines that would deprive them of their means of earning a livelihood.

A second principle of lordship and vassalage incorporated into the Charter is a lord's obligation to take counsel with his knightly tenants owing him military service. Since the barons were the king's tenants-in-chief, theoretically holding their baronies in return for supplying quotas of knights, they expected him to seek their counsel. This principle of governance by counsel had featured prominently among rebel demands, and it represents a rejection of what would be called in the reigns of John's son and grandson 'household' or 'secret' government and what is termed today in the United States 'executive privilege'. In short, the barons opposed John's habit of deciding important issues privately on the advice of intimates within his household, appointed by him without regard for their social standing. In the barons' opinion, he should take counsel with great men of distinguished lineage, suitable spokesmen for the kingdom as a whole. Two chapters of Magna Carta (12 and 14) hint at this demand for governance by counsel. In them, King John promised, 'No scutage or aid is to be levied in our realm except by the common counsel of our realm', and these chapters heralded the parliamentary politics of late medieval England.

It is sometimes asserted that these two chapters represent a step toward the principle of consent to taxation or the American colonists' cry in 1776 of 'no taxation without representation', but such an interpretation encounters difficulties. An initial problem is the two chapters' reference only to traditional obligations of lordship owed from the king's tenants-in-chief, not to general taxes paid by the whole population. John's predecessors had collected scutages without taking the barons' counsel as a substitute for their military obligation, but his imposition of scutages without spending the money on military campaigns caused the barons to consider them a new form of taxation. General levies on the whole population were still a novelty at the beginning of the thirteenth century; yet the line between the new general taxes and gracious aids or tallages was a blurred one. Often, the Angevin kings had accompanied an aid collected from the baronage with a tallage on their towns and rural communities. A second problem with these chapters is the requirement that the king only take counsel, as any lord who consulted his vassals before collecting an extraordinary aid; no reference is made to his subjects' consent or assent. In medieval terminology, counsel did not necessarily mean consent in today's sense of taking a vote, a show of hands or counting ballots. Little concept of majority rule or counting votes existed in the Middle Ages; instead, consensus was reached through long discussion with the voices of some counsellors weighing more heavily than others. Probably the unspoken assumption was that such counsel would result in compromise with an aid or scutage set at a level acceptable to all. A third difficulty is the omission of chapter 12 from subsequent reissues of Magna Carta. None the less, Henry III would continue to observe the principle and consult with great councils or parliaments before collecting new direct taxes.

Chapter 14 defines the 'common counsel of the realm' as consultation in a great council composed of the prelates of the English Church, the earls and greater barons, summoned individually by royal letters, and from 'all who hold of us in chief', who would receive a general summons from the sheriffs. The number of lesser royal tenants to be included in such a general summons was about 800, although far fewer would have answered the call. The barons were still thinking of the kingdom as a great lordship, with themselves comprising the court of their lord the king. The assembly in chapter 14 summoned to give counsel was to be a body of great men, not a band of intimates from the royal household. An assembly based on tenure, those holding lands by knight service from the king, hardly represented the whole kingdom. It did not provide spokesmen for the knightly class or other ranks of English society below the baronage, for the only knights admitted were those who happened to hold some land directly of the king.

Since deliberations of the assembled barons and bishops supposedly represented the 'common counsel of the realm', the issue of consulting other groups within the kingdom remained unsettled. With references to the 'common counsel of the kingdom' (chapters 12, 14) and the 'community [Latin *communa*] of the whole land' (61), Magna Carta reflects a radical fashion in medieval political thought that had already infected citizens of London. Originally a sworn association of townspeople to overthrow their lord and substitute self-government, the concept of 'commune' was applied by the barons to the kingdom as a whole, perhaps inspired by London's example. Their notion that all English free men formed a commune or community, a corporate body separate from the king with its own interests that could conflict with the king's ambitions, was a new one threatening to royal supremacy. The rebel barons apparently considered themselves qualified to give the king counsel on behalf of this 'community of the whole land' and capable of coercing him if he failed to heed them. The problem of giving a voice to other groups within the kingdom, whose interests might differ from those of the baronage, would not be solved until parliaments including representatives of the knights and burgesses made their appearance at the end of the thirteenth century. None the less, chapter 14 is a tentative step in that direction, the earliest assembly in Europe that spoke to the king on behalf of an entire kingdom and presented a potential mechanism for limiting royal power.

A third key aspect of the Great Charter growing out of ties of lordship linking king and baronage is its contractual nature, for a powerful strand of political thought in the Middle Ages held that governments originated in a compact between the people and their ruler. Some authors of medieval treatises concluded that on account of an original compact the people retained a right of resistance to an unjust ruler. The tie between lord and vassal strengthened this line of thought, for it had characteristics of a contract, whether verbal or written down in a charter, with each party accepting certain obligations toward the other in the ceremony of homage and fealty. The lord was obliged to proceed against one of his men only after judgement in a court composed of the lord and his men interpreted the contract's terms and adjudicated whether one party had failed to fulfil his responsibilities: in short, judgement by peers. Soon after agreement on the Charter, an essential part of the settlement was the rebel barons' renewal of their vows of fealty to King John, indicative of this understanding of the Great Charter in a context of lordship. Magna Carta represents an important stage in growth of the contract theory of government that would become such a vital element in Anglo-American political thought through the writings of seventeenth- and eighteenth-century thinkers both in Britain and in the colonies. With the Charter's liberties for all free men, the old notion of mutual obligations of lord and vassal was extended to the larger relationship of ruler and subject.

The rebel barons' difficulty lay in finding a means for enforcing their contract with King John, and their method of enforcement set forth in chapter 61, the security clause, points to a fourth principle transferring concepts of lordship and vassalage to the broader ruler–subject relationship. Although a vassal's right of rebellion against his lord had several sources, among them early Christian Fathers' teachings on the right of resistance to unjust rulers, the barons knew no way to hold John to his promises, except the threat of renewed civil war. Custom sanctioned a vassal's right to renounce formally his fealty to his lord and take up arms against him, if the lord failed to keep his part of their bargain. Of course, custom condoned only a single vassal's isolated, individual act, not collective warfare by a corporate body of barons. The rebel barons, trying to put their threat into language masking the fact of warfare against an anointed king, employed a subterfuge, turning to the legal vocabulary of 'distraint', a term for occupation of a tenant's land to force him to appear in court. This language allowed the barons to escape forfeiture of their lands by bringing their resort to force against the king within the letter of the law. The committee of twenty-five intended to act as a court capable of trying the king, and two other chapters refer to its role in judging disputes over restoration of lands and remission of monetary penalties to John's victims (52, 55). Because of bad faith by both the king and the twenty-five barons, implementation of chapter 61 proved impossible. None the less, this attempt to devise a mechanism by which the king's subjects could restrict his tyrannical acts proved to have lasting importance as a precedent for committees established by reforming magnates to restrict royal power in Henry III's reign and later.

The unmaking of the Charter

Magna Carta was an unworkable compromise between a king who accepted it only grudgingly and a group of angry, aggressive and wary barons. In John's opinion, the security clause took his crown away from him, unjustly limiting the authority bestowed by his anointing and crowning. Even lukewarm royalists viewed chapter 61 and its threat of renewed civil war as an unlawful limitation of royal authority. Extremist rebels rejected the compromise, and less hotheaded rebels reserved serious doubts about John's sincerity in agreeing to it. Most rebel barons went ahead with selecting the committee of twenty-five, however. The committee's members were longtime foes of the king, and the absence of respected moderates – not even Stephen Langton was included – did not bode well for the Charter's implementation.

John's Great Charter was in force for less than three months. Baronial distrust of the king blocked fulfilment of other agreements reached at Runnymede, and both sides were preparing for war throughout the summer of 1215. One of the agreements allowed the barons' occupation of London and Archbishop Stephen Langton's custody of the Tower to continue until 15 August, but they refused to vacate on the specified date, strengthening John's suspicion. Control of another fortification caused concern for the king, for Langton refused to allow him to resupply Rochester Castle, a royal castle, although permanently in the custody of the archbishop of Canterbury. After the archbishop's obstinacy enabled rebel forces to occupy the fortress, the pope suspended him from his office, and he left for Rome to appeal against his suspension.

Although the distance between England and Rome prevented Innocent III from keeping up with rapidly changing events in his new vassal's kingdom, reports persuaded him that the Charter infringed on John's God-given rights as monarch, and the pontiff obliged by annulling it on 24 August. While the rebel barons and their allies viewed the Charter as a restoration of ancient custom, Innocent agreed with the king that it was a break with longstanding tradition. In his August letter, the pope depicted the baronial rebels as inspired by Satan to impede his proposed crusade, rejecting his mediation, and forcing their king to agree to

Magna Carta 'by such violence and fear as might affect the most courageous of men'. He denounced the Charter as 'not only shameful and demeaning but also illegal and unjust, thereby lessening unduly and impairing [John's] royal rights and dignity'.[15]

When papal agents in England proclaimed publicly in early September the pope's excommunication of the rebels, sent from Rome in July, any hope of further negotiations between the royalist and baronial sides ended. Fighting broke out around that time, and the rebels' failure to defeat King John pushed them to the extreme step of seeking to remove him from the throne and to set aside his son as his successor. In autumn, they offered the English crown to Louis of France (the future Louis VIII), son of John's great rival Philip Augustus, although the French prince had only the slightest shred of hereditary claim to disguise what was a campaign of conquest. After Louis landed in England with a large army in May 1216, the civil war settled into a stalemate. John controlled the west of the kingdom, and he had loyal foreign mercenaries installed in some isolated strongholds elsewhere; the rebels and their French allies were confined to London, the southeast, and centres scattered about East Anglia and the north. King John fell ill and died in October 1216, after leading an army across the country to the fenlands of Norfolk and Lincolnshire.

John's death did not halt the warfare, for royalist forces managed to continue the struggle, led by faithful barons, bishops and papal representatives determined to defend young Henry III's right to the English crown. Under the leadership of the respected William Marshal, earl of Pembroke, Peter des Roches, bishop of Winchester, and the papal legate, the young king's adherents achieved military success within a year; defeat of the rebel forces at Lincoln in the spring of 1217 was followed in late summer by destruction of a fleet carrying reinforcements to their French ally. A quick reissue of Magna Carta in the name of the boy-king showed a willingness by those acting in Henry's name to compromise with reasonable rebels who bore no grudge against John's successor. The real significance of Magna Carta, then, lies not in 1215, but in the early years of John's son, Henry III.

Notes

1. Stevenson (1875), 170.
2. Hardy (1835), 130.
3. Hardy (1833–34), 1: 132; Stubbs (1913), 282.
4. Stubbs (1872–73), 2: 218; Luard (1872–84), 2: 584.
5. Warren (1978), 234, citing Hardy (1837), 209.

6. Holt (1992), 141.
7. Cheney and Semple (1953), 207-9.
8. Rothwell (1975), 311.
9. Painter (1949), 316.
10. Rothwell (1975), 316.
11. Warren (1978), 236.
12. Hardy (1835), 180b.
13. Luard (1864-69), Annals of Dunstaple, 3: 43.
14. Holt (1992), app. vi, ch. 1, 448-51; also Rothwell (1975).
15. Cheney and Semple (1953), 212-17.

chapter 4

THE FIRST CENTURY OF MAGNA CARTA

M agna Carta seemed to have failed by the summer of 1215, repudiated by the king and the pope. Following John's death in October 1216, its fate was doubtful with a nine-year-old boy as his successor and a stalemated civil war dividing the kingdom between baronial rebels and their French allies controlling some regions and royalist barons and the late king's mercenaries in others. Yet the Charter took root during the minority of John's young son, Henry III, and once he came of age in 1227 its limitations remained in force, renewed in a definitive 1225 version. In Henry's long reign, 1216 to 1272, Magna Carta, reissued and reconfirmed frequently, became embedded in the minds of the English people as fundamental law. With no constitutional means of curbing royal oppression except resort to violence, the people's calls for confirmation of the Charter at least reminded the monarch that he was bound by the law.

By Henry III's middle years, the baronage saw that the Great Charter alone could not guarantee the king's subjection to the law. Although Henry's long minority had accustomed them to advising the young king and his regents in great councils, once he came of age, he turned to counsellors of his own choosing. Yet the magnates insisted on their place as his counsellors, making their participation in governance a constitutional issue. A group of baronial reformers claiming to speak for the community of the realm challenged Henry during 1258–65, seeking to revive the 1215 Charter's provision for a committee of barons to oversee the king. In Edward I's reign (1272–1307), Parliament, speaking on behalf of the whole kingdom, grasped Magna Carta once more as a weapon against his financial demands. A century after Runnymede, parliaments would seek the Charter's reconfirmation and clarification of its meaning with supplementary chapters reinforcing its principle of the rule of law.

Reissues of the Charter during Henry III's minority

Luckily for young Henry III when he ascended England's throne in the midst of a stalemated civil war, his father's loyal supporters worked to secure the crown and country for him. Men such as the regent William Marshal and the justiciar Hubert de Burgh, who had figured in the June 1215 negotiations, took charge of securing control of the country for the nine-year-old boy. Ignoring both King John's and Pope Innocent III's earlier repudiation of the Great Charter, these royal officials, royalist barons, and the papal legate in England acting on behalf of the new king's protector and overlord, Pope Honorius III, reissued a revised version of it in November 1216, less than a month after John's death. Young Henry's protectors meant the Charter to be an expression of the principles by which he would rule, a gesture of compromise and conciliation toward the rebels, and an encouragement to wavering royalists. To keep the Irish loyal, royal letters were sent promising them the same liberties enjoyed by English subjects, and presumably copies of the 1216 Charter accompanied the letters.

The 1216 version of the Great Charter omitted a number of chapters in the original, reducing its sixty-one chapters to forty-two. The continuing civil war and the presence of French invaders on English soil account for the omission of chapters restricting the king's right to appoint foreign mercenaries to offices in England (50 of the 1215 version) and promising to remove all foreign mercenaries from the kingdom (51). Crisis conditions also caused chapters providing for release of hostages held by the king to be omitted (49, 58–59). Two other noteworthy omissions were chapters 12 and 14 of John's Charter requiring that aids and scutages be levied 'by common counsel of our kingdom', defined as a great council comprising lay and spiritual lords and also the king's lesser tenants-in-chief. An obvious omission was the final chapter (61), calling for a baronial committee to enforce John's observance of the Charter. Instead, the 1216 charter ended with a new clause (42), suspending miscellaneous matters for discussion once royal control over the kingdom was restored. Resolution of those issues would wait until 'fuller counsel' was possible, including pacified rebels, to do 'what is for the common good and the peace and estate of ourselves [Henry III] and our kingdom'.[1] Changes in wording in other chapters sought greater clarity in phrasing in order to forestall litigation, indicating that those in charge of royal government regarded Magna Carta as enacted law, enforceable in the courts. Since the new king did not yet have his own seal, the seals of the papal legate and of the regent, William Marshal, were attached to the Charter.

The aim of the 1216 Charter was to bolster the moral position of the royalists in the civil war, and the Church sought to strengthen its effect by excommunicating 'disturbers of the king's peace' who rejected the proffered compromise. The second Charter did not have its desired effect, however, for it failed to lure rebel leaders into negotiations or draw substantial numbers to the royalist side. It proved necessary to crush the rebels militarily, and by September 1217 the invading French prince and his English adherents had made peace. In young Henry's name, his protectors, the papal legate and the regent, William Marshal, swore that the barons and all others in the realm would regain all their former rights and liberties and their lost inheritances. To fulfil this oath, a great council sanctioned a second reissue of the Charter in early November 1217 along with a Charter of Forest Liberties that replaced the forest clauses in the 1215 and 1216 charters.

Future confirmations of Magna Carta or the Great Charter, so called because it was the larger of the two documents, were always accompanied by reissue of the Forest Charter. As in 1216, counsellors modified wording in the 1217 Charter with an eye to greater clarity to prevent unnecessary litigation. Some chapters were deleted and others added that treated topics absent from earlier versions, increasing the number from the forty-two chapters of the 1216 Charter to forty-seven, despite removal of the three forest clauses to a separate document. Some chapters protected baronial rights to their tenants' traditional obligations, in effect creating a new land law. One prohibited free men from giving away or selling so much of their tenures that their ability to perform services to their lords would be endangered (39), and another barred gifts of land to religious houses as a means of avoiding services to their lords (3). Another new chapter (42) addressed knights' irritation with the time that they were forced to spend attending sheriffs' courts, restricting meetings of shire courts to once a month and hundred courts to twice a year.

In the new Forest Charter, the drafters expanded the three chapters dealing with royal forests in the 1215 Charter to seventeen. These articles, all practical and specific in tone, sought to define forest law, set geographical limits to its jurisdiction, and establish regulations for forest courts. The Forest Charter forgave those who had committed forest offences in the past; it promised removal from the royal forest of lands added by John, Richard and their father, Henry II; and it allowed holders of land lying within the royal forests to clear, enclose and cultivate their holdings. Most important, this new charter brought the royal forests under the rule of law, making forest law part of the law of the land and no longer solely subject to the king's arbitrary will. It proved less successful in redefining forest boundaries, however, and contention over withdrawing land from the jurisdiction of royal foresters continued for a century or more.

Problems postponed in 1216, such as scutage, were considered in the 1217 Magna Carta. One chapter (44) declared that scutage should be levied at the rate from Henry II's time, before the rise in rates during Richard and John's wars with Philip Augustus. The clause hinted at fewer scutages at lesser rates, but lacked the provisions in the original Charter (chapters 12 and 14) requiring counsel with the great men before assessing such extraordinary levies. None the less, since the great council that approved the new charters also gave its approval for collection of a scutage, royal consultation with the magnates continued to be the practice. Worthy of note is a clarification of chapter 39 of the 1215 Charter (32 in 1216; 35 in the 1219 Charter) pledging due process; it spelled out the prohibition against the king's arbitrary dispossession of his subjects as ensuring that no one was to be 'disseised of his freehold, liberties or free customs'. One clause kept in both revised versions was chapter 60 (45 in 1217), a provision that bound the barons to observe toward their own men the commitments that the king had made to them. This provision would play an important part in later crises of Henry III's reign, as knights pressed their lords to put this promise into effect, drawing this increasingly prominent class into agitation for political reform.

No writ survives commanding the reading of the 1216 Charter, but sheriffs were commanded to publicize the 1217 Charter in their shire courts, as in 1215; indeed, the writ seems to mandate that each provision of the Charter be explained to the assembled people. Only a single copy of Henry III's 1216 Charter survives today, housed in the archives of Durham Cathedral, but three originals of the 1217 Charter are at the Bodleian Library, Oxford University. One of these is a fine copy, still possessing the legate's and William Marshal's seals, previously housed at Gloucester Abbey; the other two came to the Bodleian Library from Oseney Abbey. One exemplar of the 1217 Forest Charter survives at Durham, although badly damaged. During the thirteenth century, the Charters would be copied into cartularies, volumes that monastic houses compiled preserving copies of their charters as legal proof of their properties and privileges. Also increasing numbers of handbooks, compilations of writs and related legal texts, often containing texts of Magna Carta, appeared for the instruction of laymen employed as estate stewards or legal advisers to litigants. Such practical treatises kept the politically active classes – knights and 'law worthy' free men as well as barons – acquainted with its provisions and convinced them that it was a protector of their property rights.

Writers in the Middle Ages lacked the critical spirit of modern scholars who apply technical skills to secure the most accurate texts of historical documents. Medieval scribes did not feel compelled to copy a text exactly, but freely edited it to 'improve' it; and when making copies of Magna Carta, they frequently failed to differentiate between various versions. Roger of Wendover, first of the St Albans school of historians, writing from 1215 to 1235, saw no reason to differentiate between John's charter of liberties and Henry III's versions. His successor as historian at St Albans, Matthew Paris, had access to an authentic copy of the 1215 Charter; nonetheless, he conflated its text with the 1216 and 1217 versions. Following Wendover, he included in one of his chronicles a complete text of Henry III's 1225 Forest Charter, which he misidentified as King John's Forest Charter, a non-existent document. Most English people regarded the original grant by King John as the key document, unmindful of later versions that had superseded it as law; and with or without an accurate text, the spirit of the Great Charter survived.

As soon as possible after the restoration of peace, royal justice revived, and itinerant justices who resumed their circuits around the kingdom in 1218 and 1219 showed genuine concern for abiding by Magna Carta's clauses. A monastic annalist recorded that the royal justices in 1218 'went through all England watching over the restoration of the laws and causing them to be observed in their pleas according to the . . . charter of King John'.[2] The judges took care to enforce the Charter's clauses concerning monetary penalties, ensuring that fines accorded with litigants' ability to pay and frequently pardoning fines imposed on the poor. More striking is the royal judges' willingness to allow pleas alleging arbitrary acts by young Henry's father and grandfather to go forward. The regency council supervised the work of the common law courts, but its interventions resolutely aimed at restoration of law and order in the kingdom, not at maximizing royal income or pursuing personal vendettas.

Henry III's minority presented an opportunity for the governing classes in England, former rebel leaders, royalist barons and the late king's ministers, to establish a consensus. All accepted recovery of royal power, for they recognized that if the central government were to be strong enough to protect their rights, it needed adequate authority and income, yet it could not acquire resources for governing effectively without support from the great men of the kingdom. Just as during Richard Lionheart's long absence, the authority of the regents governing in the young Henry III's name depended on support from the magnates meeting in great councils. Indeed, one baron complained in 1220, when royal agents demolished a friend's castle, that it was done 'without the common counsel and assent of the magnates of England who are held to be and are of the chief council of the king'.[3] One of the principal demands of John's discontented barons had been baronial participation in policy-making through frequent councils, and during Henry's minority they grew accustomed to such participation, taking part in appointing great officers of state, the justiciar and the chancellor. They wished such collaboration to continue after Henry came of age, but found their prominent role curtailed once he took control of the government for himself. Once the minority ended in the early 1230s, the king's right to choose his own advisers without the magnates' consent and his tendency to turn to men in his household for counsel became points of contention. A significant baronial share in governance seemed essential for preserving Magna Carta's limitations on the royal will, and formal reconfirmations of the Charter alone would prove inadequate for protecting the barons' role during Henry III's personal rule.

Royal government bound by Magna Carta represented an awkward compromise: attempting to limit the king's power, yet allowing him the strength essential for keeping the peace and protecting his subjects. During Henry's minority, the problem worsened, for a weak regency government and powerful centrifugal forces in the countryside made the magnates stronger than at any time since the Angevin kings' accession in 1154. Both loyalists and former rebels hoped to hold on to castles, lands, offices and other sources of profit seized during the chaos of civil war to make themselves into regional potentates. With the collapse of effective central power a possibility, a number of magnates supported restoration of royal authority, even if it curtailed their own power in the shires. The chief crisis of the minority came in 1220–23, when a programme of resuming direct control over royal castles reopened the breach that the compromise of 1216 had healed between the regency government and powerful barons in the counties. In 1220, the justiciar Hubert de Burgh, with support from key earls and the episcopate, instituted a policy of castle resumption, for royal strongholds were indispensable to the central government's command over the kingdom. This required the mounting of sieges, for some powerful men resisted surrendering their fortresses. Among those resisting with violence were foreign mercenaries given custody of royal castles by John, and the demand that they surrender them heightened tensions between natives and aliens.

Successful resumption of royal castles restored the central government's supervision of the counties by 1223, but it revealed factionalism within the regency that had been concealed since the end of the civil war. Two factions with opposing approaches to governance contended for domination of the young king as he was coming of age in the 1220s. Constituting the dominant group were Hubert de Burgh and his moderate royalist allies who accepted the Charters. Opposing the justiciar were those loyal to John's authoritarian policies, mainly the late king's alien mercenaries, who rejected Magna Carta as unlawfully extorted by force. Their chief spokesman, Peter des Roches, bishop of Winchester, had been deeply implicated in John's arbitrary practices, and he had little patience with restrictions on royal power. Yet young Henry seemed to accept the limitations imposed by the Charters. When Archbishop Stephen Langton proposed that he confirm them once more in January 1223, Henry responded to those opposing reconfirmation: 'We have sworn to all these liberties and we are bound to them for that [which] we have sworn we will observe'.[4]

At the time, Henry III had little choice but to accept the Charters, for the civil war had left him penniless, and chronic poverty severely circumscribed his government's authority. The price paid for new sources of revenue, usually the percentage levy on moveable goods pioneered by John, was royal confirmation of the Charters, a bargain between young king and his subjects necessitated by his poverty. When a great council in 1225 agreed to the levy of a fifteenth, the royal government responded with revisions of the two 1217 Charters that became definitive versions. The practice of confirming the Charters in exchange for grants of revenues continued, and in 1237 Henry would again reconfirm them in return for another levy.

Another factor in issuing the 1225 Charters was Henry III's age, for he was approaching his majority and was able to attest his charters personally with his own seal, not as earlier, when the regent and the papal legate sealed royal charters as his proxies. As with the earlier versions, official copies of the 1225 Charter went out to the sheriffs, who were ordered to hold public readings for the people. One copy, sent to the sheriff of Wiltshire and later deposited at Lacock Abbey, passed to the family that acquired the abbey's property after Henry VIII's suppression of religious houses. This copy of Magna Carta remained in private hands until 1945, when a descendant presented it to the British Museum; it was sent to the US Library of Congress for two years, lent as a gesture of thanks for the Library's safekeeping of the 1215 Lincoln Cathedral copy during the Second World War. Today it is displayed in the British Library alongside another 1215 original (Additional MS. 46144) (see Plate 7). Other copies of the 1225 version survive at Durham Cathedral and in the Public Record Office at Kew (DL 10/71).

The preamble to the 1225 Charter states that the king granted its liberties 'of our own spontaneous goodwill',[5] presenting its promises as the monarch's free gift to his subjects and hiding any hint of the threat of force hanging over the 1215 and 1216 grants. The final chapter made clear that the grant was not entirely free, but resulted from a bargain, given in return for his subjects' agreement to a new general tax. The 1225 version of the Charter contains thirty-seven chapters, although a definitive numbering of its provisions only appeared with early printed editions. A few clauses were simply dropped, but the length was reduced chiefly by combining clauses; for example, chapters 44, 45 and 46 of the 1217 charter were merged into a single final chapter (37). With this reduction, the key clause in John's Charter, chapter 39, becomes chapter 29.[6] The 1225 Charter followed the 1216 and 1217 Charters in deleting the 1215 provision for a baronial committee with power to make war on the monarch; without this chapter, there was no constitutional remedy for the king's violation of his commitments. Included, however, was the king's grant of Magna Carta in perpetuity and his promise that neither he nor his heirs would 'procure anything whereby the liberties contained in this charter shall be infringed or weakened' (chapter 37); in short, any royal acts contrary to its terms were to be considered invalid. The Church seemed to possess the only threat that could compel enforcement, for it intimidated violators with the risk of excommunication, and a blanket excommunication of future violators accompanied the 1225 Charters, as it would confirmations later in the thirteenth century.

The 1225 version of the Great Charter completed the work of the royal counsellors of Henry III's minority in preserving it, and this reissue, along with the Forest Charter, meant that Henry III's will, freely exercised by his Angevin ancestors, was restricted by a written statement of the law of the land. In later generations, English kings' subjects would look to Magna Carta as a guarantor of their liberties, at the least safeguarding the Church's freedom and free men's landholdings, even though few of them knew the difference between John's 1215 grant and his son's version. By the end of the Middle Ages, John's Charter was largely forgotten, and only Henry III's 1225 version was known. Nevertheless, a vague recollection of Magna Carta as recording ancient liberties earned it the English people's veneration earlier given to the 'good old laws' of Edward the Confessor. Appeals to specific provisions of the 1225 Charter appear often enough in the plea rolls to prove lawyers' and litigants' familiarity with it. Especially common were complaints against violations of chapter 11, declaring that common pleas should not follow the king, but should be held in some fixed place; often the justices retorted that the plea touched the king, or that it was an 'uncommon plea' that merited royal attention. Reformers dissatisfied with royal mismanagement would continue to look to Magna Carta, and their demands for reconfirmation of the 1225 Charters replaced the cries for restoration of the laws of Henry I raised in 1215.

Magna Carta and the constitutional crises of Henry III's personal rule

Once Henry III took personal responsibility for his kingdom's rule, he experienced strained relations with the barons over some of the same issues that had troubled his father's reign. Henry III's relations with his barons were far from amicable, though less vicious than under his father, and for much of his reign England was a land of lawlessness, violence and civil war. Just as John appeared to place his personal and dynastic interest in recovering lost lands in France ahead of the kingdom's good, so Henry's unrealistic foreign entanglements angered the politically active classes. As in John's reign, his subjects chafed at the role in royal government exercised by the king's favourites, many of whom were aliens, and their influence at court seemed to leave native nobles outside the protection of the law. The magnates grew increasingly displeased by their declining role in governance compared to their position during Henry's minority or during Richard Lionheart's absence on crusade. Barons' suspicions of 'secret' or 'household' government had some basis, for Henry tended to bypass the great offices of state, the exchequer and chancery, that were disengaging from the royal household and developing bureaucratic routines that limited his personal control. Like his father who had relied on his chamber, a household office malleable to his will, Henry III bypassed older offices to make the wardrobe the heart of his administration. While he regularly summoned great councils and called parliaments by the 1230s, supposedly to take counsel with his magnates, he preferred the advice of intimates at court.

In the first crisis of Henry's personal rule, Magna Carta was a weapon for subjecting him to the rule of law. In his middle years, cries for reform culminated in baronial rebellion that also found inspiration in the Charter, reviving the concept of a baronial committee as a check on the king. Matthew Paris, the most important contemporary chronicler of the first half of Henry's reign, presented Henry III's troubles with his barons as largely a continuation of his father's conflicts with his great men, although Paris's chronicle stopped early in the constitutional crisis of Henry's middle years, 1258–65. Despite the magnates' ultimate lack of success in devising workable mechanisms for defending the Charter's liberties, their efforts had the effect of focusing the public's eyes on the document.

Henry III came of age by 1227, but his personal rule did not begin until he had thrown off the influence of his longtime justiciar, Hubert de Burgh. Once the king assumed full control of his government by 1230, his personality and political outlook took on new importance. Henry III was somewhat lazy, pious, perhaps overly so, too trusting, and something of an aesthete. He displayed a naïveté or simplicity that rankled his magnates, and his views seemed to be shaped by those surrounding him; as a consequence, he appeared incapable of judging the practicality of schemes that his favourites proposed to him. Henry's piety inspired him to make Edward the Confessor his model as king, a saint on the throne, but hardly an engaged ruler. His religious views reinforced exalted ideas about the sacramental character of kingship that compared his authority over England to the pope's power over the Church, and Henry concocted much of the pomp and splendour that still surround the English monarch.

Despite Henry's simplicity, he held a paternalistic notion of royal office that harked back to his predecessors' rule before 1215, contrasting with the principles set forth in Magna Carta and with the practice prevailing during his minority. Because the Charter had been reissued several times in his youth, he could not defy its restrictions, but he tried to evade them. The Great Charter was vague on certain points, and it contained no clauses spelling out a role for the magnates in the appointment of officials, patronage, or policy decisions, matters that he felt were for the monarch alone, although his great men considered his attitude incompatible with the spirit of Magna Carta. Since the 1225 document stripped away the security clause of John's charter, discontented barons and bishops had to search, without great success, for some scheme for enforcing Magna Carta. Although the English Church's threat of excommunication for violating the Great Charter's terms perhaps had a deterrent effect on officials executing the royal will, its sanctions caused Henry little anxiety despite his piety, since the papacy protected him from English prelates' sentences of excommunication.

Once the king came fully of age in 1227, it was almost inevitable that he should come into conflict with Hubert de Burgh, for a reconstituted royal household now competed with the justiciar's staff at Westminster for control of government. By 1232, Henry had moved against his justiciar, removing him from office peremptorily, seizing his lands and ordering his arrest. Henry turned to his former tutor, Peter des Roches, bishop of Winchester, who was an advocate of the authoritarian administrative practices of John's reign. An autocratic view of royal government triumphed following Peter des Roches's return to prominence in 1231, and a short-lived experiment in 'household government' ensued

(1232–34), that brought on the first constitutional crisis of the reign. Des Roches urged on Henry an expensive expedition for recovery of John's lost French lands and encouraged him to revive his father's authoritarian rule at home. Because the English baronage failed to share the king's enthusiasm for such a goal, it proved impossible to raise moneys approaching the huge amounts amassed by his father and uncle, and expeditions deployed to Poitou in 1230 and 1242 failed to win Henry III the military glory that he hoped for. Despite Henry's failure to regain lost provinces or to counter Capetian expansion into his surviving French possessions, he remained lord of some overseas territory, for the English would continue to hold Gascony in southwestern France for two more centuries.

Peter des Roches assumed the role of protector of King John's alien mercenaries still in England, and this precipitated a great crisis by 1232 that would result in a reaffirmation of Magna Carta's principles. Zealous for rehabilitation of his fellow aliens, the bishop urged Henry III to restore their possessions lost during the 1220–23 resumption of royal lands and castles. Henry obliged by annulling his own grants, earlier royal charters that had regranted the foreigners' holdings to others, thus undermining the security of the new possessors' property and threatening the very basis of landholding within the kingdom. These revocations caused upheavals that led to violent opposition by some leading magnates, resulting in Peter des Roches's disgrace by 1234. The events of 1232–34 provided a lesson in kingship for Henry, reminding him that chapter 29/39 of Magna Carta placed him under the law and reaffirming the Great Charter as England's law of the land, the standard by which good government was to be measured. Furthermore, the crisis proved that Henry's earls, barons and bishops, gathered in a great council, were willing to subject him to the law.

A great council in May 1234 overturned Henry's outlawry of Hubert de Burgh and restored the property of those displaced by the bishop of Winchester's friends. William of Raleigh, the royal justice pronouncing judgement, was an experienced royal judge and the prime mover behind the great treatise *On the Laws and Customs of England*, commonly called *Bracton*. This great survey of English law, begun in the 1220s or 1230s and completed over many years, is a difficult text with many interpolations and additions. In several passages, perhaps not original, *Bracton* stresses that the king is 'under God and under the law, because the law makes the king', and he must 'temper his power by law, which is the bridle of power'. Although it admits the monarch's moral obligation to follow the law, it proposes no plan for compelling a tyrannical ruler to do so, since the king 'has no superior except God'.[7] One passage, however, hints that an oppressive prince's subjects can find a remedy other than divine wrath, positing the possibility of the baronage taking action 'in the king's own court', as the 1234 council acted to compel Henry III to reverse his unlawful acts. Elsewhere an addition to the text spells out more clearly the magnates' responsibility to restrain a king who acts outside the law: 'The king has a superior, namely, God. Also the law by which he is made king. Also his court, namely, the earls and barons, because if he is without bridle, that is without law, they ought to put the bridle on him.'[8] This is a restatement of the barons' action in forcing King John to issue Magna Carta, a summary of their achievement in 1234, and a foreshadowing of their later attempt in the 1258–65 baronial reform movement. Texts of *Bracton* survived to circulate in the early modern era, and Sir Edward Coke cited it in one of his confrontations with the first Stuart kings.

Unfortunately, Henry III did not fully learn the Great Charter's lesson of due process during the crisis of 1232–34, and the barons had reason to fear further arbitrary royal acts. Barons could not enjoy fully the 'regular procedures' of the common law that Magna Carta guaranteed to their own tenants, for political and patronage considerations inevitably led to the king's interference in lawsuits by royal tenants-in-chief. Complaints about a lack of justice after 1234 centred not so much on disregard of Magna Carta's prohibition of the king's arbitrary seizure of person or property as on its condemnation of his sale, denial and delay of justice. Indeed, Henry's denial of justice to a longtime royal official, complaining of an unprovoked attack on his servants by retainers of one of the king's foreign relatives, would become a major factor in igniting the 1258 revolution.

Denial of royal justice was due less to Henry III personally than to powerful friends and relatives in his household, whom he allowed to corrupt the entire judicial system. Influential courtiers enjoyed royal privileges and protection that denied justice to those bold enough to bring lawsuits against them. Among those enjoying most lavish royal favour were the king's alien relatives, the Provençal and Savoyard uncles of his wife, Eleanor of Provence, and his Poitevin half-brothers, the Lusignans, who had settled in England to seek their fortunes. Country barons who did not frequent the court resented a royal government that seemed to benefit only the king's favourites, many of them aliens, and that left the native English outside the law's protection, neglecting the Charter. It appeared that Henry's judges could be bribed or intimidated into denying pleaders lacking influence redress in violation of Magna Carta's guarantees. Knights of the counties who served on local judicial commissions feared challenging the king's favourites, for they had learned that he would not listen to allegations against his friends or family. As a list of grievances against the English king submitted to St Louis of France in 1264 summarizes the situation, 'Although in the charter it is laid down that to no one shall the king sell, deny, or delay right or justice . . . after the arrival of certain aliens whom the king, scorning his native subjects, drew to his counsels, no justice could be obtained in [his] court against these men or against certain courtiers'. It goes on to state that not even wronged persons could obtain writs or other lawful remedies, 'which by custom of the realm should be granted to every petitioner'.[9] Henry proved too weak to resist such pressure from his kinsmen and courtiers; he was an 'under-mighty king' who was no match for his over-mighty subjects.[10]

If royal justice was a danger to the magnates, it was they, in turn, who denied justice to lesser men, since the tight control over the judiciary exercised by Henry III's predecessors had weakened, leaving sheriffs, barons of the exchequer and royal judges without effective supervision. In the countryside, Henry proved ineffective in imposing order, and his personal rule marks an early phase of local leaders' domination of the counties that would be characteristic of late medieval England. Power was flowing away from the central government as it surrendered local peace-keeping and dispute settlement to the magnates and their estate managers. The barons were already learning to manipulate the common law courts by methods that would become common in the fourteenth or fifteenth centuries, putting royal justices on their payroll and protecting their dependants in trouble with the law by tampering with juries or intimidating local judges.

Henry III could not give up his ambitions for his ancestors' lost French lands, despite his subjects' waning support for wars overseas. Since the king could not create a consensus among the baronage that would provide financial and political backing for his plans to recover Poitou, he had no success in overseas expeditions of 1230, 1242, or 1253; moreover, his incompetence as a military commander undermined his nobles' respect for him. A need to increase royal revenues continued, but because Henry lacked counsellors capable of managing his parliaments, he could not win the barons' consent to money-grants without redress of grievances and changes in policies perceived as threatening property rights. Although chapters 12 and 14 of John's Charter calling for imposition of aids and scutages by 'the common counsel of our kingdom' were discarded in later versions, in practice Henry had no choice but to accept the 'common counsel' of his great men before levying new taxes. Because of their reluctance to grant general levies, the king looked for other means of raising funds. An easy means for increasing royal revenues was exploitation of the common law courts, especially the itinerant justices' periodic circuits of the counties; and payments for judicial favours and fines levied on the guilty by judges visiting the counties reached a peak under Henry III, not under his father. Also his exploitation of the Jews with heavy tallages brought financial ruin to England's Jewish community, diminishing its value as a ready source of royal cash. Other revenue-raising devices included repossessing previously alienated royal lands, exploiting the royal forests, and reviving long-neglected customary payments. Yet these fiscal expedients proved inadequate, only adding to the aggravation of Henry's subjects, who regarded them as arbitrary and oppressive, violations of Magna Carta.

The magnates' price for consenting to a new levy on moveable goods in 1237 was another confirmation of the Great Charter, revocation of the most intolerable of the king's fiscal innovations, abandonment of attempts to reclaim lands formerly in royal hands, and changes in the personnel of the royal council. Also the 1237 Parliament secured the king's written statement that the new tax would not form a precedent for similar levies. Clearly, Magna Carta was considered fundamental law, a kind of contract between the king and his subjects to be renewed periodically in exchange for payments. Again when Henry needed funds for a 1253 campaign in Gascony, his magnates' grant of financial aid was followed by another confirmation of the Charters. Mere reconfirmation of Magna Carta was not adequate for curbing the abuses of Henry III's personal rule, since the 1225 Charter contained no enforcement clause. With nothing comparable to the baronial committee of twenty-five contained in King John's Charter, Henry's magnates would have to seek more radical reforms to secure for themselves a larger part in governance. Occasionally, they acted in ways that presage the 1258 reform movement, going beyond punishing the king by denying his requests for taxes and pressing for participation in central government through appointment of men of high standing to the council as 'preservers of the liberties'.

A crisis in Henry III's personal rule was building after 1250, as his ineptness inspired a major reform movement among both lay and ecclesiastical lords. The penetration of Christian piety among the nobility was pulling the two groups together, and the clergy played an important part in focusing attention on Magna Carta as dissatisfaction with Henry's rule mounted. In a solemn ceremony at Westminster Hall in 1253, the archbishop of Canterbury excommunicated violators of the Church's privileges, ancient custom and the liberties granted in the 1225 Charters, and the convocation of the clergy in 1258 drew up a list of grievances accusing the king of violating the Church's rights granted 'at the beginning of his great charter on the liberties granted to the English'.[11] Clerics complained specifically that Henry kept ecclesiastical posts vacant in order to enjoy the income for himself, a practice that they pointed out on three occasions was a violation of the Charter (1225, chapter 33). Churchmen always objected to royal interference in episcopal elections, and Robert Grosseteste, the pious and learned bishop of Lincoln, wrote to the archbishop of Canterbury as early as 1240 concerning a forthcoming election. Grosseteste suggested that the archbishop send spokesmen to explain to the electors 'the charter of King John concerning the granting of freedom of elections and the confirmation of Pope Innocent . . . and the sentence directed against all violators of the liberties granted in the Great Charter of the lord king, in which it is granted that the English Church shall be free forever'.[12]

Barons were offended by Henry III's distribution of patronage, for they saw it flowing to aliens in the royal household, not to native-born nobles. The prodigality of Henry's gifts to his four Lusignan half-brothers and to his Provençal and Savoyard in-laws alarmed even royal officials, for it threatened to dissipate the crown's resources. The king's reliance on household offices, staffed by clerks and knights of obscure or foreign origin instead of great officers of state, inspired suspicions of secret government. The misgivings had some basis, for the justiciarship remained vacant after 1232, and the chancellor no longer had charge of the king's seal after 1238. Henry was adamant about his right to control appointments of ministers and to reserve patronage and policy matters for himself. With government largely in the hands of lesser-ranking royal agents, it was easier for favoured courtiers to manipulate its machinery for personal gain and more difficult for country barons and knights, seldom at court, to master its workings or to fix blame on individual officials. Henry's failings as ruler aroused cries for reform and reconfirmation of Magna Carta, but the Charter offered no remedy for barons' powerlessness over his choice of royal officials or counsellors.

It was the so-called 'Sicilian business' in 1254 that made clear the flawed nature of the counsel that Henry III was receiving from his intimates. Lacking prudent counsellors, the king managed to entangle himself in a papal vendetta against a German family, the Hohenstaufens, that claimed imperial authority over Italy. Combining his submissiveness to the pope with grandiose dreams of dominating southern Europe from Aquitaine to Sicily, Henry accepted a papal offer of the Sicilian throne for his second son. His costly entanglement in this unlikely Mediterranean adventure brought dissatisfaction in England to a boiling point, for it afforded no advantage to the kingdom. It exemplified Henry's flaws as ruler: failure to consult the magnates, putting family interests above

those of the kingdom, exercising poor judgement, and taking on commitments without considering the consequences.

Personal factors proved almost as important as policy matters in
fomenting a reform movement as rival factions formed at court to influence Henry III. Winners in the contest for royal generosity rallied around
the king, while resentful losers turned to plots for reform. Barons
frequenting the court to promote their personal projects sought to preserve royal prerogatives, and they formed a faction centred on Queen
Eleanor and Henry's brother, Earl Richard of Cornwall, greatest of the
magnates. A rival court faction, less lucky at the game of patronage,
formed around Henry's son, the Lord Edward, who resembled other
royal heirs in chafing at his lack of independent resources. Barons lacking
or losing influence in the competition among court factions advocated
reforms to regain their rightful place as the king's natural counsellors.
They resented what they saw as private or secret government not in the
best interest of the kingdom, but for the benefit of Henry's kin, powerful
courtiers and foreign favourites. The most prominent opponents of
the king were former royal favourites, notably the French-born earl of
Leicester, Simon de Montfort, a foreigner who had profited from royal
favour, marrying the king's sister and winning high office, and then lost
the king's friendship. At first, his enmity toward Henry owed more to
personal grievances than to political principles, but he soon committed
himself to broad reform beneficial not only to the baronage, but to the
knightly class as well. Like the magnates, knights feared government
under the household's sway that isolated the king and permitted insiders
at court to exploit their position for personal advantage.

By 1258, the second great crisis of Henry III's personal rule had
begun, a baronial movement to restrain his authority, to place the bridle
of the law on him. While thwarted baronial ambitions figure in the
opposition to the king, they are no more a full explanation for the strife
of 1258–65 than of the earlier rebellion against John. Constitutional
questions played a prominent part, and the reforming barons' criticisms
of Henry's government grew out of the previous generation's experience
in the 1215–17 rebellion and events of Henry's minority. In their
view, Henry's early years had shown the merits of ministers responsible
to great councils, and they wished to move beyond Magna Carta to
machinery for permanent baronial participation in governance that would
place the king firmly under the rule of law. The reformers hoped to
convert the great officers of state from personal servants of the king into
public servants accountable to the political community by reserving key
posts for men of baronial rank. They favoured frequent parliaments as
a means of presenting their views and imposing accountability on the

king. Previous parliaments, meeting at irregular intervals for short sessions, had proven inadequate for controlling royal servants in constant attendance on the king. The discontented barons also wished to create a formally defined royal council, with mandatory baronial membership, that could be held accountable for the advice it gave the king.

By spring of 1258, the Sicilian imbroglio had deepened many magnates' disgust with Henry III, and a small group of plotters organized a sworn confederation or commune committed to opposing jointly his war in Italy. Once the great men of the kingdom, led by the earls Richard de Clare of Gloucester and Simon de Montfort of Leicester, began to demand change, Henry could not ignore the danger, since clergy, minor barons and country gentry shared the magnates' outrage. The reformers faced a dilemma, for they could hardly compel a crowned and anointed monarch to accept their demands without threatening force, violating their fealty and running the risk of treason. Almost any limitation on royal power would have been unacceptable to Henry III and his courtiers, and the rebels' experience against King John had shown the difficulty of devising any workable mechanism for restricting the monarch's authority. Opposition magnates sought to avoid accusations of treason by treating Henry as a simpleton, a mental incompetent, led astray by 'evil counsellors' in his household, and they sought to remove them and to place the king under the great men's wardship, as in his minority. Soon the small band of rebel barons expanded into a body calling itself *le commun de Engleterre*, usually translated by English historians as 'the community of the realm', that is, a society or corporation capable of speaking for the whole kingdom. For many in the Middle Ages, the word 'commune' aroused fear, recalling revolutionary associations in continental towns that had seized power with violence. Indeed, the baronial reformers challenged hallowed assumptions about royal authority, and their programme culminated in radical political experiments not to be seen again in England until the seventeenth century.

Clearly, this sworn band of reforming barons was familiar with Magna Carta, and they held that their proposed innovations grew out of the Charter, necessitated by the king's resistance to its constraints. Matthew Paris wrote that one of the demands made by the Oxford Parliament of June 1258 was that the king 'should faithfully keep and observe the charter of the liberties of England, which his father, king John, had made and granted to the English and sworn to keep; and which he, king Henry the third, had many times granted and sworn to keep'.[13] The Parliament insisted on appointment of a committee to reform the government, with the king and the commune each nominating twelve members. In June 1258, the committee crafted the Provisions of Oxford, initiating a period of political experimentation lasting until 1265 that searched for a way to limit royal power and broaden the base of England's government.

The Provisions adopted at Oxford proposed to limit Henry III by creating two councils sharing power with him: a council of fifteen appointed jointly by the king and the barons, and a second council of twelve appointed by the barons alone 'to treat of the common business of the kingdom and of the king likewise'.[14] The reforming barons demanded restoration of the great offices of justiciar and chancellor and their separation from the royal household; in acknowledgement of their 'public' nature, the new council of fifteen would share in their selection and supervision. Reform of the exchequer followed in an effort to prevent the king's expenditure of funds diverted to his household offices. If implemented, such a programme would have wrested execut-ive power from the king, changing England's pattern of governance from a monarchical model to rule by aristocratic councils similar to the Italian city-republics.

The movement soon took on characteristics of a moral crusade, for preachers of the new mendicant orders and scholars at Oxford Univer-sity condemned 'modern princes who oppress poor country folk',[15] and bishops were prominent in debates of the 1258 reforming Parliament. The English clergy were well acquainted with Magna Carta, for they constantly cited it in their protests against Henry's infringement of the Church's liberties. Nearly all monastic chronicles written during the period of the baronial struggle show their authors' bias toward the barons' cause. The most important of them, Matthew Paris until he stopped writing in 1259, favoured attempts by the community of the realm to limit royal power through turning to the Great Charter and other charters of liberties. He condemned the king for violating his oaths and for showing 'little regard for . . . the tenor of his Great Charter so many times paid for'.[16]

The *Song of Lewes*, probably written by a friar in celebration of the barons' 1264 victory, sets forth the ideals of good governance held by such reformist barons as Simon de Montfort. They had three chief concerns, first of which was placing the king firmly under the law, echoing Magna Carta and *Bracton*. As the *Song* states, 'If the king be without this law, he will go astray; if he hold it not, he will err shame-fully. Its presence gives right reigning, and its absence the disturbance of the realm', and it cites the Old Testament, 'King Saul is rejected because he broke the law; and David is related to have been punished as soon as he acted contrary to the law'. Second, the king must choose his counsellors carefully, placing 'natives at his side, whether as councillors or as the greater men of the realm, not strangers nor favourites who supplant others and the good customs'; and he ought not raise up newcomers to court at the expense of native nobles. The third principle is the magnates' responsibility for the best interest of the realm when the king fails to choose suitable counsellors; in the Song's words, 'it is the duty of the magnates of the kingdom to see what things are convenient for the governance of the kingdom, and expedient for the preservation of peace'.[17]

Once the Provisions of Oxford had reformed the central administration, the desire for reform spread throughout the countryside, and free men of middling and lesser rank pressed for changes in local government. Minor barons, knights and lesser freeholders in the shires shared the magnates' dissatisfaction with Henry III. As evidence from the 1258–59 judicial circuit shows, victims of local officials, far from court and lacking influence to approach the king with their complaints, had little recourse; one plaintiff protested that he was unable to prosecute his action of debt 'on account of the favour in which [his debtor] stood with William de Valence, the queen's uncle'.[18] The 'community of the bachelors of England', speaking for the rural gentry in the shires, protested to Parliament that the reforming barons had done nothing 'for the utility of the republic', remedying only matters concerning themselves. In October 1259, the knights secured passage of the Provisions of Westminster, often conflated with the Provisions of Oxford. It reaffirmed Magna Carta, setting forth that 'the charters of liberties and of the forest are to be kept and maintained',[19] and it sought to placate the knights by limiting the office of sheriff to knights native to the county, who were to be elected annually and paid a stipend. More crucial were the restrictions that the Provisions of Westminster placed on lords' authority over their private courts, extending Magna Carta's guarantees of 'due process' to free men subject to their jurisdiction as had been earlier promised but never implemented. When members of the council prepared to go on circuits to hear the people's complaints in 1259, their instructions called for them to hear the people's complaints against injuries inflicted in breach of the Charter's liberties.

England struggled under the new constitution for two years, but co-operation between king and councils proved impossible, and it crumbled by April 1261, when Henry III obtained the pope's absolution from his oaths to support the Provisions. Although the king repudiated the Provisions of Oxford, he sought to reassure his subjects by declaring his continued acceptance of the Charters. By 1263, his heir, the Lord Edward, was recruiting a royalist party among the baronage, and civil war threatened. As was frequently the case in thirteenth-century confrontations, the two sides sought to avoid war by agreeing to a complicated scheme for arbitration. Louis IX of France, renowned for his saintliness, wisdom and justice, agreed to arbitrate, but his exalted view of kingship ensured that he would find the Provisions in conflict with the English king's sacred and ancient rights. The French monarch did assert, however, that Henry III was bound by 'royal privileges, charters, liberties, establishments and praiseworthy customs of the kingdom of England existing before the time of the same provisions' – in other words, by Magna Carta.[20]

Once news of the French king's ratification of Henry III's position arrived in January 1264, warfare was inevitable. By this time, the most formidable resistance to Henry's recovery of power lay in the counties among the gentry, knights and lesser-ranking free men, who were more willing to move to outright rebellion than the barons with their stronger sense of personal loyalty to the monarch. Simon de Montfort, earl of Leicester, who had become leader of the militant opposition, stood steadily for the Provisions of Oxford. Despite possessing his share of aristocratic arrogance, pride and selfishness, he possessed a streak of idealism, and political principles springing from his Christian faith won him friends within the Church's hierarchy. He could look beyond narrow noble advantage to appeal to the knightly and commercial classes that had seldom participated in English politics previously. His sympathy for the common people encouraged peasants to see themselves as part of 'the community of the realm' and fight on the Montfortian side, when warfare erupted in the spring of 1264.

Montfort's resounding victory over the royalist army at the battle of Lewes brought another quest for a mechanism for limiting royal power. Although the earl of Leicester had stalwartly supported the Provisions of Oxford with its pattern of baronial councils, after his victory at Lewes he was the over-mightiest of subjects, wielding dictatorial power over England. Yet it was politically impossible to depose an anointed monarch, and the victor had no means of legitimizing his authority. Montfort governed in the captive king's name through a series of councils, an undertaking that marked the most radical attempt at redistributing power in the English kingdom before the seventeenth-century civil war and Cromwellian experiments in republican governance. He soon made a bid to broaden his base of support by ordering four knights elected from each county to come to a parliament, and in 1265 he summoned knights to another parliament along with representatives of the boroughs. Montfort's expansion of representation in Parliament was hardly likely to be followed by Henry III after the reform movement's defeat. None the less, inclusion of representatives of the knights of the counties and merchants in the boroughs encouraged a wider definition of the community of the realm, and in the fourteenth century their presence would be a permanent feature of parliaments.

Simon de Montfort's rule did not last long, for he could not keep his following united, and some reformers came to consider him an obstacle to reconciliation with the monarch. A royalist army defeated the reformers' force, leaving Montfort dead on the battlefield at Evesham in August 1265; and within days, most reform measures were nullified and Henry III restored to full power. The reforms and the strife of 1258–65 had failed to put a bridle on the king, but the royalist victory did not signify displacement of Magna Carta from its central position in English law and politics. As part of the Dictum of Kenilworth that formally ended the period of civil war in 1266, the king promised once more to observe the Great Charter and the Forest Charter. His heir, the Lord Edward, who had sympathy for some aspects of the reform movement, became *de facto* ruler of the kingdom on his father's behalf, and in 1267 he secured enactment of certain measures of the 1259 Parliament in the Statute of Marlborough. Included in this statute was a clause declaring that 'The Great Charter shall be kept in every one of its articles, as well in those pertaining to the king as those pertaining to others'.[21] The English people continued to assign a high value to Magna Carta, and their appeals to it both as a premise for political reform and as a practical defence in the law courts guaranteed its perpetuation in the next century.

Edward I and new confirmations of Magna Carta, 1272–1307

Edward I's governance of England resembled closely that of his father and grandfather, for all three followed Angevin tradition in their dedication to preserving and expanding the ruler's power. Unlike Henry III or John, however, Edward largely succeeded in bolstering the crown's position, insisting on exercising his rights to the fullest extent. Coming to the throne not as a minor like Henry III, but as an adult experienced in ruling, he proved more capable in maintaining efficient administration. A warrior-king, far away on crusade at the time of his father's death in 1272, he conformed more closely to contemporary ideals of kingship than either his father and grandfather. Warfare characterized Edward's reign, for he dedicated himself to the defence of Gascony, the last of the English kings' French possessions, and to the extension of England's authority over the entire island of Britain, undertaking the conquest of Wales by 1277 and making war on the Scots after 1296. His costly warfare, like that of his Angevin forebears, demanded arbitrary revenue-raising measures that oppressed his subjects, for his aims proved too ambitious for the income of a thirteenth-century monarch. Resistance to his constant pressure for money would arouse cries for the confirmation of the Charters in the last decade of his reign.

While Edward I is traditionally held up as the model of a Christian prince, combining Christian piety and chivalric conduct, the inhabitants of Wales and Scotland, victims of his repeated invasions aimed at crushing them, would hardly have accepted such a characterization. Nor would modern scholars, who speculate that had Edward lived longer, he could have turned England in a direction similar to the absolutist path followed by French monarchs. Yet Victorian scholars treated Edward I with respect, anointing him the father of the English Parliament because his reign proved to be a decisive period for the constitutional and legal spheres, with Parliament taking shape. They saw him shaping parliaments into genuine national assemblies that shared in governing the kingdom on behalf of all ranks of the English and enacting statutes bringing order to English land law to protect private property. Regardless of the validity of the Victorians' view, a large assembly including spokesmen for knights and townspeople replaced committees of barons as the favoured instrument for reining in the king and his chosen counsellors. With such a forceful ruler as Edward I, earlier reforming schemes under his father for putting the government into the hands of baronial committees or commissions appeared impractical. Such programmes would not resume until the reign of Edward's weak son, Edward II.

Edward I confirmed Magna Carta and the Forest Charter as early as 1276, and no political crises clouded the first half of his reign, a time that is often identified as the high point of medieval English monarchy. In the second half of Edward's reign, however, his practice of personal government was violating the spirit of Magna Carta. His chief problem was financial, caused by his military campaigns throughout the 1290s against the French, the Welsh and the Scots, with fighting sometimes raging on two or three fronts simultaneously. After 1294, his warfare seemed to have no end, and heavy taxation undermined his previous popular support. No longer was the king requiring new taxes intermittently to meet emergencies; instead, his need for money, military service, and supplies seemed to be perpetual. Edward's demands for funds aroused such opposition from his barons and bishops, lesser clergy and merchants that a political crisis erupted by 1297, and almost a century after 1215, Magna Carta again took centre stage. Parliaments would take up the Charter as a weapon, demanding its reconfirmation and clarification of its chapters with supplementary clauses to impose the rule of law on the king, ending his arbitrary collection of taxes and requisitions of supplies.

The Great Charter was widely known at the end of the thirteenth century, with copies circulating in legal handbooks owned by lawyers and landholders. The propertied classes could grasp its significance, since increased emphasis on written proof such as charters in the law courts attracted them to Magna Carta with its explicit clauses as a defence of their lands and liberties. Because of its promise of freedom for the English Church, ecclesiastics valued the Charter, and churchmen were the first to raise complaints against Edward I's arbitrary demands. In 1279, the archbishop of Canterbury quarrelled with the king over ecclesiastical reforms opposed by Edward because they endangered his use of church livings to reward royal clerks. To make a point, the archbishop had the Charter read out at an ecclesiastical council and threatened to excommunicate anyone threatening its promise of freedom for the English Church. At the same council, he sought to ensure the people's access to the Charter and ordered copies, 'well and clearly written', to be posted in a prominent spot in all cathedrals and collegiate churches.[22] Edward objected to these decrees, however, ordering the archbishop to repudiate them, and the copies of Magna Carta were taken down from church doors.

Edward turned to the English Church in his quest for funds, taking half its income, a demand allegedly so shocking to the dean of St Paul's Cathedral that he died of apoplexy on hearing of it. The English clergy promptly appealed to Pope Boniface VIII, last of a series of aggressive thirteenth-century popes, and the opportunity to demonstrate papal superiority over a secular prince delighted him. In 1296, he issued a papal bull forbidding kings from taxing their clergy without the pontiff's prior permission. This presented the English clergy with a dilemma, forcing them to disobey one lord, either their secular master, the English king, or the pope, their spiritual sovereign. When they refused to disobey the pope by paying taxes to Edward, he placed them outside royal protection, in effect outlawing them. Eventually, Boniface VIII had to back down from his ban on lay taxation of the clergy, for he faced more formidable opposition from the French ruler, Philip IV. The pontiff agreed to a face-saving compromise in 1297 that allowed princes to tax their clergy in time of emergency without papal permission, leaving the definition of an emergency to the monarchs. Boniface's surrender marks the onset of a long period of papal weakness that would free Edward to tangle with the English clergy without fear.

By 1297, Edward I's excessive demands for funds for his wars united the clergy with the laity in opposing him. Driven to mobilize all the kingdom's resources for military needs in 1294, the king had increased the customs duties, enraging the merchants of the kingdom, who dubbed this unpopular new levy the *maltote* or evil toll. Edward's financial impositions initiated a period of political crises that would last for several years, and Magna Carta with its companion Forest Charter took centre stage once more. The trigger was the king's order in July for a new tax on moveable wealth and compulsory sale of merchants' wool to him for resale at a profit in preparation for a Flemish campaign. Fuelling the barons' anger was his demand that they fight in Flanders, a land where their ancestors had never performed military service. Edward won agreement to the new levy, not from a full parliament, but from a select group of magnates, or 'those standing about in his chamber' in the malicious words of a chronicler.[23] The king tried to disguise the questionable approval of the tax, declaring in his writs that it had been granted by the merchants of the kingdom. He followed this levy with another on the English clergy's goods, collected without the Church's counsel or consent on grounds of its necessity for defence of the realm. Popular opposition to the new taxes was widespread; men of one county declared that they would not pay until they were granted the liberties promised in Magna Carta and the Forest Charter.

The king's opponents, meeting in late July at Stratford near London, drafted demands to be presented to him, the *Monstraunces* or Remonstrances, a long list of grievances that included a request that the liberties granted to the English people in Magna Carta be observed. The Remonstrances complained that Edward's subjects were so burdened with taxation that they could neither afford military service in Flanders, even if they owed such an obligation, nor pay additional taxes, singling out the evil toll on wool for special mention. Furthermore, the document stated that 'all the community of the land feel themselves greatly aggrieved that they are not treated according to the laws and customs of the land by which their ancestors used to be treated, nor have they their liberties which thy used to have, but are arbitrarily put out'; and it went on to say that they 'feel themselves greatly aggrieved in that they used to be treated according to the clauses of the great charter, whose clauses are all neglected to the great loss of the people'.[24]

The situation was so tense that Edward, before sailing for Flanders in late August 1297, took care to reinforce royal castles in case of civil war. However, the king reportedly told the archbishop of Canterbury that 'If the clergy will give me a satisfactory portion of their goods for my war, I will have the old charters of liberties and of the forest firmly observed'.[25] To strengthen the magnates' opposition to the royal extortion, two earls came to the exchequer with an armed band and forbade collection of the tax and the wool crop, in the name of 'the whole community of the realm'. In Edward's absence, his council and his heir, Edward of

Caernarvon, had to deal with the crisis, and they summoned a parliament that agreed to a confirmation of Magna Carta and the Forest Charter in early October 1297, countenanced by the king overseas. They could not agree on adding new clauses to the Charter, and additional articles were placed in a separate text, a document containing six promises that became known as the Confirmation of the Charters. The first article committed Edward to keeping Magna Carta and the Forest Charter, made 'by common assent of all the realm' and confirmed by his father, Henry III. It included provision for publicizing the Charters, ordering that local royal officials 'cause the aforesaid charters to be published and have it declared to the people that we [Edward] have granted that they be kept in all their points'. Another article (3) ordered that the Charters be sent to cathedrals throughout the kingdom, 'and be read before the people twice in a year'.[26]

Among the most important clauses in the Confirmation of the Charters were promises that the contested tax levies would not constitute a precedent (article 5) and that the king would levy neither new general taxes on moveables nor export duties without 'the common assent of all the realm and for the common profit of the same realm' (6).[27] This had the effect of extending to newer forms of taxation the requirement in chapters 12 and 14 of John's 1215 Charter for counsel before levying aids and scutages that was omitted in later versions of Magna Carta. Left unaddressed was the question of who constituted 'all the realm', although it appears that knights and burgesses were to be included alongside the lay and ecclesiastical magnates. Another issue left unaddressed was the means by which 'all the realm' should register its assent. Since parliaments did not yet have exclusive authority to commit the kingdom to new taxes, it would have been possible for the king to seek consent from other assemblies.

An unofficial document, the so-called statute *De Tallagio non concedendo* (No tallage to be imposed), apparently dating from around this time, seems to point to Parliament as the appropriate agency, although it appears to be a statement of opposition demands, not an actual statute. Its first article declares that no tallage or aid is to be collected by the king 'without the will and common assent of the archbishops, bishops and other prelates, earls, barons, knights, burgesses and other free men of our realm'.[28] Antiquaries in the Tudor and Stuart eras accepted this document as genuine, although they dated it centuries earlier, and lawyers such as Sir Edward Coke would find support in it for their belief in Parliament's antiquity and its power over taxation.

Implementing the Confirmation of the Charters were royal letters recording that the king had viewed and verified the 1225 Charters; by these letters, Edward I approved and confirmed his father's promises for himself and his heirs and admitted that 'some articles . . . hitherto have perhaps not been observed'.[29] His letters went out to the counties, accompanied by copies of the newly confirmed Charters for public reading. As a result of Edward's letters, the two 1225 Charters took their places as the first of the English statutes, and it is the text of the two Charters in these 1297 letters that the first publishers of printed editions of the statutes followed in the sixteenth and seventeenth centuries. Four originals of these copies of Magna Carta survive, two preserved in former British colonies overseas, lands unknown to the late-thirteenth-century English, one at the National Library of Australia in Canberra and another purchased by an American billionaire businessman, Ross Perot. Perot bought the copy sent to Buckinghamshire that had belonged to one of the county's knightly families until it came on the market in 1981. He placed it on permanent loan at the National Archives in Washington, where it is now exhibited at the Archives alongside the Declaration of Independence and other American charters of freedom.

The 1297 crisis left both the king and his great men embittered and suspicious of each other, and their mutual mistrust endured for the rest of Edward's reign. Before the magnates left on a Scottish campaign in 1298, they insisted on a public reading of the Charters. Again at a parliament in March 1300, the archbishop of Canterbury and baronial leaders asked for reconfirmation of the Great Charter and the Forest Charter, for Edward's continued need for money for his war in Scotland had brought renewed complaints. Another confirmation followed, and a public reading of Magna Carta took place in Westminster Hall. The account of this reading makes the first specific mention that the Charter was read to the people in the English language.

Along with his 1300 confirmation, Edward had to make additional concessions in the Articles upon the Charters, or *Articuli super Cartas*, twenty articles supplementing the Confirmation of the Charters. The first article stipulated steps for solving the problem of enforcing the 1225 Charters, calling for three upstanding men to be chosen in each shire to hear complaints about violations of the Charters in cases where the common law offered no remedy. It also insisted on wide publicity for the Charters, mandating sheriffs to hold public readings in the county courts four times a year. To remedy abuses in the central administration, the Articles upon the Charters directed the king to govern through the traditional great offices of state, not through his household officials. Several articles safeguarded the integrity of the common law justices, preventing royal interference in their judgements and restricting other royal officials from usurping their judicial authority. They limited the king's steward and the marshal to hearing pleas concerning offences within the royal household (article 3), barred the exchequer from hearing common pleas 'contrary to the form of the great charter' (4), and restricted the constable of Dover Castle to disputes over upkeep of the castle (7). These articles are foreshadowings of sixteenth- and seventeenth-century rivalry between the common law courts and the conciliar or prerogative courts. Another article restricted the king's issuance of writs concerning the common law under his personal seal, his privy seal or household seal (6), for the chancellor, the official keeper of the great seal, had detached himself from the royal household. A point of major contention treated in the Articles was the royal right of *prise* or purveyance, the requisitioning of foodstuffs, carts and horses, or other supplies for the royal household; supposedly reimbursement was to be made later, though often much later or possibly never, and at rates below market prices, if paid. Although chapters 19 and 21 of the 1225 Charter had meant to protect the king's subjects from this abuse, they provided little relief; detailed regulations in the Articles of 1300 (article 2) placed real restrictions on the royal household's abuses of purveyance.

At the Lincoln Parliament in early 1301, a knight put forward a bill making the accustomed call for the king's observance of the Charters, but also calling for annulment of statutes contrary to the Charters. When the bill was ratified, Edward I was angered, but the Lords' request that he seek their common consent when naming his chief ministers irritated him even more. Apparently, a compromise concluded the parliamentary session, with the king again confirming Magna Carta and Parliament authorizing another tax levy. This time, Edward acknowledged that statutes enacted contrary to the Charters were to be emended 'by the common counsel of our realm . . . or even annulled', a statement that clearly validated the Great Charter's status as England's fundamental law.[30]

Edward's attempts to free himself from the limitations of the Confirmation of the Charters and the Articles upon the Charters constitute one of the themes of his last years, alongside the Scottish war. When he negotiated an agreement with England's merchants to increase the customs duties in 1303, such negotiation with a single group within the kingdom instead of the whole community in Parliament clearly violated the spirit of the 1297 Confirmation of the Charters. By the end of 1305, the king had largely freed himself from both the 1297 Confirmation and the 1300 Articles. With a more pliable pontiff on the papal throne, Edward won papal absolution from his promises to observe the Confirmation and the Articles in exchange for his consent to the pope's levy of a tax on the English Church. Despite the king's disavowal, the confirmations of Magna Carta in 1297 and 1300 remained fixed in his subjects' memories.

Edward I's reign marked a move in the direction of modern legislation with parliaments enacting numbers of statutes, many of them aimed at bringing order to the land law by strengthening noble lords' rights over lands of their knightly tenants. Since numerous provisions of Magna Carta treat the king's privileges in his relationship with his tenants-in-chief, three of Edward's statutes – Westminster I and II and Gloucester – refer to clauses of the Charter, restating or elaborating their provisions. The Statute of Westminster I repeats in large part the 1225 Charter's chapter on wardships (4) and states that matters concerning wards should be dealt with 'as is contained in the Great Charter of Liberties'.[31] Westminster I also expands Magna Carta's prohibition against exorbitant fines (chapter 14), extending it to tribunals of boroughs and cities and specifically prescribing that the offender's peers set the amount. Westminster III, enacted in 1290, builds on chapter 32 of the 1225 Charter, a provision not in the 1215 Charter that prohibited free tenants from granting away or selling so much of their holding that they could no longer perform services owed to their lord. The perpetuation of certain clauses of Magna Carta in Edward's legislation meant that it would continue to be cited in the common law courts, discussed in legal treatises, and studied by youths preparing for legal careers.

The Statute of Mortmain, enacted in 1279 as part of Westminster II, was Edward I's way of punishing ecclesiastics for defending the Great Charter, which he regarded as meddling. Yet it is an outgrowth of chapters in the 1217 and 1225 Charters (43 and 36), outlawing gifts of knightly tenures to monastic houses without a royal licence. Lords complained that their tenants' grants of land to religious institutions were often fraudulent, cheating them of the 'feudal incidents' and other privileges of lordship once the land passed into the 'dead hand' (*mort main*) of the Church. Not surprisingly, the clergy resented limitations on gifts and objected that the statute violated the first chapter of Magna Carta, quoting its promise that the English Church 'shall have all its rights undiminished and its liberties unimpaired'.[32]

Despite the volume of new legislation, little attention was given to making official copies of statutes, not even copies for royal judges. When the chancery began to keep a statute roll by 1299 or so, the first statute enrolled was the Great Charter. Although most lawyers and judges had access only to unofficial manuscript collections of statutes, these made available copies of the Charter, occasionally in French translation, that followed the 1225 text confirmed by Edward I in 1297 and copied on to the Parliament Rolls. Although the goal of the Edwardian statutes was the simplification of the land law, it grew steadily more complex with technical legal language that contrasted with the straightforward and succinct guarantees in Magna Carta, and litigants needed specialists' assistance. As early as the 1220s, professionals were assisting litigants in the common law courts, and an organized legal profession had taken shape in England by the end of the thirteenth century. Two types of legal professionals appeared in the royal courts: attorneys, authorized substitutes for absent litigants, and serjeants, pleaders who accompanied suitors to court and spoke on their behalf. By 1300, these new lay professionals had gained official recognition, and the inns of court in London had evolved apart from the clerically dominated schools to train 'apprentices of the Common Bench', youths preparing for careers in the common law.

Private petitions to Parliament or the chancellor complaining against unjust royal acts record citations of the Charter more often than do the rolls of the common law courts. For example, the archbishop of Canterbury complained in a 1284 letter to the chancellor against royal writs denying him custody of Dover Priory, 'contrary to the liberties that the lord king conceded to the magnates'.[33] Doubtless, the prelate was referring to chapter 33 of the 1225 Charter that confirmed to patrons of religious houses custody of their monastery's property whenever the post of abbot or prior was vacant. When the old issue of criminous clerks, cause of the conflict between Henry II and Thomas Becket, rose again in 1284 as a result of the murders of two ecclesiastics, the Church defended its right to try clerics accused of secular offences. Taking shelter under chapter 29/39 of Magna Carta, it argued that since free men ought not to lose their rights without judgement 'much more so should the church not be despoiled of its rights and liberties'.[34] When the issue of crimes by clerics appeared again in 1297, the bishop of London appealed to the Charter, petitioning the king to stop the London sheriffs from arresting members of the clergy for crimes belonging to the Church's jurisdiction.

Some lay persons with complaints against the king or his ministers turned to the Great Charter in pleas before the common law courts. Apparently, they or their legal advisers knew the Charter well enough to appeal to specific chapters, not simply its general principles. In Edward I's reign, lords of private courts still took advantage of its ban on the writ *praecipe* (chapter 24, 1225) to reclaim cases before royal justices for their own courts. Since chapter 27 limited the royal right of wardship to tenures held by knight service, a widow sought wardship of her eldest son 'according to the form and tenor of Magna Carta', claiming that the boy's inheritance was not an estate held by military service to the king.[35]

In a 1302 case, a knight charged with a felony raised objections to his jury on grounds derived from Magna Carta's promise of trial by peers. First, he protested that it was the same jury that had indicted him, and second, that the jurors were not knights and therefore not his peers. The justices rejected his first objection, for trial juries were sometimes selected from juries of presentment or grand juries before the mid-fourteenth century, but they accepted his second objection and summoned new jurors of knightly rank. Although neither the defendant nor the judges cited the Charter, chapter 29/39 was the obvious inspiration for his second complaint.

The plea rolls and the year books, law reports for students, give evidence for litigants' citations of Magna Carta in private pleas not involving actions by the king or his servants, sometimes groundless or frivolous mentions. As early as 1221, widows were turning to chapter 7 in suits for their dower lands, the portion of their husbands' property allotted to them during their widowhood. When a widow in Edward I's time complained against her lord's suit to recover lands that she held by dower-right, she ignored clauses relating directly to dower to turn at once to chapter 29/39's majestic promises. She maintained that a judgement against her would amount to unlawful seizure of her land, 'inasmuch as it is contained in the Great Charter of the liberties of England that no one shall be disseised of his free tenement without lawful judgment'.[36] In a 1292 plea, the plaintiff lost his suit because he was found to be unfree, and only free men were entitled to common law procedures. His attorney then insisted on his client's free status and claimed that the jury's contrary finding had caused him to lose his land, 'against common laws and against the tenor of the Great Charter of the lord king'.[37]

By Edward I's time, the newly established inns of court required books for law students. The massive early-thirteenth-century treatise *Bracton* proved impractical, but it provided a model for treatises condensing it and incorporating Edward's legislation. Lawbooks written in the late thirteenth century were primarily practical manuals by authors without *Bracton*'s breadth of learning. They did not treat Magna Carta in any depth, and they did not always follow *Bracton* in reminding readers of the king's subjection to the law, but their exposition of procedures in a step-by-step fashion strengthened the concept of due process of law. One book, labelled *Britton*, masqueraded as a law code issued by Edward I for England and Ireland, and the author expressed his view that these laws could be amended by the king with the consent of his earls, barons and other members of his council. Presenting the writs and procedures of the common law courts in French instead of Latin, *Britton* proved popular throughout the later Middle Ages and was one of the first English lawbooks to appear in a printed edition. Less popular was a book known as *Fleta*, written shortly after 1290, containing over twenty references to Magna Carta, including one to chapter 29/39. It defines law, not as the king's will, but as measures adopted with the magnates' advice, and it follows *Bracton* in asserting the king's subjection to the law, paraphrasing the famous statement that the barons must put the bridle of law on the king.

The legal tract from Edward I's time treating Magna Carta most fully is *The Mirror of Justices*, an anonymous work dating from around 1290, although authorship is traditionally attributed to Andrew Horn, chancellor of the city of London. It impressed neither contemporaries nor modern authorities, who today find it uncritical, filled with misinformation and myths borrowed from miscellaneous sources. In the seventeenth century, however, such believers in England's 'ancient constitution' and immemorial law as Sir Edward Coke accepted the *Mirror*'s fictions as true. It endorsed their tracing of English laws, customs and institutions – even Parliament – to a past lying beyond Alfred and Arthur, among alleged Trojan colonists.

Whoever was the author of the *Mirror*, he managed to twist clauses in Magna Carta, misconstruing their true meaning for his own purposes, for example arguing that chapter 40 of John's Charter, banning sale, delay or denial of justice, prohibited fees charged by the royal chancellor for issuing writs. Yet he recognized Magna Carta as England's fundamental law, stating that 'the law of this realm [is] founded upon the forty articles of the Great Charter of Liberties'; in his view, it was 'damnably disregarded by the governors of the law and by subsequent statutes'. Listing 155 abuses of the law, he gave first rank to the doctrine that 'the king is beyond the law, whereas he ought to be subject to it, as is contained in his [coronation] oath'. Furthermore, the *Mirror* declares that laws ought not be made by the king and his clerks, aliens, or others who dared not contradict him, but by common consent of the king and his barons. It echoes *Bracton* in concluding that monarchs had 'companions to hear and determine in the parliaments, all the writs and plaint concerning wrongs done by the king, the queen, their children and their special ministers'.[38] It is not surprising that on the *Mirror*'s publication in the 1640s it won popularity among parliamentary opponents of Charles I.

Although Parliament would replace Magna Carta as the focal point for political conflicts in the later Middle Ages, the Charter's position as a guarantor of the rule of law was still strong. As fourteenth-century parliaments took up the task of subjecting the king to the 'bridle of the law', they continued to seek royal confirmations of the Great Charter and to draft statutes that reinforced its promises. The document's ties to the common law and to the emerging legal profession were secure enough to preserve its pivotal place in England's law. Late medieval common lawyers, products of practical training outside the universities, disdained Roman and canon law and gloried in the distinctiveness of native English law.

Notes

1. Rothwell (1975), 327–31.
2. Stenton (1965), 31, citing the Waverley Annals.
3. Carpenter (1990), 4, 209.
4. Carpenter (1990), 296–7, citing Matthew Paris, *Chronica majora*.
5. Rothwell (1975), 341.
6. Henceforth this chapter will be labelled 29/39.
7. Thorne and Woodbine (1968–77), 2: 33, 305.
8. Thorne and Woodbine (1968–77), 2: 43, 110.
9. Treharne and Sanders (1973), 270–3, doc. 37C, ch. 3.
10. Coss (1989), 28, quoting K.B. McFarlane.
11. Thompson (1925), 74–5, quoting Matthew Paris, *Chronica majora*.
12. Thompson (1925), 72.
13. Rothwell (1975), 123.
14. Rothwell (1975), 3, 366.
15. Carpenter (1999), 339; Maddicott (1994), 353–5.
16. Rothwell (1975), 118–19.
17. Rothwell (1975), 899–912.
18. Maddicott (1984), 57.
19. Rothwell (1975), 373; Treharne and Sanders (1973), 150–5.
20. Stephenson and Marcham (1937), 148.
21. Rothwell (1975), 386.
22. Thompson (1925), 96.
23. Prestwich (1980), 29, citing Matthew of Westminster, *Flores Historiarum*.
24. Rothwell (1975), 472, 482.
25. Thompson (1925), 78.
26. Rothwell (1975), 485.
27. Rothwell (1975), 486.
28. Rothwell (1975), 486.
29. Rothwell (1975), 487–8.
30. Rothwell (1975), 512.
31. Thompson (1925), 56.
32. 1225 Charter, Rothwell (1975), 341.
33. Maitland (1887), 3: 263–4.
34. Prestwich (1988), 256.
35. Thompson (1925), 40–1.
36. Thompson (1948), 71.
37. Thompson (1948), 71.
38. Whittaker (1893), 175, 155 and 7.

chapter 5

MAGNA CARTA IN THE LATER MIDDLE AGES AND THE TUDOR PERIOD

Although rulers as late as Henry V (1399–1413), continued to confirm Magna Carta, it slipped into the shadows of high politics by the mid-fifteenth century to remain in the background until the seventeenth century. England under Edward II (1307–27), witnessed a halt to the progress toward powerful monarchy that had characterized Edward I's reign and a revival of baronial efforts to bridle kings seen as unfit for the crown. By the fifteenth century, the king's subjects gave greater priority to confronting rapid economic change and endemic lawlessness than to preserving restraints on royal power, and their cries for confirmation of the Charters ceased. After more than thirty confirmations in the fourteenth century, Magna Carta was confirmed only eight times in the next century.

Late medieval English history seemed to Tudor historians and Shakespeare an age of lawlessness with factionalism, civil strife and uncertainty over the succession that led to the toppling of kings in 1327, 1399, 1461, 1470, 1471, 1483 and 1485. The conflicts that became known as the Wars of the Roses centred on a simple question of who should wear the crown, not on constitutional liberties. Despite interests and ideals shared by king and aristocracy, uncertainty about the succession weakened royal authority, and under the later Plantagenet and Lancastrian monarchs great nobles filled the power vacuum in the countryside, often ignoring, intimidating or corrupting local royal officials and common law judges. Eventually, the people's desire for renewed and expanded central government would outweigh concern for Magna Carta's liberties, and stronger royal authority under the Yorkists and Tudors aroused little resistance.

Yet Magna Carta continued to resound in parliamentary debates and in judicial proceedings throughout the late Middle Ages. Parliaments during Edward III's long reign (1327–77), enacted a series of measures known to seventeenth-century critics of Stuart absolutism as the 'six statutes', spelling out precisely the Charter's promise of what was coming to be called 'due process of law'. As late as Henry VI's time, Parliament passed a statute reciting chapter 29/39's promise of due process in more precise language: 'No freeman shall be taken or imprisoned, or be disseised of his freehold, or liberties, or free customs, or be outlawed or exiled, or in any other way destroyed; nor will we pass upon him, nor condemn him, but by lawful judgment of his peers, or by the law of the land'.[1]

As lay literacy widened, lawbooks listing the Charter as the first of the statutes taught not only the lawyers but also the country gentry the common law tradition of due process. Thousands from the landholding classes learned that legal expertise was essential for defending their landholdings, and they considered the Great Charter and the common law their surest protection for property rights. The late-fourteenth-century religious radical John Wycliff even advocated that instruction in 'the king's statutes, and namely the Great Charter' replace Roman and canon law in the curriculum at Oxford and Cambridge.[2] Not even the sixteenth-century Tudors' emphasis on their subjects' obedience could overshadow Magna Carta's principle of the rule of law. A 1587 pamphlet warned of the danger of disobedience, but concluded by citing chapter 29/39 and adding that Elizabeth I was pleased to be bound by the law, 'as other her noble progenitors have done'.[3]

The Great Charter and the rise of Parliament

The reigns of Edward I and Edward III mark key stages in the growth of Parliament as a permanent part of England's government. Magna Carta with its implied compact between the king and his subjects limiting royal authority played a part in the appearance of an assembly representing the three estates of the kingdom, lords spiritual and temporal and the commons, sharing power with the monarch. Once Parliament came to contain spokesmen for ranks below the magnates, it became the protector of the people's liberties promised in Magna Carta. Members of fourteenth-century parliaments were aware of a link between the Charter and their right to consent to new taxation, and the first petition presented to the monarch by the Commons at each new parliament was a request that the Great Charter and the Forest Charter be firmly kept. Royal confirmations of the Charters, recorded on the statute rolls, impressed on the English political classes that these documents were unique, above simple statutes as fundamental and perpetual law.

Although scholars have spilt much ink trying to define Parliament and its place in England's governance, its origins lie in the notion of governing 'by counsel', which barons opposing King John saw as a remedy for his tyrannical rule. The weak government during Henry III's minority gave reality to baronial desire for frequent consultation in great councils that were assumed to speak for the 'community of the realm'. Young Henry III's magnates became accustomed to participating in the kingdom's governance, and the periodic great councils were increasingly called parliaments, although the word had not yet taken on precise meaning. Henry III's clerks in 1244 even described the assembly of barons that had imposed the Charter on his father in 1215 as the *parleamentum de Rumened* [Runnymede].[4] In the king's view, Parliament was not so much a means of seeking his great men's consent as a way of achieving unity and consensus, not merely voting proposals up or down. Chapters 12 and 14 of John's 1215 Charter had required the king to take counsel with his barons before levying scutages or aids, and these two clauses play a key part in the growth of Parliament into a representative body. Although they disappeared from subsequent versions of Magna Carta, Henry III found it prudent to take counsel in parliaments before collecting a general tax, and the custom of securing consent to taxation became permanent after he came of age. Such consent was usually coupled with a royal reconfirmation of the Charters. By Edward III's reign, parliaments had expanded to include knights and townspeople, and its exclusive right to speak for the entire realm in giving or withholding consent to taxation became firmly fixed.

Representation appears a basic element in defining Parliament for most persons today, yet no notion of representative government is set forth in chapters 12 and 14 of King John's Charter. None the less, an idea of representation, a concept that communities must give their consent to measures affecting them directly, with their chiefs or elders making binding decisions on their behalf, survived into the Middle Ages from earlier societies. By the mid-thirteenth century, the English baronage and episcopate thought themselves entitled to speak for the 'community of the realm', a notion that first appeared during King John's time. The great men of the kingdom felt themselves capable of recognizing and protecting the common good of the king's subjects as 'virtual representatives' for all classes. Their right to bind all the English people by their decisions was not questioned, and parliamentary acts were issued in the name of the whole kingdom. Yet a pretence prevailed during Henry III's reign that general taxes approved by the magnates alone had the consent of knights and free men; a writ authorizing a percentage levy in 1237 even listed the unfree among the groups allegedly agreeing to it.

Throughout the thirteenth century, the growing role in local governance of knights of the counties and burgesses in the towns was drawing them into the kingdom's political community. Occasionally, even in John's time, the king had summoned delegations of knights to give information or to hear his commands, although they were not precisely representatives of their shires. Certainly, Magna Carta took into account the knightly class's increasing importance, and by Henry III's middle years there was some sense that the knights required representation in great councils or parliaments. As early as 1227, 'knights and honest men' of each county were commanded to elect four knights to present grievances to the king 'on behalf of all the county'. Then in 1254, two knights were elected from each shire to come to the king's council to state 'on behalf of everyone in the county' the level of tax that the shires would grant. This was not a precedent for future parliaments, for the knights rarely had authority to make binding commitments for their fellows in the shires.

While the reformers of Henry III's middle years struggled to find a means for the magnates to take part in determining great matters of state, the problem also arose of integrating the knightly class into the political community. In 1264, when Simon de Montfort's grip on the baronage was weakening, he made a bid for broader support by turning to the knights and burgesses. After the battle of Lewes, he ordered each county court to elect four knights to represent their county in parliaments, and the next year Montfort again summoned knights to a parliament, also summoning spokesmen for the towns in a foreshadowing of the Commons. This 1265 precedent was followed only in one or two parliaments in Henry III's last years, but such assemblies including knights of the counties and men from the boroughs would give a wider meaning to the term 'community of the realm' in his son's reign.

Under Edward I, the attendance of representatives of the shires and boroughs, along with delegations of the lower clergy, became commonplace. Perhaps his parliaments did not fully embody a new principle of representation, yet writs in 1295 summoning knights and burgesses stated clearly that their decisions were legally binding on their communities. When Edward's Confirmation of the Charters in 1297 raised the question of the consent of 'the whole community of the realm' to new taxation, the response was to summon spokesmen for knights of the counties and townspeople along with magnates. The last parliament to meet without representatives of the knights and burgesses was in Edward II's last years; under his son Edward III, all parliaments would include them, and they began sitting apart from the peers in their own chamber.

Since the Middle Ages made little distinction between giving judgement and legislating, the great council did not act simply as an advisory assembly, but as a law court. John's baronial opponents had sought to have their disputes with him heard before their fellow barons, and merging with their idea of governance 'by judgement' was the idea of judgement 'by peers', settlement of disputes by a panel of one's equals as promised in chapter 29/39 of Magna Carta. It was not a great leap from Parliament's acting as a judicial body to its enacting new legislation in response to people's petitions seeking justice. Much of the early parliaments' work centred on hearing petitions of those who had failed to find remedies for their grievances elsewhere, and petitions that individuals presented to parliaments in the reigns of Edward III and Richard II often appealed to Magna Carta's provisions. Once Commons had become a separate body in Edward III's parliaments, private petitions gave way to common petitions, statements of general grievances drafted by the Commons, chiefly complaints for which the common law courts offered no redress. Common petitions became a major source of legislation, in effect bills that became statutes once accepted by the lords, the king and his council.

In the fourteenth century, Magna Carta, the Forest Charter and Edward I's Confirmation were seen as sacrosanct, and statutes conflicting with them were held to be invalid. A statute enacted under Edward III in 1369 declared that 'If any Statute be made to the contrary, that shall be holden for none',[5] and it called for an examination of the statutes to ensure that they did not conflict with the Charter. Periodically, Commons asked for a reading of the Charters before themselves and the Lords assembled together, and new statutes were passed that reinterpreted and expanded Magna Carta's provisions, the so-called six statutes of Edward III's middle years.

Despite Parliament's growth in the later Middle Ages into an institution with the power of the purse, the king still possessed a large measure of independence, a domain for discretionary activity unrestricted by Parliament or common law courts that became known as 'the royal prerogative'. The two spheres of royal and parliamentary authority remained unclear, potentially raising the issue of sovereignty or ultimate authority over the kingdom, although medieval politicians and political theorists in an age of divided or shared sovereignty hesitated to raise it openly. They accepted an ideal of shared power, the supremacy of 'the king in parliament'; as Henry VIII would express it later, 'We as head and you as members are conjoined and knit together into one body politic'.[6] This combination of monarch and representative assembly contained seeds for conflict, however, since the king insisted on setting policy in consultation with advisers of his own choosing, yet depended on parliamentary grants for funds to carry out those policies. By the seventeenth century, more assertive parliaments would insist on defining and demarcating the royal prerogative, raising the dreaded question of sovereignty and finding support in Magna Carta for parliamentary equality with the monarch, if not supremacy.

The Charter and the last Plantagenets: Edward II, Edward III, Richard II

Difficulties had plagued Edward I's last years as his ambition outreached his resources, and he left serious problems for his son, Edward II (1307–27), chiefly an unresolved war to subjugate the Scots and heavy debts. Under Edward I's successors, the situation under Henry III repeated itself, as the baronage resisted 'household government' that weakened its influence on the king. Two parallel and related movements to enforce Magna Carta's clauses curbing arbitrary royal authority were under way in the fourteenth century. One was a revival under Edward II and again under Richard II at the end of the century of baronial proposals for committees of magnates to supervise royal government, reminiscent of mid-thirteenth-century reform movements. Another was Parliament's prominence as an enduring political institution by Edward III's reign, claiming to be the protector and interpreter of the Great Charter. Often the first item of parliamentary business was a public reading and reaffirmation of the Charter, and as in the previous century, royal confirmation of the Charters was the price that parliaments demanded for approving general taxes. With a representative assembly permanently in place, it eventually would replace periodic baronial commissions as the favoured mechanism for guaranteeing aristocratic participation in the central government.

One of the new king's earliest acts brought him into conflict with the guarantees set forth in Magna Carta by the summer of 1307. Edward II arrested his father's treasurer, Walter Langton, bishop of Coventry and Lichfield, tossed him into the Tower, confiscated his lands and personal goods, and prepared to put him on trial before special commissioners, none of whom ranked as a peer. After Langton was freed in January 1312, he petitioned for a large sum as compensation for his losses in 1308, appealing to chapter 29/39 of the Charter. The ex-treasurer complained that he had been seized 'without being arraigned, or called in judgment, against the form of the law of the land, and against the points of the great Charter, suddenly taken and imprisoned, and held in prison a year and a quarter'.[7] Langton's entreaty had no effect, however, and he never received payment for his lost property.

Edward II had shown himself before his father's death to be susceptible to the charms of handsome and ambitious young men, and he proved incapable of separating his private life from his public position, upsetting the whole system of royal patronage. Showering gifts and offices on personal friends without regard for their political usefulness, he neglected to build up a 'court party' of loyal magnates and capable royal servants. One of Edward II's first acts as king was to recall to court a particular friend, Piers Gaveston, a young Gascon knight whom his father had banished, and his favours to Gaveston soon outraged native nobles. Soon a group of barons was demanding the Gascon favourite's exile, and arguments over his influence at court disrupted the new king's first years.

The chief conflicts of Edward II's reign centred on his magnates' mistrust of his favourites at court and their campaign to regain what they considered their rightful place as his counsellors. In the bitter struggles between the king's friends and their baronial opponents, constitutional principles proved less important than personal rivalries and competition for power and patronage. Both factions were willing to resort to violence in the contest to control the king and the royal household, and their hatred erupted in armed conflict. Soon after Edward's succession, a baronial spokesman presented articles that treated boldly the problem that the struggle for Magna Carta had raised a century before: how to place the king under the law? These articles claimed that 'the dignity of the crown' must be protected from a king 'who is not guided by reason', and they drew a distinction between the king's person and the crown, stating that 'homage and the oath of allegiance are more in respect of the crown than in respect of the king's person'. This document declared Piers Gaveston 'a man attainted and judged', and begged the king to carry out his subjects' will, 'since he is bound by his coronation oath to keep the laws that the people shall choose'.[8]

In 1310, a group of barons intent on broad reform arrived at a meeting of the great council in armour and with weapons at hand. They pressed Edward II to submit to another reforming committee, twenty-one barons known as the Lords Ordainers, who would present a series of ordinances in 1311 for reordering the kingdom's government. Forty-one detailed articles comprise the Ordinances, a long document aimed at securing for the baronage a greater role in government with Parliament as their voice. Indeed, one article (29) called for annual parliaments, even twice yearly if necessary, and two articles claimed parliamentary control over the king. Article 9 stated that 'the king shall not go out of his kingdom or undertake against anyone the act of war without the common assent of his baronage, and that in Parliament'; and another (14) bound the king to make appointments to the great offices of state

Plate 1 King John's Purbeck marble tomb sculpture in the choir of Worcester Cathedral, probably carved only a few years after his death. Courtesy of the Conway Library, Courtauld Institute of Art, London.

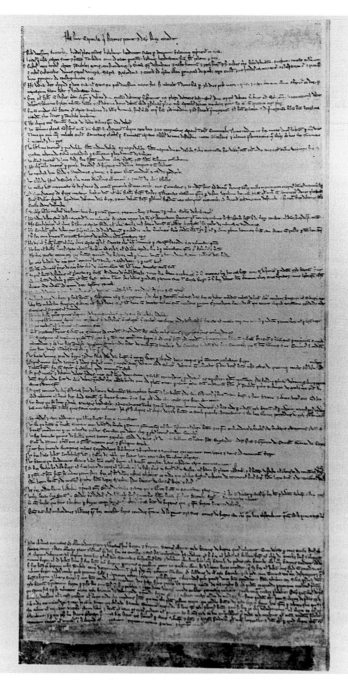

Plate 2   The Articles of the Barons, displayed at the British Library, London, Additional MS 4838. Sealed by King John at Runnymede a few days before Magna Carta in June 1215, it provided a basis for negotiating the terms set forth in the Charter. By permission of the British Library.

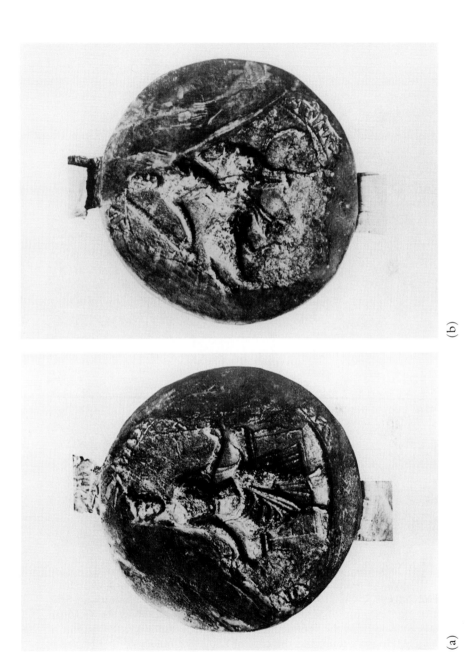

(a)

(b)

Plate 3 King John's seal, obverse (a) and reverse (b), attached to the Articles of the Barons, but since separated, displayed at the British Library with the Articles. By permission of the British Library.

Plate 4 'John's Fury at Signing Magna Carta', a painting by M. Dovaston specially for Walter Hutchinson (ed.), *Story of the British nation*, 4 vols (London: Hutchinson & Co., 1922–24), vol. 1, 385. It is a vivid illustration of the Whiggish interpretation of 'Bad King John' in popular histories in the Victorian age that continued into the twentieth century. Hutchinson is now an imprint of the Random House Group, but the current copyright holder of this picture is unknown.

7 *Exemplification of King John's Magna Carta, 1215*

Plate 5   One of two original exemplars of Magna Carta granted by King John in June 1215 now at the British Library, Cotton MS, Augustus ii.106. This copy is in better condition and is the one that is displayed to the public. By permission of the British Library.

Plate 6 The Lincoln Cathedral exemplar of the 1215 Magna Carta seen leaving the Library following the United States' entry into World War II in December 1941. On display at the New York World's Fair when the war broke out in 1939, it was placed at the Library of Congress in Washington for safekeeping, then transferred to Fort Knox, Kentucky, where it remained throughout the war. Photo courtesy of the Library of Congress Archives, LC-USP-359C.

Plate 7   The Lacock Abbey copy of Henry III's 1225 reissue of Magna Carta that became the definitive version. It passed into private hands after Henry VIII's dissolution of the monasteries, but is now at the British Library, Additional MS 46144, displayed alongside the 1215 Charter. By permission of the British Library.

Plate 8 Sir Edward Coke, common lawyer, royal judge under Elizabeth I and James I, and member of Parliament, whose doctrine of the 'ancient constitution' revitalized Magna Carta during struggles against the absolutist tendencies of the first two Stuart kings. Courtesy of the Library of Congress.

ROBERTVS COTTON
MILES ET BARONETVS
CVIVS HÆC
EFFIGIES.

Plate 9   Sir Robert Cotton by an unknown artist. This seventeenth-century
antiquary saved two of the four surviving 1215 copies of Magna Carta, including the one displayed today at the British Library. His manuscript collection
passed to the British Museum in the eighteenth century to form one of the
British Library's core collections. Courtesy of the National Portrait Gallery,
London.

Plate 10   Sir William Blackstone by an unknown artist. His *Commentaries* made the common law accessible to a wide public, especially in the thirteen North American colonies, educating both laymen and law students in the English legal tradition. His critical edition of Magna Carta, published in 1759, gave an accurate text of the original 1215 Charter, no longer confused with later versions. Courtesy of the National Portrait Gallery, London.

Plate 11   Arthur Beardmore, a radical politician charged in 1762 with seditious libel, who arranged to be arrested while instructing his son in Magna Carta. A 1764 print illustrating the incident proved popular with the public. © Copyright the British Museum.

Plate 12   1769 print of John Wilkes, a radical politician and journalist who appealed to Magna Carta in his frequent skirmishes with the British authorities. Beneath his portrait are scrolls labelled Magna Carta and the Bill of Rights. © Copyright the British Museum.

Plate 13 1810 print of the arrest of Sir Francis Burdett, who imitated Beardsmore in arranging to be arrested while instructing his son in Magna Carta. He was arrested on orders of the House of Commons, angered by a 'libellous and scandalous' piece that he had authored. © Copyright the British Museum.

Plate 14 'King John Signing Magna Carta' by J.W.E. Doyle, from an 1856 history of England for children in the 'sixties style' of engraving popular from the 1850s to the 1870s. The depiction of John signing the Charter with a pen is an obvious anachronism. Courtesy of the Bodleian Library, University of Oxford, 226c.3, p. 71.

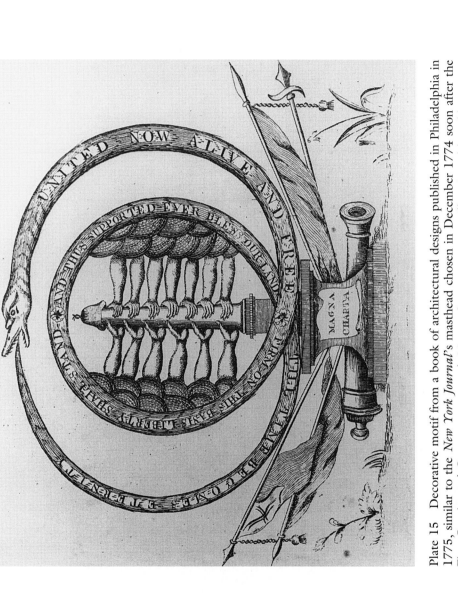

Plate 15 Decorative motif from a book of architectural designs published in Philadelphia in 1775, similar to the *New York Journal*'s masthead chosen in December 1774 soon after the First Continental Congress convened. Magna Carta supports a pillar topped by a liberty cap, braced by twelve arms symbolizing the colonies. The encircling snake represents the colonies' unity, for a segmented snake earlier had signified colonial disunity. Courtesy of Rare Books Division, The New York Public Library, Astor, Lenox and Tilden Foundations.

Plate 16   The Magna Carta Memorial at Runnymede erected by the American Bar Association in 1957; the inscription reads, 'To commemorate Magna Carta symbol of freedom under law'. Photo by Suzanne Hole, copyright © Runnymede Borough Council.

and royal household posts 'with the counsel and the assent of his baronage, and that in Parliament'.[9] The Ordinances' key demand was dismissal of the king's evil counsellors and Piers Gaveston's banishment from the kingdom along with several other unpopular friends of the king (20, 21, 22 and 23).

Magna Carta occupied an important place in the Ordinances. Two articles (6 and 38) acknowledged that the Charter bound the monarch, demanding that it be kept 'in all its points' and that the Ordainers or the next parliament clarify any points that are 'obscure or doubtful'. Another (31) made the Charter the standard for legislation, declaring that statutes were to remain in force 'provided that they are not contrary to the great charter or to the charter of the forest'; if in conflict with the Charter, they were to be 'held for nought and utterly undone'.[10] The Ordinances also acknowledged London's 'liberties and free customs' (chapter 13 in the 1215 Charter, 9 in the 1225 Charter), abolishing all new customs dating after Edward I's coronation as 'contrary to the Great Charter and contrary to the liberty of the city of London' (article 11).

Like similar measures under Henry III and Edward I, the Ordinances had no effective means for enforcement. Edward II's opponents among the baronage were men with few new political ideas, and they could think of nothing more meaningful than demanding that the king confirm the Ordinances and Magna Carta. Under the Ordinances Edward II was still head of government as well as chief of state, in charge of day-to-day administration, yet he considered their limitations crippling to royal authority, just as his grandfather had viewed the Provisions of Oxford. After 1312, the capture and execution of Piers Gaveston by a group of barons poisoned any possibility of co-operation between the king and his magnates, and Edward determined to secure release from the Ordinances. A 'middling party' of moderate royalist barons and bishops patched together a truce in 1318 lasting for two years, and a reissue of Magna Carta formed part of the settlement, yet Edward was resolved to avenge his friend's murder.

Soon Edward II found another favourite, Hugh Despenser the Younger, a noble from the Welsh Marches, thirstier for power than Gaveston and with a greedy father. The Despensers' influence and their aggressive acquisition of lands in Wales and on the Welsh Marches fuelled new baronial resentment of royal patronage policy, for they exploited their influence over the king to secure his armed assistance for their land grabs on the Welsh borders. In the view of their enemies, this was a violation of chapter 29/39 of Magna Carta, for the king was literally 'going against' and 'sending against' his subjects with force and violence. In the summer of 1321, a parliament dominated by the

Despensers' enemies sentenced both young Hugh and his father to exile and forfeiture of their lands, despite their appeals to Magna Carta. This 'trial by peers' hardly proceeded by law of the land, for it was conducted by armed opposition magnates in the absence of any ecclesiastical lords. Edward himself turned to the Charter to protect his favourite, protesting that to banish young Despenser 'would be contrary to the tenor of the great charter of the liberties of England and the common law of our realm'.[11] Soon Edward II moved against his favourites' persecutors with open warfare, and his forces were victorious, defeating the baronial party in battle at Boroughbridge by 1322. Following the royalist victory, Edward's vanquished opponents endured travesties of trials similar to the proceeding that had exiled the Despensers, with the captives' notoriety or past record determining their guilt. The result was a bloodbath, and twenty-five defeated barons were executed and others imprisoned or heavily fined. With summary executions once more the rule, whether the killing of Piers Gaveston by the king's baronial foes or the deaths of barons at the hands of royalists, Magna Carta's guarantee that punishment must be preceded by judgement took on renewed importance. Its promise of trial by peers was also significant for the baronage, since the trials staged by the clique surrounding the king after Boroughbridge were little more than judicial murders.

Parliament met at York in the spring of 1322 under firm royal control and reversed its earlier judgement against the two Despensers, acting on their petitions. The document repealing their conviction cites both Magna Carta's pledge of procedure by 'the law of the land' and its promise not to delay or deny justice. The Statute of York repudiated the Ordinances of 1311 and rejected baronial claims to decide what was best for the king and the kingdom. The statute affirmed that in future regulations treating the exercise of royal power should be issued only 'in Parliaments by our lord the king and by the assent of the prelates, earls and barons and the community of the realm'.[12] The revocation of the Ordinances did not affect the validity of the 1225 Charters, which remained in force, periodically reaffirmed in response to parliamentary petitions.

Edward II's triumph in 1322 exposed the kingdom to almost five years of exploitation by his courtiers and councillors that stoked his unpopularity. Yet he would not be overthrown in another baronial uprising, but in a sort of tragicomedy engineered by his neglected queen, Isabelle of France, and her lover, Roger Mortimer, a lord of the Welsh marches. When she and Mortimer launched a rebellion from Flanders in September 1326, Edward's support soon ebbed, and he fled into Wales with the Despensers; but the king soon fell into rebel hands, and the queen's forces seized power in the name of her fourteen-year-old son,

Prince Edward. Although the victors could hardly disguise the unlawful and revolutionary nature of their deposition of an anointed monarch, they needed theoretical justification for their usurpation. In January 1327, the queen and her party summoned a special parliament to proclaim her son King Edward III and approve six articles setting forth reasons why the senior Edward should no longer be England's king. These articles declared him incompetent, but more significantly, claimed that he had violated his coronation oath, a hint at contractual notions implicit in earlier baronial thinking surrounding the Great Charter of 1215. The barons viewed the coronation oath as a compact by the monarch with his subjects, and breach of promises made at the coronation constituted grounds for stripping him of his crown. To take no chance that Edward's deposition should appear unlawful, the rebel leaders also forced him to abdicate. A delegation to the captive king threatened that unless he agreed to abdicate, his son would be repudiated and replaced by another ruler not of the blood royal. Completing Edward II's humiliation was his murder at Berkeley Castle, the first English king to suffer such a fate since the Norman Conquest.

The young Edward III's first parliament confirmed Magna Carta, but Roger Mortimer, ruling the kingdom in the name of the new king, exacted bloodthirsty revenge on his enemies, continuing the extra-legal violence that had characterized the conduct of both Edward II and his baronial opponents earlier. Mortimer was soon urging Edward to march with armed forces against nobles perceived as posing a threat to the new regime. This brought a rejoinder from the archbishop of Canterbury, reminding the young king of Magna Carta: 'It is commonly known that in the Great Charter it is contained, that you shall not go nor send nor ride against any of your realm, and this was afterwards ratified by several Popes, and established as a law of the land, and confirmed by you yourself, and you are bound by your said oath to maintain it'.[13]

In 1330, when Edward III was eighteen, he took power for himself, banishing his mother from court and executing Lord Mortimer, her lover. Warfare characterized Edward's long reign (1327–77), for he invaded France with the goal of recovering his Plantagenet ancestors' lands, and he outdid his predecessors, laying claim to the French crown through the right of his Capetian mother. Although Edward's launching of the Hundred Years War (1338–1453), earns him the condemnation of some historians, it won him popularity with his subjects and ensured him the co-operation of his barons, who shared his chivalric outlook. They considered warfare a prince's proper occupation, and their own hope of gaining glory and plunder in France spurred their enthusiasm for his war. Because Edward III's political priority was securing funds for warfare, he was willing to surrender royal privileges to Parliament in return for money grants. As a result, his long reign proved to be a great age for growth of Parliament's powers.

Few clashes occurred under Edward III to cause his subjects to rally around Magna Carta, and only one confrontation brought the Charter forward as a focus for complaint. In 1340–41, it played a part in a conflict between the king and royal officials left in charge in England during his overseas adventure. With a king once more absent from the kingdom fighting for long periods, the old problem of effective government by the king's agents without his personal supervision had re-emerged. Conflict arose between Edward's household following him on campaign and his viceroy at home, John Stratford, archbishop of Canterbury. Edward returned to England after his first expedition greatly angered, convinced that Stratford and other royal officials had contributed to its failure by sending insufficient funds and supplies. To reassert personal control, he dismissed several royal servants, charged them with numerous offences and imprisoned them in the Tower. When clerics among the disgraced royal servants claimed ecclesiastical immunity from secular jurisdiction, Edward was outraged, and Archbishop Stratford sought sanctuary from royal wrath among his monks at Canterbury. A war of words between the king and the prelate ensued, and Stratford elevated the quarrel into a constitutional conflict, appealing to Magna Carta. In a letter to the king in January 1341, the archbishop reminded him of the fate of his father, who had 'caused to be taken, against the law of the land and of the Great Charter, the peers and other people of the land, and put some to shameful death . . . and what happened to him for that cause you, sire, know well'. He warned Edward: 'And now, by evil counsel . . . , you begin to seize various clerks, peers, and other people of the land, and to make unseemly process against the law of the land, and against the Great Charter, which you are bound to keep and maintain by the oath made at your coronation'.[14]

Stratford sought a hearing before Parliament, and when Edward III was forced to summon it in the spring of 1341, the archbishop again accused the king of violating Magna Carta's provisions. As a lord spiritual, he demanded trial by his peers in Parliament. Doubtless, the archbishop was over-dramatizing the situation, for Edward was doing little more than exercising his privilege of removing ministers who had displeased him. The king's arbitrary arrests of them had reminded the Lords in Parliament of the Charter's promises, however, and they supported Stratford's claim to trial by peers, objecting to several royal councillors' presence among them. Parliament enacted a statute specifying that peers were to be tried only before their fellow Lords and also that royal ministers accused of official misconduct must not be arrested or otherwise punished until judged by Parliament. Edward agreed to appoint royal councillors only with the Lords' approval, a provision undercutting previous monarchs' insistence on their right to choose freely their own councillors. The monarch realized that he had weakened the royal prerogative, and once the crisis abated, he declared the statutes invalid, and a new Parliament in 1343 sanctioned his declaration. Despite Edward's repudiation of his concessions, chapter 29/39 of Magna Carta still stood as a support to the Lords' privilege of trial by their peers in Parliament.

During Edward III's reign, parliaments passed several measures that clarified the meaning of the term 'law of the land' in chapter 29/39 of Magna Carta, and they became known to seventeenth-century common lawyers opposing the Stuart monarchs as 'the six statutes'. The Parliament of 1331 enacted the first of these statutes, probably in reaction to Isabelle and Mortimer's arbitrary acts following Edward II's deposition. It decreed that 'no man from henceforth be attached by any accusation, nor forjudged of life or limb, nor his lands, tenements, goods, nor chattels seised into the king's hands against the form of the Great Charter, and the law of the land'.[15] The second of the six, enacted twenty years later, extended the meaning of the Charter's expression 'law of the land' in an effort to curb extraordinary criminal proceedings before prerogative courts or special commissions not bound by the common law. This second statute prohibited any person's imprisonment or dispossession 'by petition or suggestion made to our lord the king, or to his council', and it required that such punishment result from 'indictment of good and lawful people of the same neighbourhood where such deeds be done, in due manner, or by process made by writ original at the common law'. The third statute, enacted in 1354, is important for expanding those protected by chapter 29/39, replacing the phrase 'no free man' with more inclusive language, 'no man, of whatever estate or condition he may be', and it promised that no one would be dispossessed, imprisoned, or put to death without 'due process of law', the first use of that phrase in the statutes. The fourth measure labelled a statute in the seventeenth century is actually a 1362 petition for a general confirmation of the Charters, important because it protests against arrests by the king's special command, that is, detention in disregard of established common law procedures. The fifth statute complained of arrests made by 'suggestion' to the king and provided that when such an accusation proved false, the accuser should undergo the same punishment that the accused would have suffered. The last of the six, enacted in 1369, strengthened earlier guarantees against irregular arrest, ensuring that 'no man be put to answer without presentment before justices, or matter of record, or by due process and writ original, according to the old law of the land'. Furthermore, it declared that 'if any thing from henceforth be done to the contrary [of the old law] it shall be holden for none'. Although the sixth statute does not cite the Great Charter, its enactment followed another royal confirmation, and its phrase 'old law of the land' clearly referred to chapter 29/39.

Much legislation in Edward III's reign dealt with specific provisions of the Charter, not great matters of individual liberty, problems arising in part because of the king's prerogative of dispensing with the law in individual instances, and in greater part because of royal agents or local lords' misdeeds, a consequence of feeble royal power in the countryside. Complaints of the chancery's exorbitant fees charged for writs prompted frequent petitions by the Commons to Edward, protesting that such charges constituted 'sale of justice' barred by Magna Carta. The king's usual response to such common petitions was simply a vague command to the chancellor to be 'reasonable' or 'gracious' with his fees. Another subject of petitions was a plea for enforcement of standard weights and measures throughout the kingdom called for in the Charter, and seven statutes between 1340 and 1497 dealt with this matter. Edward's parliaments also legislated limits on some prerogatives of the king's lordship that Magna Carta had previously regulated, acts that he did not oppose since the feudal incidents were losing significance as sources of royal revenue. In 1340, Parliament barred collection of tallage and scutage for the rest of Edward's reign, and in 1352 the king agreed to collect feudal aids only after securing parliamentary consent.

Outside the legislative sphere, Magna Carta continued to play an important part in legal processes, whether lawsuits or petitions to Parliament. By the mid-fourteenth century, a number of the Charter's chapters were either uncontroversial or no longer relevant, and records reveal more references to chapter 29/39 than to any other article. Its precept that persons must pursue their claims against others in accordance with the 'law of the land' was implanted in the common law, as was the analogous axiom that no one was to be deprived of life, liberty or property without 'due process of law'. A number of cases centred on seizure of landed property without lawful judgement, some of which involved prominent ladies. When the widow of Piers Gaveston presented a petition in 1318 seeking restoration of the earldom of Cornwall and other estates seized from her murdered husband, she thought it useful to cite the Great Charter. She turned to chapter 7, which declared that a widow's inheritance and dower land shall be turned over to her immediately after her husband's death, and to chapter 29/39's protection against ouster from one's freehold without the award and judgement of 'the law of the land'. It is no surprise that her ploy failed, and her petition for restoration of the confiscated Gaveston estates was denied.

Appeals to other provisions of the Great Charter appeared most often in private proceedings in which the king or his servants had no place. Throughout the reigns of the three Edwards, lords continued to claim cases for their private courts, sometimes with success, based on the Charter's prohibition of the writ *praecipe*. The Charter's protection against disproportionate fines or monetary penalties imposed in the royal courts was also a subject for appeals. By the time of Edward II, that protection extended to baronial courts; those who felt that their lord's court had assessed too large a sum could obtain a writ of *moderata misericordia* challenging their fine. In registers of original writs circulating widely among lawyers, a number of writs, including this one, are described as 'founded on' Magna Carta.

The citizens of London were jealous guardians of their liberties guaranteed by Magna Carta, and the Guildhall housed copies of it with subsequent royal confirmations of the city's liberties. A new royal charter granted to London at the beginning of Edward III's reign gave greater liberties than ever. In his middle years, however, the king secured passage of a statute authorizing heavy fines on city officials convicted of wrongdoing, and Londoners were incensed that their officials were to be tried by 'men of foreign counties', not by the city's own citizens. In a 1357 petition, they reminded Edward that London's right to its franchises and customs was recorded in the Great Charter. The extension of royal protection to foreign merchants in Magna Carta conflicted with the privileges granted to London, and Londoners' petitions against foreigners' favoured position often cited the Charter. Sometimes appeals to the city's liberties confirmed by Magna Carta could border on frivolous courtroom manoeuvring. In 1312, the mayor sought to stop a suit over London property claimed by the king as escheat, arguing that the Court of King's Bench lacked jurisdiction; he claimed that London's ancient liberties granted by 'the Great Charter of the liberties of England' required that such a plea be heard before itinerant justices at the Tower.[16]

By the last years of Edward III's reign, the war in France was no longer going well, waves of plague racked the country, and high taxes sharpened popular discontent. The king was in his dotage, no longer capable of asserting authority, and greedy courtiers controlled the royal household, enriching themselves. The result was demands for sweeping reform, voiced at the Good Parliament of 1376. This parliament introduced a new mechanism for holding the king's counsellors to account, a limitation on the monarch found neither in Magna Carta nor in baronial reformers' schemes. It authorized the removal of royal ministers by process of impeachment in the Commons and trial before Lords, first employed against several of Edward's courtiers.

Succeeding Edward III on his death in 1377 was his ten-year-old grandson, Richard II. His reign (1377–99), witnessed a return to conditions that had marked the reigns of Henry III and Edward II, with the nobility suspicious of a king perceived as governing through a household filled with evil counsellors and fawning favourites. In attempts to limit Richard to the rule of law, his great men would revive earlier baronial projects for committees or councils sharing power with the monarch. In 1386, he had to accept a reform commission, the Lords Appellant, similar to the reforming councils of Henry III's middle years or to the Lords Ordainers in Edward II's reign. Richard shares other characteristics with Henry III, for he came to the throne as a minor and was something of an aesthete; but also he shares qualities with King John, for he proved to be suspicious of his nobles, demanding their subservience and needlessly cruel to them. Unlike John, however, Richard had little enthusiasm for military expeditions; indeed, he sought peace in the Hundred Years War, a policy unacceptable to his nobles, who had benefited financially from the fighting. Once Richard II came of age, he voiced authoritarian views of royal power, making statements suspiciously similar to Roman law doctrines that the emperor is above the law. Instead of emphasizing his responsibility for protecting his subjects' rights, Richard stressed the royal obligation of preserving the privileges, prerogatives and other rights of the crown. In an address to Parliament in 1397, his chancellor lectured members on their duty to restore lost royal rights so that 'the king may be in his liberty and power as his progenitors have been before him, and as he ought to be of right, notwithstanding any ordinance to the contrary'.[17]

Following young Richard II's coronation in 1377, Commons petitioned for a reading of the Great Charter before the assembled parliament, and it admonished him 'to keep and observe said Charter as at his coronation he had been charged to do'.[18] Again in 1380, the Charter was read to early arrivals at a parliament at Northampton. After this, confirmations of Magna Carta were intermittent, and in the fifteenth century they stopped entirely, despite frequent transgressions of its guarantees; instead, parliaments requested confirmation of all previous statutes without specific mention of the Charter. Richard's later parliaments followed a formula that hinted at restricted liberties, simply asking that all communities 'have and enjoy their liberties and franchises from henceforth, as they have reasonably had and enjoyed in the time of his noble progenitors Kings of England'.[19]

Richard II faced his first crisis when the Peasants' Revolt of 1381 broke out among the peasantry of counties surrounding London. Beaten down by economic difficulties that had followed the outbreak of the Black Death, imposition of an inequitable poll tax or head tax sent them on a rampage. The rebel peasants occupied London, but the young king's appearance before them awed them into withdrawing from the city and dispersing. Influenced by a radical Christian tradition, they made egalitarian demands for personal freedom, abolition of harsh labour laws, and reasonable rents. The rebels never cited Magna Carta, and their hostility to lawyers and the law courts reveals their lack of confidence in the common law. Yet fourteenth-century peasants had some awareness of the Charter; tenants on a manor of the prior of Christchurch, Canterbury, complained that financial penalties imposed in his manorial court were 'against reason and Magna Carta'.[20]

Just as Richard II approached his majority, he had to face an attempt by a small number of magnates to impose on him a supervisory commission, similar to earlier baronial committees. By 1386, this group, the Lords Appellant, moved him to assert authority over the royal government. In an attempt to free himself from the Appellants' supervision, Richard put ten questions to royal judges at Nottingham in 1387. The first asked whether the statute establishing a baronial commission was unlawful because 'derogatory to the regality and prerogatives of the lord king'. They answered in the affirmative, and their responses to the other questions supported Parliament's subjection to the king's will, severely limiting its initiative in legislation. The judges' replies rank among the boldest statements of the royal prerogative ever made in medieval England. After this judicial endorsement, references to the royal prerogative, rarely encountered earlier, occurred frequently, and promoters of royal sovereignty would confront Magna Carta's principle of the subjection of the king to the law.

After Richard II was forced to submit to the Lords Appellant at the Merciless Parliament of 1388, he dedicated his energies to regaining full power. He soon succeeded and erected a despotic regime, hounding his enemies either into exile or to their execution. It is surprising that the king's arbitrary pursuit of the former Lords Appellant inspired no appeals to Magna Carta's protections. By the end of the fourteenth century, most English free men trusted that the Charter's 'judgement by peers' guaranteed their right to trial by jury, and the great lords of the realm believed that it ensured them trial before their parliamentary peers. Yet Richard enforced his will with military tribunals, the courts of the Constable and the Marshal that were more susceptible to his control than the traditional common law courts. Furthermore, he maintained for the first time in England's history a standing army, a force of 2,000 men capable of intimidating Parliament and the peers. Finally, the king's extra-legal actions went too far, and he pushed the magnates into rebellion by disinheriting his cousin, Henry Bolingbroke, threatening the security of the aristocracy's property rights. Bolingbroke was the eldest son of the king's uncle, John of Gaunt, and heir to the great duchy of Lancaster; but Richard had forced him into exile, and on John of Gaunt's death, confiscated all his estates. The king's high-handed treatment of the greatest peer of the realm signalled to others the precariousness of their own property holdings, and when the would-be duke of Lancaster returned to England with a band of warriors in summer 1399 to reclaim his inheritance, many barons rallied to his banner.

Richard II had no significant support, and by autumn 1399 a process of deposition was under way in Parliament. Supposedly, the king abdicated by his own will, but to strengthen the case for deposing him, Henry Bolingbroke's first parliament drafted articles listing his many offences. One article summarized the arbitrary nature of Richard's rule and set forth Magna Carta's principle of the rule of law, condemning his 'refusal to keep and defend the just laws and customs of the realm, but according to the whim of his desire he wanted to do whatever appealed to his wishes'. It accused him of stating 'with harsh and determined looks, that the laws were in his own mouth, . . . [or] were in his breast, and that he alone could change or establish the laws of his realm'. Two other articles made direct reference to the Great Charter. One quotes chapter 29/39 without mentioning its source, recalling that 'it is established and ordained that no freeman shall be seized, etc., or in any way destroyed, and that the king will neither go against him nor send against him, except by the lawful judgment of his peers, or by the law of the land'. The article accuses Richard of trying many persons in 'a military court', instead of the common law courts, and forcing them to prove their innocence in trial by battle, not by common law procedures. Another article complains of the king's writs of prohibition that diverted purely spiritual cases from the ecclesiastical courts, 'wickedly violating the ecclesiastical liberties approved in Magna Carta'.[21]

An ex-king alive and free was too great a threat to any usurper of the throne, and the victorious Bolingbroke imprisoned Richard II at Pontefract Castle, where he died in 1400 after four months, likely worn down by the harsh conditions of his captivity. Since Richard left no son, his nearest heir was his cousin who had overthrown him, Henry Bolingbroke, whose father had been the fourth son of Edward III. Bolingbroke ascended the throne as Henry IV, first of the three Lancastrian kings. Another claimant to the crown existed, however, the eight-year-old earl of March, descended from Edward III's third son, though his claim was clouded by passing not through males only, but through a female. None the less, doubts about the succession clung to the new monarch, and uncertainty about Henry IV's right would weaken the Lancastrian kings and result in the Wars of the Roses by the mid-fifteenth century.

The Charter in the fifteenth century: the Lancastrian and Yorkist kings

The English monarchs' custom of periodically confirming Magna Carta ended early in the reign of Henry VI, last of the Lancastrian kings. The traditional explanation for the waning of the Charter is England's fall into a century of disorders and disasters beginning with the Lancasters' usurpation of the crown in 1399 that was ended by the Tudors' restoration of authoritarian rule. This version of fifteenth-century history was an invention of Tudor-sponsored historians, and through William Shakespeare's history plays it still influences views, although historians' recent tendency is to downplay the disasters of that age. Shakespeare depicted Henry IV's reign (1399–1413), as unhappy because he was a usurper who had violently overthrown a lawfully anointed and crowned monarch, and his usurpation brought competition between the Lancastrians and Yorkists for England's crown that eventually unleashed the Wars of the Roses (1455–85). According to the Tudor histories, it was Henry Tudor's victory at Bosworth Field that restored good order to the kingdom, although historians today doubt that the years between the 1399 deposition and 1485 were disastrous for the English people. They reject over-emphasis on conflict in the years between Edward II and Richard III that ignores the common concerns that united kings and their great men. Looking at death and destruction during the Wars of the Roses, they find them less devastating than the civil war of John's reign or Henry III's struggles against his barons.

Henry IV found his position as monarch shaky because he came to the throne by overthrowing his predecessor, and he and his two Lancastrian successors dared not risk antagonizing their great men. This led seventeenth-century opponents of Stuart monarchy to laud them for sharing power with Parliament, and some historians later showed similar admiration, hailing them for 'premature constitutionalism' and contrasting them with the supposedly proto-absolutist Yorkist and Tudor 'new monarchs'. It is difficult to find any constitutional principles underlying Lancastrian rule, however; royal power was weak, not because the monarchical principle was questioned, but simply because the Lancastrian kings' right to the crown was contested. Since other nobles of royal blood could challenge their claim, they had little choice but to share power with the magnates to prevent their transfer of loyalty to another claimant. In the late Middle Ages, neither the monarch nor the magnates could survive without the other. The Lancastrians needed aristocratic participation in the administration, exercised through the council and supported by magnates' bands of armed retainers. Also under the Lancastrians, Commons grew more outspoken, insisting on cheap government, and demanding that the king 'live of his own'.

Henry IV's first parliament asked for confirmation of Magna Carta and the Forest Charter, along with all other ordinances and statutes, and the king confirmed the Charters a half-dozen times during his fifteen-year reign. After a quarter-century of Lancastrian rule, the custom of beginning common petitions with a request for confirmation of the two Charters ended, although parliamentary petitions protesting against abuses of the royal prerogative continued. Henry IV bowed to parliamentary authority in the legislative arena, admitting in a letter to the pope that English statutes could not be annulled or amended without the assent of representatives of the kingdom's three estates. Members of Parliament remembered Magna Carta, and a statute of 1442, extending the peers' right to trial by the Lords in Parliament to peeresses, quoted chapter 29/39's entire text.

Fifteenth-century churchmen also continued to show interest in the Great Charter, and the first convocation of the clergy under Henry IV requested royal confirmation of all the Church's privileges, liberties and rights, 'especially those contained in Magna Carta'.[22] The archbishop of Canterbury, one of Henry IV's adherents, addressed the Lords at a 1404 parliament after dissatisfaction with the royal household had surfaced. He admitted that 'there had not been such good government in [the king's] household nor about his person, as there could have been if it had been well supervised in good time', and he explained Henry's criteria for governing the kingdom in a manner that would heed the Great Charter's principles. The archbishop told the Lords that the king wished 'that the laws should be kept and observed; that equal right and justice should be administered to poor and rich alike; that, on account of any letters under the secret seal or the privy seal, or on account of any command or signed instruction whatsoever, the common law should not be disturbed, or the people in any way delayed in their pursuit [of justice]'.[23] A later archbishop of Canterbury revived the Church's periodic imposition of general excommunications of violators of the Charter, a practice dating back to Henry III's minority. Such ecclesiastical censures apparently continued in the Yorkist period and under the early Tudors, for a 1534 statute outlawing a number of pre-Reformation practices also banned general excommunications of violators of the Great Charter.

The Great Charter no longer appeared as an essential protection against arbitrary government because an increasing number of statutes spelled out its principles in new enactments binding the king to act 'according to law' or by 'due process' or 'process of the law'. Fifteenth-century legal records reveal litigants resorting less frequently to Magna Carta than in earlier centuries. Although they were more likely to cite legislation reinterpreting the Charter than its original clauses, a sufficient number of citations can be found to indicate that Magna Carta was far from forgotten. Pleaders were more likely to appeal to its technical provisions than to underlying principles, and lawyers or judges occasionally cited it for frivolous purposes, perhaps simply to display their legal learning. The absence of appeals to the Charter's guarantee of due process becomes noticeable during Richard II's arbitrary rule, continues under the three Lancastrian kings and becomes more apparent under the Yorkists. In an atmosphere of lawlessness and *coups d'état*, broad interpretations of the Statute of Treasons and Parliament's passage of bills of attainder legitimized extra-legal pursuit of the king's enemies in clear violation of chapter 29/39.

Great lords occasionally pressed their right to trial by their peers, although rarely referring to Magna Carta. Yet the learned justice Sir Thomas Littleton took note of the Charter during Edward IV's reign, rendering a decision that 'the statute of Magna Carta rules' in a lord's indictment for felony or treason and that he must be tried by his peers in Parliament. In another opinion, Littleton interpreted the Charter's term 'law of the land' to mean the common law procedures, 'process made by writ original at the Common Law'.[24] As author of a treatise on the land law that became a classic textbook of English law, Littleton's opinion carried great weight. Although he barely mentioned the Charter in his book, *Tenures*, his references to it in judgements would appeal to seventeenth-century opponents of Stuart oppression.

During the reign of Henry V (1413–22), renewal of the Hundred Years War largely overshadowed constitutional issues, and his victories in France won him popularity. Although Shakespeare depicted the second Lancastrian monarch as a model ruler, his preoccupation with making himself king of France and his premature death at the age of thirty-five meant that nothing was done to solve economic and social troubles facing his English realm, and the accession of his infant son Henry VI in 1422 brought no solution to mounting problems. As in most royal minorities, court factions fought to control the young king for their own advantage; but their conflicts continued after Henry VI came of age, for his periodic spells of madness required reinstatement of his status as a minor.

The only constitutional issue in the Wars of the Roses was the absence of any lawful, peaceful means of designating the rightful claimant to the throne once the king's incompetence became clear. Since the kingdom's stability depended on a capable king, the need to control an unfit king in the person of Henry VI spawned rivalry between the Lancastrian and Yorkist factions at court that degenerated into armed conflict. Although historians writing under Henry VII's patronage depicted the Wars of the Roses in dark colours as disastrous for England and brightened only by Tudor victory in 1485, the so-called wars actually consisted of a few battles between small bands of combatants, barely touching the mass of the population. Since the rivalry was not about abuses of royal authority, but primarily a struggle to ensure effective central government, neither side could turn to Magna Carta for support. A contender against Henry VI with a strong hereditary claim was Richard, duke of York, who was descended from King Edward III through both his father and his mother. He first claimed the right to rule as regent during Henry's intermittent madnesses, then claimed the crown for himself. After the duke of York was killed in battle at the end of 1460, his eldest son took up his claim, was crowned King Edward IV the next year, and ruled England until his death in 1483, although forced off the throne in 1470 briefly by a Lancastrian recovery. Edward left as heir a young son, but the boy's uncle, Richard, duke of Gloucester, soon took the throne for himself as Richard III. The boy-king and his younger brother became 'the little princes in the Tower', allegedly murdered by their uncle, whom Tudor historians portrayed as a Richard 'Crookback', a tyrant, usurper and villain deservedly killed in battle by Henry Tudor's forces.

Amid the changes in later-fifteenth-century England, Magna Carta no longer occupied a central place in political life. Indeed, Edward IV and Richard III are sometimes classed as 'new monarchs' along with their Tudor successors, allegedly moving England toward early modern absolutism. In fact, their goal was limited mainly to regaining the power that Edward I had held before central authority had declined in the fourteenth and early fifteenth centuries. The English people did not reject reassertion of royal sovereignty, nor did they rally around Magna Carta in defence of their liberties, yet they never entirely forgot it. Thousands of them took part in common law procedures, notably trial by jury, that inculcated the Charter's principle of due process of law. As the chief baron of Henry VI's exchequer court said: 'The law is the highest inheritance that the king has: for by the law he himself and all his subjects are ruled, and without the law there would be no king and no inheritance'.[25] The Great Charter occupied a central place in the legal system as a protector of property rights, studied at the inns of court and cited by lawyers and judges. It gained wider circulation than ever by the end of the fifteenth century with expanding lay literacy and printed books widely available.

Lawyers formed the only lay profession in late medieval England with its own institutions for training novices, the inns of court that had grown up in London apart from the cleric-dominated universities at Oxford and Cambridge. Students learned the law from the year books, accounts of cases taken down as study aids that contained justices' citations of the Great Charter. As apprentice lawyers observed court proceedings at Westminster, held moots or mock trials at the inns and listened to lawyers' lectures or 'readings' of statutes, they encountered references to Magna Carta and to the thirteenth-century legal classic *Bracton*. The influence of common lawyers extended beyond the law courts, for they were also a managerial group, acting as administrators in royal agencies and stewards of great men and rich merchants. Like the United States today, fifteenth- and sixteenth-century England was strongly 'law minded', preoccupied with legal issues, judicial processes and lawful rights.

The prerogative or conciliar courts, created under the Yorkists and expanded by the Tudors, seemed to threatened the common law courts, for they took on the task of enforcing law and order more vigorously and efficiently than the traditional tribunals. The common law courts with their complex procedures and jury trials were sometimes slow and ineffective in convicting criminals, as well as susceptible to local magnates' corruption of judges and intimidation of juries. The new tribunals were intended to complement the common law courts, to give swift justice, punish offences left uncorrected under common law, and awe even the mightiest of the king's subjects. To accomplish these goals, they adopted authoritarian procedures derived from Roman law. Following the ecclesiastical courts' inquisitorial methods, they did not limit their prosecutions to persons indicted by grand juries, but arrested suspects on the basis of 'information' or 'suggestion' by shadowy informants; and they borrowed their method of proof from Roman law, relying on judicial examination of witnesses and documents, not jurors' collective testimony. Extraordinary tribunals circumventing the common law courts were not an invention of the Yorkist kings, however, for their predecessors had employed special commissions combining judicial and administrative functions. In 1415, the people of Sandwich had presented a parliamentary petition protesting against such a royal commission named by Henry V to punish some Sandwich men's piracy, arguing that it was against common law and Magna Carta's provision that no one should be judged except by English common law.

Fifteenth-century England was hardly a time of flourishing intellectual life, but in the midst of the Wars of the Roses, the lawyer and judge Sir John Fortescue composed treatises on English law and government. An ardent supporter of the Lancastrian side, he was the victim of an act of attainder by the victorious Yorkists in 1461 and spent the next decade writing while in exile in France. Fortescue's book *In Praise of the Laws of England* takes the form of a dialogue in which the author instructs the Lancastrian heir, and it praises the English pattern of governance as a 'political and regal' monarchy, superior to the purely 'regal' French model. Fortescue continued his topic of tyrannical monarchy versus limited monarchy in two other treatises, *On Regal and Political Lordship* and *The Governance of England*.

Although not an original thinker, Fortescue set forth two concepts that became fundamental for Anglo-American political thought. First, he celebrated the principle of the rule of law, acknowledging as a true king only one who rules in accordance with the law, although making no mention of Magna Carta. Second, he expressed a preference for mixed government with the law's authority coming from the will of the people, who give their assent to laws through Parliament with the king's approval. Fortescue contrasted England's limited monarchy with the absolute or 'regal' rule of the French king, who 'may rule his people by such laws as he makes himself' and 'may set upon them such taxes and other impositions as he wishes himself, without their assent'. Echoing the Great Charter, he pointed out that the English king could not seize his subjects' possessions unless in accordance with law; nor could he 'rule his people by other laws than such as they assent to'.[26] Like most medieval political thinkers, however, Fortescue proved incapable of proposing practical remedies against a monarch who refused to submit voluntarily to the law. Also like his fellows, Fortescue had little historical perspective. He assumed that the English pattern of mixed government monarchy was continuous from time immemorial, brought by mythical Trojan settlers, who had constituted a community living under laws enacted with the assent of all. His imagined mixed polity, supposedly existing in England before the Roman or Saxon settlements, would strike a chord with early-seventeenth-century opponents of the Stuart kings, reinforcing their myth of an 'ancient constitution'.

Neglect of the Charter under the Tudors?

Under the Tudors' rule in the sixteenth century, Magna Carta occupied no larger place in England's major political controversies than it had in the previous century. After enduring a series of weak rulers since 1399, the English people sensed a need for strong government, and many found some sacrifice of liberties a small price to pay for good order in the kingdom. Histories have presented Henry VII and his successors as 'new monarchs' or practitioners of 'Tudor despotism', and it once was popular to hail them as early examples of the absolute monarchy that would characterize sixteenth- and seventeenth-century European states. Such a view of the Tudors seems less plausible today. Although supposedly seeking royal sovereignty by gathering more and more power into their hands, in their own day such limitless power was deemed to belong to God alone, and neither rulers nor their subjects dared enquire openly about the source of monarchical authority over the kingdom.

In practical terms, the Tudors could never have exercised truly despotic dominion because they lacked adequate resources. They had neither a standing army nor a police force, and, suffering from the same lack of money that had plagued their medieval predecessors, they depended on the propertied classes' support for parliamentary approval of new taxes. Indeed, the Tudor monarchs claimed that ultimate authority in England belonged to 'the king in Parliament', that is, to king and Parliament jointly; and they attempted to manipulate their legislature to secure support and to avoid confrontations over the constitutional questions raised by Magna Carta. To cloak their arbitrary acts in law, the Tudors acknowledged the crown's obligation to maintain at least an appearance of due process, and judges and lawyers in their service protected the crown's privileges in the courts. Despite the skill of most Tudor monarchs in public relations, especially Elizabeth I, the expanding jurisdiction of conciliar or prerogative courts generated discontent among common lawyers, who viewed them as potential rivals to their jurisdiction. Some of the new tribunals, such as the Star Chamber or Court of Requests, dated from the Yorkist kings, created as branches of the royal council to enforce law and order more effectively than the common law courts.

The Great Charter played little part in the political controversies of Henry VIII's reign (1509–49); and he often violated his subjects' rights in enforcing his religious settlement that made the Anglican Church independent of Rome. He persecuted those suspected of questioning his supremacy over the Church by imprisoning them for long periods without pressing charges. Only occasionally did victims of imprisonment without indictment or bail claim 'the benefit of [an English] subject' or 'the liberty of an Englishman', guaranteed them by Magna Carta.[27] Although a few prominent Catholics persecuted by Henry VIII sought protection in the Charter's first chapter promising freedom for the English Church, most turned to the theology of universal papal authority for arguments against royal supremacy over the spiritual sphere.

After experiments with militant Protestantism under Edward VI, Mary Tudor (1553–58), attempted to restore Roman Catholicism as England's official faith. Some Protestants, radicalized by the reformed religion of John Calvin, wished to replace the Anglican Church with a more thoroughly reformed church on the Calvinist model, and they wrote tracts urging resistance to the new ruler that would win favour later among seventeenth-century Puritan zealots. Among the authors was the former bishop of Winchester, John Ponet, living in exile on the continent, who stressed traditional English themes of the rule of law set forth by Fortescue a century earlier. Ponet wrote in a 1556 treatise reprinted in the seventeenth century that kings should be 'obedient and subject to the positive laws of their country' and that laws required 'the consent of the people' expressed by Parliament. He expressed more extreme views, however, and in a chapter entitled 'Whether it be lawful to depose an evil governor and kill a tyrant?', he answered firmly in the affirmative.[28] By Elizabeth I's last years, Puritans presented a greater threat to royal supremacy over the Church of England than did Catholic supporters of papal sovereignty. A new ecclesiastical tribunal, the Court of High Commission, armed with the Roman and canonical procedures of the earlier prerogative courts, was the queen's chief instrument for suppressing the Puritans. The High Commission's practices alarmed the common lawyers, a number of whom held Calvinist religious beliefs and made common cause with Puritan militants.

Although Tudor government was hardly a 'new monarchy', the English kingdom's social and economic structure was no longer medieval, and political influence was drifting away from the aristocracy. English aristocrats found themselves squeezed by rapid economic change in the sixteenth century as commerce replaced agriculture as a major source of new wealth, and fast-rising inflation increased the costs of luxuries essential for maintaining their proper state. Penury forced a number to flock to the king's court to become courtiers in the hope of impressing him favourably and winning his patronage. As the fortunes of the peerage fell, the significance of the gentry, descendants of the medieval knights, rose; numbers of them won election to the House of Commons, where they expressed their political and religious concerns. With the Protestant Reformation under way by the 1530s, many gentry in Commons had converted to Puritanism, and they were free with advice to Elizabeth about the religious settlement, even about her marriage plans, which she neither sought nor desired from them.

Another sixteenth-century novelty was Humanism, a new cultural current flowing from Italy that influenced both the aristocracy and the gentry. Its ideal of the 'gentleman', weaving together martial qualities of the chivalric knight with the learning of the philosophers and statesmen of classical Greece and Rome, won over the prosperous laity. Enthusiasm for classical antiquity inspired a revival of the ancient Roman ideal of the active life dedicated to public service, and the English gentry rejected the Church's model of the contemplative life of monks. The gentry, having long taken part in governing the countryside, seized on this new Italian standard of conduct and found a means of fulfilling the classical ideal in political activity, holding local office, serving at court or in Parliament.

Subjects of the Tudors felt that they were living in a new age, rescued from the chaos of civil war between Lancastrians and Yorkists, restored to peace and order by a rejuvenated monarchy, delighted by the new learning from Italy and liberated from papist superstition by the new truths of Protestantism. Italian humanists' praise of history as the best preparation for leadership inspired native English antiquaries or amateur historians. Motivated by national pride, they expanded the Italians' preoccupation with the classical past to a search for the glories of the English past, and soon learned amateurs among the gentry became collectors of old manuscripts and authors of histories written in the English language imitating the humanist style. The native English lacked a critical approach to their sources, however, accepting unreliable medieval chronicles that conflated history with myths, such as the Anglo-Saxons' descent from the Trojan refugee Brutus, or the Church of England's foundation by Joseph of Arimathaea. Even the best scholars misdated the origin of Parliament, placing it in Henry I's reign. Eventually, the new interest in England's early history would prove subversive to Tudor-style authoritarian monarchy, encouraging myths of the English people's immemorial liberties.

The official Tudor version of England's history, set forth in works such as Edward Hall's history of the Lancastrian, Yorkist and Tudor reigns (1548) or in Ralph Holinshed's *Chronicle* (1578, 1586), still circulates today through Shakespeare's history plays. Historians writing under Tudor sponsorship presented Henry VII rescuing England from almost a century of anarchy following the Lancastrian usurpation of 1399. According to Tudor propaganda, tyranny, though evil, cannot excuse rebellion; and to avoid chaos, obedience to the ruler must be English subjects' highest obligation. This point of view coloured the picture that historians painted of all rebellions, including the baronial rising against King John to win Magna Carta.

Propagandists supporting Henry VIII's rejection of papal supremacy recognized the value of medieval materials for supplying ammunition against papist opponents. Certainly his attempt to challenge papal authority and to bring the Church in England under royal control presented parallels with the authoritarian regime that the early Plantagenet kings had tried to construct. Although most apologists for the king's break with Rome viewed King John in a positive light as a hero struggling against the papacy, they showed little sympathy for the Great Charter or the rebel barons. Protestants found that Magna Carta, with its first article confirming the English Church's liberties, afforded them no advantage in the struggle to end papal authority over England. In Holinshed's account, the lesson of John's reign was not the subjugation of a tyrannical prince to the law, but 'the palpable blindness of that age wherein King John lived, as also the religion which they reposed in a rotten rag'.[29] Shakespeare's history plays spread the Tudor propagandists' message of the wickedness of rebellion against an anointed and crowned king, and his drama *The Life and Death of King John* makes no mention of the Charter.

Fascination with England's history was spurred by Henry VIII's suppression of the monasteries, which dispersed their libraries filled with materials for medieval history. While many medieval manuscripts were lost in the looting of religious houses or destroyed by later Protestant zealots, numbers fell into the hands of antiquaries. English gentry with antiquarian interests became avid collectors of monastic chronicles, including manuscripts crucial to reconstructing Magna Carta's early history. The Tudor monarchs saw the new curiosity about English history as a means of strengthening their regime, and they offered patronage for antiquarian and historical studies. Henry VIII gave one of his librarians, John Leland (d. 1552), a commission to search monastic and collegiate libraries for historically important manuscripts, and his recovery of medieval masterworks laid the foundations for study of English medieval history in the Tudor era. He added medieval manuscripts to the Royal Library, among them the Barnwell Chronicle, a previously unknown thirteenth-century source that counterbalanced the St Albans' chroniclers' hostile view of King John.

Also important for medieval studies was Leland's contemporary, John Bale (d. 1563), whose life is unlike that expected of a bibliophile, resembling rather that of the hero of an adventure novel. A friar who converted to Protestantism, he became a dramatist, authoring plays and leading a company of strolling players. One of Bale's plays was *King John*, possibly the first history play in English, written in the 1530s. Despite his knowledge of medieval sources, he made the play a vehicle for anti-papal propaganda, omitting any reference to Magna Carta; his *King John* typifies Tudor antipathy toward rebels with its talk of the 'base rebellion' by the baronage.[30] Because of Bale's pronounced Protestant views, he fled England during Henry VIII's last years to return after young Edward VI's accession. He won nomination to an Irish bishopric, but the Irish, angered by his attempts to protestantize their church, chased him from the country, and he went into exile again, only returning to the British isles after Elizabeth I's accession. He was an avid collector of books, and he had amassed a large collection of medieval manuscripts before he lost them on his flight from Ireland.

The dispersal of monastic libraries coincided with the growth of a printing business in England, and soon antiquaries were collaborating with printers to publish editions of medieval manuscripts in their collections. Even though Tudor political doctrine discouraged sympathy toward the baronial rebels against King John, the introduction of the printing press to England by the late fifteenth century made copies of Magna Carta more widely available. As early as the 1480s, printers had begun publishing such popular lawbooks as Littleton's textbook of land law, and legal works made up a large portion of the earliest books printed in England. Among the early printers was Richard Pynson, an immigrant from Normandy named the official 'king's printer', and his 1508 edition of Magna Carta was perhaps the first to be published in full. His book *Magna Carta cum aliis Antiquis Statutis* was often reprinted and became the basis for an English translation. Another early printed work that made Magna Carta available was a 1527 collection of statutes, the *Great Abridgement*, by the brother-in-law of Thomas More, John Rastell, a lawyer who ventured into the printing business. His book, arranged by legal topics, did not include a full text, but it covered twenty-four chapters of the Great Charter.

By Elizabeth I's time, men prominent in royal government such as her chief minister, William Cecil, Lord Burghley, and Matthew Parker, archbishop of Canterbury (d. 1575), as well as men of less lofty rank such as Sir Robert Cotton, were amassing libraries of manuscripts from England's medieval past. Archbishop Parker's interest in medieval materials sprang from his quest for weaponry against papal authority and armament for defending the Elizabethan religious settlement. He took advantage of his post as primate of England to build the most important of sixteenth-century libraries of medieval manuscripts, which he left to his Cambridge college and to the University Library. As a result of Parker's efforts, Matthew Paris's history, the *Chronica Majora*, a narrative of John and Henry III's struggles against their barons with a strong anti-royalist bias and a crucial source for the Great Charter's early history, was published in 1571. It belonged to the medieval manuscript collection of Lord Burghley, an enthusiastic book collector who lent it to the archbishop, and because Parker found Matthew Paris's anti-papal attitude appealing, he edited the chronicle for publication, despite his meagre editorial skills. Parker also authored a book sketching English ecclesiastical history that followed the St Albans monk's account of the quarrel between King John and Stephen Langton.

With Parker's work, the St Albans chronicler's somewhat inaccurate text of the 1215 Charter was made accessible, restoring it to the premier position long occupied by Henry III's 1225 Charter. Earlier, few had any awareness of Magna Carta's connection with King John's reign, for they knew it only from the statute books in its 1225 version. In 1576, Richard Tottell prepared a more accurate version of the Charter for his edition of the *Antiqua Statuta*. The first printer to produce an English translation of the Great Charter's full text, along with other early statutes, was George Ferrers (d. 1579), a noted poet and politician, who was also a common lawyer. Ferrers's translation is often clumsy and verbose, giving words and phrases in incorrect sequence, but it succeeds in conveying the document's general meaning. The recovery of the Great Charter of 1215 contributed to a new appreciation of the baronial conflict with King John by the early seventeenth century.

The foundation of the Society of Antiquaries in 1572 gave added impetus to the study of original documents and chronicles. A number of the society's members were common lawyers, whose profession required familiarity with record evidence and predisposed them toward historical studies, particularly such subjects as growth of legal institutions and procedures. They steered clear of abstract questions concerning the character of monarchy, England's constitution, or English liberties, properly fearing that discussion of such issues was dangerous. Despite the Society's interest in old records, it failed to produce improved care for the government's archives, which were in a chaotic state, scattered in several castles and threatened with loss. Luckily, in the first Elizabeth's reign some depositories were placed in the hands of capable scholars with a genuine interest in preserving the public records. John Agard (d. 1615) at the exchequer, for example, worked to catalogue its records. A member of the Society of Antiquaries, he combined a passion for antiquarian research with a legal education. Agard laid down instructions for preserving records in the introduction to one of his catalogues, listing the four dangers to documents' safety: fire, water, rats and mice, and misplacement.

Another early archivist was William Lambarde (d. 1601), appointed keeper of records at the Rolls Chapel by Elizabeth in 1597. A lawyer whose interest in the early laws led him to learn Old English, he published what he thought were law codes of the Anglo-Saxon kings and William the Conqueror. These apocryphal laws would encourage an

identification of the common law with immemorial custom, contributing to seventeenth-century antiquaries' myth of an 'ancient constitution'.
In Lambarde's treatise on the duties of justices of the peace, he 'planted
precedents here and there' and sought to add 'some delight of history
and record'. Among his precedents was Magna Carta's promise of trial
by peers, which he equated with jury trial, 'the verdict of twelve good
and lawful men of the country . . . according to the ancient liberty of the
land'. Another of Lambarde's treatises discusses the Great Charter, which
he labelled 'the first letters of *Manumission* of the people of this *Realm*,
out of the *Norman* servitude'. Although aware of Matthew Paris's chron-
ficle, he made no mention of John's Charter, but focused on the 1225
version, which he described as made 'by the common consent of the
whole realm, . . . by the King, Peers, and Commons of this land', in
other words, by Parliament.[31] In the same treatise, Lambarde examined
a fourteenth-century treatise on Parliament, *De Tallagio non concedendo*,
incorrectly dating it to Edward the Confessor's time; this supposed
statute convinced parliamentarians in the next century of the antiquity
of England's representative body. Through the work of antiquaries
such as Lambarde, raw material for medieval English constitutional and
legal history was in print before the death of Elizabeth I, handing on to
adversaries of her Stuart successors a mixture of fact and myth about
England's ancient law and immemorial custom.

If Magna Carta, originating in rebellion, figured little in the high
politics of the Tudor age, it never lost relevance for the common law
courts, and legal treatises, year books and lessons for law students at
the inns of court contained references to its provisions. An example
is *Doctor and Student*, a guide to the chancery court by Christopher
St German that quotes chapters 29/39 and 40 as confirmation of 'the
old custom of the kingdom'.[32] Most Tudor 'readings' or lectures at the
inns of court analysed the Charter's individual chapters and neglected
its overall import as a constitutional document. Illustrating this approach
is the work of one of the most learned Elizabethan common lawyers,
Edmund Plowden (d. 1585), who pioneered the shift in reporting
cases from year books to modern law reports. In his *Commentaries and
Reports*, he cites Magna Carta in five cases, but these citations show that
he viewed the Charter as no more than another statute chiefly relevant
for private law. His contemporary, Sir James Dyer (d. 1582), also contributed to the modern method of law reporting, but in at least one
passage showed himself capable of seeing in the Charter general principles. Citing a case from Henry IV's time, he wrote that any of the king's
subjects has the right to seek redress from him 'for injuries done to him
in goods lands or person' against anyone else of whatever rank or status;

and he added, 'And the king being personally in the Chancery, said to no one will we sell, to no one will we deny or defer justice or remedy as Magna Carta says'.[33]

Throughout the Middle Ages, suits before the common law courts had centred on disputes over land, but as England advanced toward a capitalistic economy in the sixteenth century, lawsuits over mercantile matters multiplied. The prerogative courts were claiming jurisdiction over commercial cases, forcing the older courts to compete with them for business. In the common lawyers' minds, these special tribunals not only presented competition for cases, but also posed a threat to the people's liberties, for they did not afford native English legal protections to the accused, but borrowed authoritarian Roman law procedures. Common lawyers objected to the absence of trial by jury in the prerogative courts, a right that the English had considered protected by Magna Carta since the fourteenth century. They also complained that the prerogative courts prosecuted suspects without indictment by a grand jury, trying them on mere suspicion because of supposed 'ill-fame' as in Roman and canon law. Furthermore, common lawyers objected to the courts' use of the *ex officio* oath that compelled defendants to testify about the charges against them, forcing them to risk incriminating themselves.

In the Tudor era, perhaps those who most clearly grasped Magna Carta's meaning were the Puritans, who were experiencing the Anglican hierarchy's pressure for religious conformity under Elizabeth I. They complained about enforcement under the Court of High Commission's procedures, which they considered violations of the law of the land. Some ardent Puritans who sought to separate from the Anglican Church argued that the Charter's first chapter, guaranteeing the English Church's freedom, applied not to the official Anglican Church, but to 'the true church of Christ'. One questioned the royal prerogative's exemption from the law, declaring that judges 'are bound by law to administer justice and equity unto the poor subjects, notwithstanding that the prince's letters be directed to the contrary'.[34] Since lawyers practising before the common law courts feared the prerogative courts as rivals and threats to traditional English liberties, a number were willing to take the cases of Puritans summoned before the High Commission. Late in Elizabeth's reign, common lawyers defending their Puritan clients resurrected the Great Charter's promises, and pamphleteers publicized the liberties that it guaranteed. Robert Beale (d. 1601), an antiquarian, civil servant and member of Parliament, and Sir James Morice, another member of Parliament, both composed treatises depicting Magna Carta as basic and unalterable law, 'the law of laws', above all royal writs. Morice, in a reading at one of the inns of court, declared the teaching that the king governed 'at his will and pleasure' and not by law to be 'altogether repugnant to the wise and politic state of government established in this realm'.[35]

Chronicles, statutes and legal treatises convinced the common lawyers defending Puritans hauled before the High Commission that Magna Carta afforded protection against its procedures. One ingenious lawyer turned to Magna Carta to protest against the *ex officio* oath, subjecting the accused to the possibility of self-incrimination. He gave a strained reading of chapter 28, which actually treats the ancient process of wager of law or proof of innocence by 'compurgation', the collective oath of neighbours of the accused, limiting wager of law to those accused by credible witnesses. This enabled the counsel for the defence to argue that 'By the statute of Magna Carta and the old laws of this realm, this oath for a man to accuse himself was and is utterly inhibited'.[36] The common lawyers' conflicts with civil lawyers defending this Roman law practice of forcing accused persons to testify against themselves contributed to the Great Charter's elevation from a mere statute to a 'liberty document'.

To counter the Court of High Commission's Romano-canonical procedures, counsel for accused Puritans turned to chapter 29/39 of Magna Carta and to the six statutes of Edward III, maintaining that only common law processes constituted the 'law of the land'. They argued that the phrase 'by law of the land' denoted trials sanctioned by common law or by parliamentary statute and that the High Commission's proceedings, authorized only by the queen's prerogative, were no part of the law of the land. They petitioned the common law courts for writs of prohibition barring the ecclesiastical tribunal from prosecuting persons accused of non-conformity to Anglican liturgical formulas. The Puritans and their legal representatives, upholding Magna Carta as fundamental law above the royal prerogative or parliamentary statutes, were preparing the way for seventeenth-century parliamentarians who would take up the Charter as a shield against Elizabeth's Stuart successors.

Notes

1. Doe (1990), 31.
2. Thompson (1948), 130.
3. Brooks (1993), 80.
4. Treharne (1970), 75–6.
5. Thompson (1948), 16–17.
6. Elton (1982), 277.
7. Thompson (1948), 80.
8. Rothwell (1975), 525.

9. Text, Rothwell (1975), 527–39.
10. Rothwell (1975), 538.
11. Thompson (1948), 78.
12. Rothwell (1975), 544.
13. Thompson (1948), 78.
14. Myers (1969), 72.
15. For quotations, Thompson (1948), 90–4.
16. Thompson (1948), 107.
17. Myers (1969), 405–6.
18. Citation, Hindley (1990), 181.
19. Thompson (1948), 18.
20. Musson (2001), 25.
21. Myers (1969), 407–14, articles 16, 27, 29.
22. Thompson (1948), 131.
23. Myers (1969), 456–7.
24. Thompson (1948), 85–6, 87.
25. Doe (1990), 27–8.
26. Myers (1969), 419.
27. Thompson (1948), 142–3.
28. Weston (1991), 194–5, 280.
29. McKisack (1971), 119.
30. Hindley (1990), 187.
31. Thompson (1948), 184, 186, 187, 188.
32. Plucknett and Barton (1974), 49.
33. Thompson (1948), 174.
34. Thompson (1948), 228.
35. Brooks (1993), 72.
36. Thompson (1948), 222.

chapter 6

MAGNA CARTA'S REVIVAL IN THE SEVENTEENTH CENTURY AND AFTER

S hortly before Charles I's 1628 Parliament met, one of its members said, 'I should be very glad to see that good old decrepit law of Magna Charta, which hath been kept so long and lain bedrid, as it were – I shall be glad to see it walk abroad again, with new vigour and lustre, attended and followed with the other six statutes [of Edward III]'.[1] In the seventeenth century, the Great Charter again claimed a central position as common lawyers and parliamentarians wielded a mythical ancient constitution as a weapon against the royal prerogative reasserted by the Stuart king. The English tradition of subjecting royal power to the rule of law enshrined in Magna Carta was an anomaly in seventeenth-century Europe, for trends supported divine-right doctrines. Religious wars, noble revolts and social strife had convinced other Europeans that their only alternative to anarchy was submission to an absolute monarch's God-given authority.

When James VI of Scotland came south to become King James I of England (1603–25) on the death of Elizabeth I, he brought with him notions of divine-right monarchy that combined with Tudor authoritarianism to threaten Parliament's role in the kingdom's governance. James I had authored a defence of divine-right monarchy, titled *The True Law of Free Monarchies*, meaning by a 'free monarchy' one unrestrained by such rival bodies as Parliament. James argued that his authority came directly from God, to whom he was solely responsible. Although he did not deny monarchs' obligation to obey divine law and accustomed moral principles, he contended that the only recourse for subjects enduring unjust rule was passive resistance. Notions of royal power espoused by James and by his son Charles I (1625–49) were hardly pleasing to members of Parliament, already growing restive in Elizabeth I's last years.

The antiquarianism flourishing in the sixteenth century continued in the new century, and historians, lawyers and members of Parliament found in the common law and Magna Carta ammunition against arbitrary

Stuart rule. Chief among those recognizing the Charter's potential as a weapon against royal sovereignty was the learned jurist and antiquary Sir Edward Coke (d. 1634), who would play a major role in adding it to the arsenal of anti-absolutist arguments. By the 1640s, opponents of Charles I faced the same dilemma that had confronted King John's barons: what was the remedy for a monarch who refused to respect the law? The answer was the same as in 1215 – war against the king – this time waged by Parliament rather than rebel barons. The civil war of 1642–48 set in motion by seventeenth-century advocates of the Great Charter moved further than that in 1215–16, resulting in military dictatorship, the execution of the king and a decade of experiments in republican government.

In 1688–89, the Glorious Revolution marked an end to debates over England's constitution, settling sovereignty on Parliament. With the emergence of the cabinet system in the eighteenth century, Great Britain would become the only European kingdom to have strong and effective government that was not headed by an absolute monarch. The Charter's resuscitation by opponents of Stuart oppression coincided with the founding of the first English settlements across the Atlantic, and the colonists were confident that they carried to North America all rights and liberties conferred by Magna Carta on English subjects. This combination of circumstances ensured that the document's seventeenth-century revival would survive into twenty-first-century political thought.

Historians' rediscovery of England's medieval past

Under the Tudors, antiquarian curiosity had combined with the printing business to publish texts of old English laws and history; and by the seventeenth century, antiquaries inaugurated the first great age for the study of English legal history. Supporters and opponents of absolute monarchy alike combed through old legal documents seeking support for their arguments. Most important for adversaries of the Stuarts was Magna Carta, hailed by the noted historian Sir Henry Spelman (d. 1641) as 'the most august document and a sacrosanct anchor to English Liberties'.[2] Just as hazy notions of the laws of Edward the Confessor had inspired and justified the baronial rebels of John's time, so the Great Charter would supply opponents of the Stuart kings with a mythical ideal of English liberties. The Charter presented a programme for reform to safeguard the people's rights through bending the king's will to the rule of law.

Some seventeenth-century writers continued to spout the Tudor propagandists' view that armed resistance to an anointed king is always wrong, repeating earlier unfavourable depictions of the baronial rebellion against King John and Magna Carta. An example is John Speed's *History of Great Britain*, written in 1611, in which he wrote that the barons rose in revolt in order to 'attain the shadow of seeming liberties'. He commented on the baronial committee of twenty-five authorized by the 1215 Charter: 'Thus one of the greatest sovereigns of Christendom was now become the twenty-sixth petty king within his own Dominions'.[3]

With the 1571 publication of Matthew Paris's thirteenth-century chronicle, historians had an anti-royalist view of the baronial rebellions of John's and Henry III's reigns that questioned Tudor condemnation of all revolts against legitimate rulers. They also had a printed text, though imperfect, of the original Magna Carta in addition to Henry III's 1225 Charter published in the statute books. John Selden (d. 1654), who stands alongside Sir Edward Coke as the leading seventeenth-century authority on English legal history, took advantage of Matthew Paris's text to publish an edition of John's Charter. While still a student, Selden authored an account of English law that included a chapter on 'King John and his Grand Charter', comparing the text of the 1225 Great Charter with the 1215 Charter and calling attention to chapters in the original omitted from later versions. None the less, the most frequently cited version of Magna Carta throughout the seventeenth century continued to be Henry III's Charter. Selden also published an edition of the so-called laws of William I that buttressed common lawyers' belief in the antiquity of the common law, reinforcing the myth that England's ancient laws and customs stretched beyond the Norman Conquest.

The other key figure for the intellectual origins of England's seventeenth-century revolution is Sir Edward Coke, attorney-general to Elizabeth I and James I. Later as chief justice of Common Pleas and King's Bench and a member of parliament, he became a stout defender of England's 'ancient constitution', defending English common law, as the protector of English subjects' property, inheritance and birthright. In his writings, Coke revived Magna Carta, reconfirmed many times, as historical precedent for opposing the first two Stuarts' absolutist doctrines, which he decried as alien imports. He regarded Magna Carta not as new law, but as 'declaratory of the principal grounds of the fundamental Laws of England, and . . . additional to supply some defects of the Common Law', that is, confirming longstanding law and custom.[4]

Coke's views bolstered the doctrine of the 'ancient constitution', a body of laws and customs thought to have existed since the pre-Roman settlement of Britain to limit the king's power and hold him to account for his actions. His depiction of England's past marks a major step in

fashioning the Whig interpretation of history, and his distortions of
the English past reconfigured people's understanding of Magna Carta
and medieval England. Like his contemporaries, he had no concept of
a constitution in the modern sense of a document outlining an organiza-
tional chart for government. Coke's ancient constitution was a bundle
of immemorial custom, legal principles and precedents contained in the
common law, 'the birthright and the most ancient and best inheritance
that the subjects of this realm have'.[5] In eleven volumes of *Reports* on
cases and in his four-volume *Institutes on the Laws of England*, Coke
imposed order on the common law. The second volume of the *Institutes*
setting forth his teaching on the Great Charter was not published until
after his death on the eve of civil war, the final volumes appearing in
1644; but his views on the Charter were already widely known, scattered
throughout the earlier *Reports*. The title page of his *Eighth Report*, published in 1611, cites the king's promise in chapter 29/39 not to sell,
deny or defer right or justice.

Sir Edward Coke made two chief contributions to his contemporaries'
understanding of Magna Carta. First, he convinced them that it formed
a link in a chain of royal confirmations of English law, stretching back
to the laws of Edward the Confessor and beyond. Coke's notion of
the English constitution's timeless character minimized the Norman
Conquest's revolutionary effects and made the Charter merely a reaffirmation of liberties enjoyed by the English people from time immemorial.
In his view, William of Normandy had become king of England not
only by his victory at Hastings, but also by a coronation ceremony that
was a form of election, a compact with his new subjects binding him
to the laws of Edward the Confessor. For Coke, the Great Charter was
a confirmation of this fundamental contract, reaffirmed through its many
confirmations in the thirteenth and fourteenth centuries, and a weapon
for limiting the royal prerogative far beyond the attempts of baronial
rebels or late medieval parliaments.

Second, Coke reinterpreted or misinterpreted Magna Carta to give
it relevance, misconstruing its clauses anachronistically and uncritically.
Coke convinced his contemporaries that a thirteenth-century document
protected private property and secured Parliament's rights, for he overlooked the Charter's 'feudal' features, attaching little significance to the
barons' ties of personal loyalty and dependent landholdings that made
the king their lord. In his discussion of chapter 29/39, Coke took the
phrase 'by the law of the land' to mean 'due process of the common
law'.[6] He and his followers assumed that this clause guaranteed such
perpetual rights of the English people as *habeas corpus* and trial by jury,
thought to be contained in early law codes and royal charters predating

King John's 1215 grant. Since a representative assembly did not yet exist, chapters 12 and 14 of John's Charter had nothing to say about parliamentary consent to taxation. Coke's school, none the less, construed the call for 'common counsel' before levying aids or scutages as meaning Parliament's consent. Despite such anachronisms, Coke and his fellow lawyers grasped Magna Carta's essential meaning, that the king must be under the law.

Coke and his followers held a mythical view of Parliament's origin that surpassed their anachronistic interpretations of Magna Carta; indeed, Coke believed that the 1225 Charter's validity derived from its enactment 'by authority of Parliament then sitting'.[7] He and his friends imagined representative bodies in England from time immemorial, while some less insular contemporaries located the origin of representation among the 'Goths', their label for the Anglo-Saxon settlers. Following the notoriously unreliable thirteenth-century *Mirror of Justices*, Coke concluded that an assembly in King Arthur's time was the precursor of Parliament, the result of a compact between pre-Roman settlers and their earliest kings. Even the most careful scholars misdated Parliament's founding by a century or more to the reign of Henry I. Not only was the antiquity of Parliament assumed, but the presence of Commons from its beginning was taken for granted with no awareness of knights' and burgesses' intermittent attendance before the fourteenth century. The myth of Parliament's antiquity enabled parliamentarians to maintain that the Stuart kings were absolutist innovators, while parliamentarians were simply seeking to preserve an ancient tradition of shared authority by king, Lords and Commons, with sovereign power belonging to 'the king in Parliament'. Coke's belief in the supremacy of law caused him to hint at judicial review of statutes; he wrote in his *Reports* that 'in many cases, the common law will control Acts of Parliament, and sometimes adjudge them to be utterly void'.[8]

The early Stuarts had confidence that the royal prerogative could override the common law and the statutes during war or other emergencies, a view confirmed by royal judges. This inspired supporters of Parliament to argue all the more for its central place in a 'mixed' English constitution and stimulated scouring of medieval manuscripts by opponents of royal sovereignty that alarmed royal officials. When Sir Edward Coke was committed to the Tower in 1621 for being too outspoken in that year's Parliament, the authorities seized manuscripts of his uncompleted legal works. Eventually, all were returned except three, most likely drafts of the final volumes of his *Institutes of the Laws of England*. He published the first volume, known as *Coke on Littleton*, in 1627, but his books and papers were again confiscated in 1631 to forestall publication of detailed discussions of Magna Carta. On the learned lawyer's death in 1634, Charles I again had his papers impounded. Members of the Long Parliament saw the value of Coke's survey of England's laws for pro-parliamentary propaganda, supporting its increasingly revolutionary position. As civil war approached in the early 1640s, Parliament pressed the king for release of Coke's papers; once they were returned to his family, other volumes of the *Institutes* were published, with his account of the Great Charter appearing in 1642.

Another antiquarian who found himself in trouble for his scholarly activity was Sir Robert Cotton, a collector of manuscripts who knew the contents of royal record depositories better than their official keepers. In 1629 the government sealed Cotton's library, fearing that its contents constituted a threat to the crown, and he died in 1631, broken-hearted at being locked out of his own library. He was generous in allowing access to his collection, and it attracted opponents of Charles I in search of historical precedents for attacks on his absolutist programme. Cotton's library survives today as the core of the British Library's medieval manuscript collection, a gift of his grandson to the nation in 1700 that includes Cotton's two originals of John's Magna Carta.

Members of the Long Parliament saw the value of publicizing Magna Carta and sponsored writings asserting its prominent place in the English constitution. In 1643, Parliament authorized the printing of *Sovereign Power of Parliament and Kingdom* by William Prynne, a Puritan pamphleteer punished for earlier writings against Charles I's high Anglicanism by having his ears cut off and his cheeks branded. He began *Sovereign Power* by acknowledging his debt to Sir Edward Coke for showing that both the Great Charter and the Forest Charter were fundamental, permanent and immutable. He gave a tortured interpretation of chapter 29/39 of the Charter, making the king's promises applicable to Parliament as well as the people in an attempt to strengthen its authority. He wrote of royal refusal to approve a bill passed by Parliament:

> It is point blank against the very letter of Magna Carta (the ancient fundamental Law of the Realm, confirmed in at least sixty Parliaments) Chapter 29 *We shall deny, we shall defer . . . to no man* (much less to the whole Parliament and Kingdom, in denying or deferring to pass such necessary public Bills) *justice or right*, a law which *in terminis* takes clean away the King's pretended absolute negative voice to these Bills we now dispute of. [9]

Prynne's propaganda pamphlet points to the aim of the Long Parliament's radical members to seize sovereign power, supplanting either monarchical sovereignty or the co-ordinate power of king and Parliament. Another book appearing the same year, the anonymous *Brief Collections Out of*

Magna Carta; or, The Known Good Old Laws of England, presented a similar argument.

The Charter revived as a weapon against the early Stuarts

Although the conflict between the Stuart kings and their subjects affords parallels with thirteenth-century struggles by the baronage against King John, Henry III and Edward I, much had changed in the intervening centuries. Opposition to arbitrary royal rule no longer centred on a great council of barons, but on Parliament, and particularly the lower house. Once educated and articulate gentry took their places in the House of Commons in the Tudor era, Parliament had a more plausible claim than had medieval councils of magnates to speak for the kingdom as whole. Gentry in the seventeenth-century Commons, many of them experienced in the common law and devout Puritans, were no longer as deferential toward the king or the House of Lords as in earlier centuries.

In an age when absolutism was the dominant political doctrine throughout Europe, the problem of defining the proper spheres of king and Parliament became a major issue in England's political life. Many feared that the new Scottish kings would try to govern their English kingdom alone and that Parliament could follow continental representative assemblies into oblivion; indeed, James I managed without parliaments between 1614 and 1621, and Charles I from 1629 to 1640. With limits on royal authority ill-defined, the monarch possessed broad discretionary powers in several spheres of governance that traditionally were free from parliamentary oversight. Parliament had never gained exclusive control over enactment of new law, and the king could issue ordinances or proclamations that had the force of law; also he had the power of dispensing with statutes or suspending them in certain situations. Nor did Parliament have complete control over royal revenues, for the monarch had considerable independent resources, such as profits from his own estates, surviving feudal payments by the great nobles, and the customs duties. Once the early Stuarts set their minds on exploiting the royal prerogative to the full or expanding it, conflict with Commons and the common law courts was bound to follow.

Early in James I's reign, a focus of contention between king and Parliament was revival of several old royal privileges. One was the king's issue of patents for monopolies over the sale of certain goods; these were granted to favourites, angering business rivals who considered such grants unlawful restraints on trade. Generating more grievances was the monopolists' power to enforce their privileges by arresting and imprisoning infringers, and victims charged that such actions were contrary to chapter 29/39 of the Great Charter. A bill was introduced in Commons 'for the better securing of the subjects from wrongful imprisonment, and deprivation of trades and occupations contrary to the 29th Chapter of *Magna Carta*', but it never reached the House of Lords.[10] A proclamation by James I cancelling some monopolies did little to remedy the situation, and Parliament enacted a statute limiting royal monopolies in 1624. Another royal privilege that had aroused complaints since the later Middle Ages was purveyance, requisitions of goods for stocking royal castles and supplying the king's household. When the Stuart kings turned to purveyance as a means of raising revenue without parliamentary consent, protests soon followed, and members of Commons cited chapters 19 and 21 of Magna Carta and related late medieval statutes treating it. Appeals to the Charter against the royal right of purveyance did not produce any new legislation, however, for the House of Lords was unwilling to provoke a confrontation with James I.

Strife between the monarch and the Commons over supervision of the Church of England continued after Elizabeth I's death. Both she and her Stuart successors regarded their authority over the Church as part of the royal prerogative, but Puritans, who were more and more prominent in the Commons, challenged the Elizabethan ecclesiastical settlement. The Calvinist Puritans abhorred the episcopal pattern of ecclesiastical governance, which James I strongly supported, and Charles I favoured an elaborate liturgy too closely resembling Catholic ceremonial for their comfort. In their zeal for total eradication of 'papism' and reconstruction of the Anglican Church along Calvinist lines, they asserted Parliament's right to legislate in the spiritual domain.

By Charles I's time, the nature of constitutional debates was changing, and some parliamentarians feared that the traditional theory of a mixed constitution was an insufficient restraint on Stuart absolutism. The question of where sovereignty or ultimate authority over the kingdom resided could no longer be sidestepped. According to early modern political theorists, only one agency – king or representative assembly – could command the people's undivided allegiance. This issue had never arisen before, since Roman concepts of sovereignty had faded in the Middle Ages, and medieval political theorists hailed God alone as the sole sovereign power. Politicians and political thinkers in late medieval England had upheld the ideal of co-operation between the crown and the representative assembly, holding the realm to be a mixed 'body politic', an organic unity with the king as head and the subjects, represented by Parliament, as the body. Because head and body could not survive apart from one another, the two parts shared sovereignty, with paramount power belonging to 'the king in Parliament'. The ideal of mixed monarchy seemed to be fulfilled under the Tudor monarchs, whose skill in manipulating Commons made government seem to be functioning through co-operation between 'head' and 'body'.

Henry VIII had associated Parliament with his break with the papacy and establishment of a national church, and his children had sought parliamentary sanction for their shifting religious policies. By Elizabeth I's last years and in her Stuart successor's reign, parliamentarians were growing more assertive, however, insisting on debating matters not previously within their purview, pressing Elizabeth to marry or questioning James I's passive foreign policy. Commons revealed its newly aggressive character not only by debating matters that James I did not wish discussed, but also resuscitating the fourteenth-century practice of impeaching royal officials. If the king had immunity from the law, royal officials did not, and impeachment was a way to attack him by striking at his servants, as in 1621 when the Commons accused Sir Francis Bacon, then lord chancellor, of bribery.

By Charles I's accession, most members of Parliament still clung to a notion of mixed monarchy, declaring the king in Parliament supreme. This doctrine did not resolve the debate over sovereignty, and any suggestion of parliamentary parity with the monarch, much less superiority, was viewed by the early Stuarts as a radical innovation. Parliament pushed forward its own definition of the ancient constitution, proclaiming its unfettered right to make or unmake any law. Once Charles admitted the mixed nature of England's constitution by 1642, parliamentary leaders no longer trusted that pattern to constrain royal absolutism, and they moved to advocacy of fully co-ordinate parliamentary power. With the outbreak of war between king and Parliament in 1642, revolutionary arguments surfaced that openly embraced parliamentary sovereignty, and tendentious interpretations of such historical documents as the Great Charter supported this radical new opinion. Mixing anachronistic and uncritical interpretation of the Charter's clauses with the ancient constitution myth, the Stuarts' opponents painted themselves as defenders of long-held liberties, while pursuing limits on the monarchy unimagined in 1215 or 1225.

Another arena for conflict was the law courts, for the common lawyers viewed the Stuarts' prerogative courts, branches of the king's council created under the Yorkists and Tudors, as rival tribunals threatening traditional English liberties guaranteed in Magna Carta. Not bound by common law procedures, such bodies as the Star Chamber or Court of High Commission borrowed from Roman law in order to move with greater speed and efficiency. Since the High Commission was a powerful instrument for enforcing conformity to the Anglican Church, hostility to it united Puritans and common lawyers. Particularly distasteful to the common lawyers was its discarding of trial by jury in favour of the ecclesiastical courts' inquisitorial procedures, and they found equally offensive its practice of requiring accused persons to testify against themselves under oath. The early Stuarts were not content with controlling the prerogative courts, but intervened in the common law courts as well. James I took an active role in proceedings before Common Pleas and King's Bench, moving to adjourn or dismiss suits, discussing cases with the justices, even claiming a right to revoke them for his personal judgement.

Sir Edward Coke clashed with the king in conflicts between the common law courts and the ecclesiastical courts. When Coke adjudged that the common law courts could issue writs of prohibition, stopping proceedings in the church courts, James I claimed the right to determine which matters belonged to ecclesiastical jurisdiction. Coke denied his claim in 1607, boldly explaining that 'His Majesty was not learned in the laws of his realm of England and causes which concern the life or inheritance or goods or fortunes of his subjects [are decided by] judgement of law – which law is an art which requires long study and experience, before that a man can attain to the cognizance of it'. James then replied that if that were true, the king 'should be under the law – which was treason to affirm', and Coke responded by quoting the thirteenth-century legal treatise *Bracton*, which stated that 'the king ought to be under no man, but under God and the law'.[11]

When James I later attempted to intimidate common law justices by meeting with them individually before they handed down judgements, Sir Edward Coke protested vigorously. In a 1615 case, Coke maintained that the king could consult with his judges only as a body, not with individual justices. The two clashed again the next year, when the attorney-general ordered Coke and his fellow justices to adjourn another suit until the king could be consulted, but the judges rejected his right to stay a lawsuit. James then compelled the judges to come before him, and he lectured them while they were on their knees, awing all except Coke into yielding. Coke told the king that he would do whatever was fit for a judge to do, an audacious answer that led to his dismissal from the King's Bench in 1616. He won election in 1620 to the House of Commons, where he continued waging combat on behalf of Magna Carta's liberties.

Royal finances exacerbated the early Stuarts' conflicts with their subjects, for seventeenth-century England was experiencing economic depression and decreasing royal revenues, yet Commons balked at new taxes, expecting the king to 'live of his own'. The early Stuarts saw in their power to regulate foreign commerce a source of income independent of Parliament, and James I unilaterally raised the 'tunnage and poundage' or customs duty on imported currants in 1605. A proceeding known as Bates' Case followed, when John Bates was prosecuted before the Exchequer Court for refusing to pay the increased tariff. His lawyers argued that chapter 30 of the 1225 Charter, allowing merchants to enter and leave England free from 'all evil tolls', barred the king from arbitrarily raising the customs rates, and they cited fourteenth-century statutes buttressing their contention that parliamentary consent was required. The king won a favourable judgement, however, when the exchequer ruled that setting import duties was part of the royal prerogative, for regulation of overseas trade for the kingdom's welfare was the ruler's responsibility not shared with Parliament. One justice rejected limitations on customs duties imposed by Magna Carta, Edward I's Articles upon the Charters or Edward III's statutes, arguing that judgement must be given following the exchequer's precedents, not according to common law. Another found that the case concerned 'material matter of state and ought to be ruled by the rules of policy', adding that 'all commerce and affairs with foreigners . . . are made by the absolute power of the king'.[12] Bates' Case did not end discussion of chapter 30 of the Great Charter, and debates in Commons on extra-parliamentary impositions continued.

James's successor in 1625, Charles I, was a less skilful politician than his father. His paramount principle was a belief in his mission as monarch set above his subjects by God, and he possessed a streak of obstinacy that made him reject compromise and confuse inflexibility with adherence to principle. Charles became brazen in his attempts to boost royal revenues because Commons, alarmed by his divine-right doctrines and mistrustful of his alleged Catholic leanings, rejected any new money grants. Commons refused to grant the new king the customs duties or 'tunnage and poundage' for life, as was customary, but renewed them for only one year. Yet Charles issued a royal ordinance to collect the customs fees without parliamentary authorization after their expiration, and his subjects paid without serious protest.

Another of Charles I's attempts to add to his income without parliamentary approval was a forced loan in 1626, leading to a legal action, the Five Knights' Case or Darnel's Case. The king's incarceration of five knights without charges for refusing his demand raised the issue of arrest by the king's 'special mandate'. The knights applied to the courts for a writ of *habeas corpus* for their release on grounds that they had not been charged with any specific offence. This was a novel use of the writ of *habeas corpus*, a fourteenth-century procedural writ for securing the appearance of persons in court. By the fifteenth century, the common law justices had employed the writ to defend their jurisdiction, issuing it to release persons imprisoned by the prerogative courts. The gaoler rejected the five knights' writs, however, replying that they had been imprisoned 'by special command of the king'.

Counsel for the knights then argued that imprisonment by 'special command' without specifying charges enabled the king to arrest anyone he pleased, an alarming prospect. Representing one of the knights was John Selden, the prominent antiquary, who turned to chapter 29/39 of Magna Carta to defend his client; he declared that 'no freeman whatsoever ought to be imprisoned but according to the laws of the land; and . . . the liberty of the subject is the highest inheritance that he hath'.[13] Selden was the first person to link *habeas corpus* with the Great Charter, arguing that his client's detention by royal command without cause violated the Charter's guarantee of due process of law. The attorney-general responded that the monarch had incarcerated persons without bail for centuries without challenge and suggested that the prisoners' only recourse was a petition to the king, for no writ against the king was possible, since all writs were issued in his name. When the Court of King's Bench ruled on Charles's detention of prisoners by his command, a majority, bound by the precedent of many previous detentions, decided in his favour. The justices stated that when the monarch gives no specific cause for imprisonment, it is presumed to be 'a matter of state, which we cannot take notice of'.[14] They found that the same fundamental law protecting the king's subjects also safeguarded the crown's rights, reserving for it a sphere of authority. Although the justices' support for the royal prerogative apparently strengthened the king's hand, it inspired opponents of absolutism to stronger opposition, armed with *habeas corpus* as a new weapon.

By the early 1620s, members of Commons, inspired by Sir Edward Coke's veneration of Magna Carta, called for its reconfirmation, and their calls continued after Charles I's accession. Coke saw royal confirmations of English liberties as a recurring feature of the kingdom's history, stretching from late medieval confirmations of the Charter back to William the Conqueror's acceptance of Old English laws. For the Stuarts' opponents, the Norman king's confirmation hinted at the 'original contract' between king and people that would occupy a central place in eighteenth-century Enlightenment political thought. By the 1628 Parliament, Charles was willing to confirm Magna Carta alone without any additions, but resisted parliamentary attempts to reinterpret it. Not content with a simple reconfirmation of the Great Charter, Commons presented the Petition of Right, a new challenge to the traditional balance of power between king and Parliament. Central to their petition, chiefly authored by Coke, was chapter 29/39 of Magna Carta, which it restated along with statutes of Edward I and Edward III that extended its due process guarantee to any man 'of whatever estate or condition that he be'. The Petition elaborated on the Charter's liberties to ensure that no one should be compelled to give gifts, make loans or pay taxes to the king 'without common consent by act of Parliament'. It complained of denial of *habeas corpus*, protesting detention 'by your majesty's special command . . . without being charged with anything to which they might make answer according to the law'.[15]

When the Petition of Right went to the House of Lords, some peers supported it fully, but others sought to insert some protection for the royal prerogative. Many in the upper house felt that the king possessed sovereign power in certain spheres on which neither Parliament nor the law courts could intrude. Coke strongly spoke against the Commons' acceptance of the Lords' proposed amendment:

> I know that prerogative is part of the law, but 'Sovereign Power' is no Parliamentary word. In my opinion it weakens Magna Carta, and all the statutes; for they are absolute, without any saving of 'Sovereign Power'; and shall we now add it, we shall weaken the foundation of law, and then the building must needs fall. Take we heed what we yield unto: Magna Carta is such a fellow, that he will have no 'Sovereign'.[16]

When the petition reached Charles I, he refused to approve it with the traditional French expression of royal approval, *Le roi le veut* (the king desires it); instead, he adopted a formula implying passive acceptance, *Soit droit fait come est desiré* (let it be done as desired). The king soon revealed his true opinion of the Petition of Right, when he had several leaders of Commons arrested and tried before the Star Chamber, some of whom did not survive their imprisonment. The 1628 Petition of Right marks the most significant supplement to Magna Carta's liberties since the Articles on the Charters in 1300 or Edward III's six statutes. Even Charles's guarded statement conceded that the Charter in its new inter-pretation was a constitutional constraint on the monarch.

Parliament's assertiveness over the Petition of Right convinced Charles I to try governing alone, and no parliament met during the 'eleven years' tyranny' from 1629 to 1640. He was convinced that he could give England good government if not distracted by disputes with his parliaments, but he would have to find new revenues to replace parlia-mentary grants. He tried reimposing old, half-forgotten obligations, for example fining gentry who refused to be dubbed knights or extending the royal forests in violation of the Forest Charter. Charles also exploited 'ship money', an old payment by port towns for coastal defence that he extended to the entire kingdom on grounds that all England benefited from the royal navy. In 1637, his judges endorsed the extension of ship money, stating that 'When the good and safety of the kingdom in general is concerned and the whole kingdom is in danger, your majesty may . . . command all the subjects of this your kingdom at their charge to provide and furnish such number of ships . . . as your majesty shall think fit'.[17] A test case came the next year, when John Hampden was put on trial for refusing to pay ship money. A majority of King's Bench justices ruled that royal responsibility for the kingdom's defence entitled Charles I to take all necessary steps. They made extravagant claims for royal sovereignty and belittled Parliament's authority, defining it as a body where 'peers and commons . . . make known their grievances . . . to their sovereign and humbly petition him for redress'. One judge added, 'I never read nor heard that Lex was Rex [law was king]; but it is common and most true that Rex is Lex [king is law], for he is . . . a living, a speaking, an acting law'. A minority of the tribunal found ship money to be an illegal general tax, 'expressly contrary to divers statutes prohibiting a general charge to be laid upon the commons in general without consent in Parliament'.[18]

By such expedients as ship money, Charles I could raise revenues to cover peacetime expenses, but could not afford the costs of war. Unfortunately, he provoked fighting in Scotland in an attempt to impose an Anglican pattern on the Scottish Church (1639–40), and war debts forced him to resummon Parliament. Two parliaments met in 1640; the first, the Short Parliament, was dissolved after three weeks, since it had no interest in solving Charles's financial problems until his subjects' liberties were assured. Although Sir Edward Coke was no longer alive to lead the fight for Magna Carta, one member of Commons echoed his thoughts:

> The Charter of our Liberties, called Magna Carta, . . . was but a renovation and restitution of the ancient laws of this kingdom . . . and in the third year of [Charles I], we had more than a confirmation of it; for we had an act declaratory passed, and then, to put it out of all question and dispute for the future, his Majesty . . . invested it with the title of Petition of Right. What expositions contrary to that law of right have some men given to the undermining the liberty of the subject with new-invented subtle distinctions, and assuming to themselves a power . . . out of Parliament to supersede, annihilate and make void the laws of the kingdom?[19]

Since the Short Parliament proved to be intractable, a second soon succeeded it. Known as the Long Parliament, it would sit until dissolved by Oliver Cromwell in 1653, and it had no more interest in solving the king's financial problems than its predecessor.

The Long Parliament's first meeting brought the conflict over sovereignty to a head, impeaching royal officials and passing statutes that undercut the basis for Charles I's arbitrary rule during the eleven years' tyranny. When a massive uprising in Ireland against the Protestant population in 1641 required the king to raise an army to restore order, the Commons feared giving Charles a weapon that he later could turn against them. They sought to place the military under parliamentary control with a militia ordinance, a clear challenge to royal sovereignty and to the king's traditional responsibility for the kingdom's defence. With Parliament dismantling machinery for enforcing the royal prerogative and denying the king's right to reject or amend legislation, Charles decided that he must take drastic steps. In January 1642, the king turned to force against radicals in the House of Commons, dispatching troops to arrest five of its leaders. The five were forewarned and fled, but the king's attempted violence against one house of Parliament brought on civil war.

The warfare between forces of the king and the Long Parliament that began in 1642 required Parliament to function both as a legislature and as an executive body directing a war, a desperate situation that encouraged new doctrines of parliamentary sovereignty. By 1648, the king was defeated, but a second civil war soon broke out between the largely Puritan Parliament and radical Protestant soldiers in the New Model Army that had fought on its behalf. The victorious soldiers installed an ill-disguised military dictatorship that put Charles Stuart on trial in January 1649. At the ex-king's sentencing, the president of the tribunal turned to thirteenth-century baronial rebellions for precedent, describing a time 'when the nobility of the land did stand out for the liberty and property of the subject, and would not suffer the king that did invade to play the tyrant freer but called them to account for it',[20] and he cited passages of *Bracton* to reinforce his view of English history. The revolutionary step of beheading an anointed monarch as a 'tyrant, traitor and murderer, a public enemy of the commonwealth' frightened many inside and outside England, who considered Charles I's execution a violation of both the divine and natural orders.[21] Earlier, treason had been a crime committed against the king, but the new regime defined it as a prince's crime against his own people.

The country experienced a decade-long Interregnum, 1649–60, when it underwent experiments with republican regimes under radical Protestants, the Commonwealth and the Protectorate headed by Oliver Cromwell. Recalcitrant parliaments caused Cromwell almost as much frustration as the Long Parliament had spawned for Charles I, and critical conditions forced him into exercising extraordinary powers to cope with emergencies. He too collected customs duties without parliamentary consent and imprisoned persons without showing due cause. When an opponent appealed to Magna Carta, Cromwell is alleged to have ridiculed the revered document in crude language as 'Magna Farta'.[22] By Cromwell's death in 1658, the revolutionary attempt to institute a godly regime had clearly failed.

The Cromwellian interregnum marks the time when the idea of individual liberty was first linked with concepts of democracy or popular participation in governance. Slowly the connection between liberty and democracy strengthened, as a few political thinkers recognized that the English people's liberty under the law depended on their participation in governing the country. Earliest circulation of such ideas occurred when religious radicals in the parliamentary army, opposed to monarchy, an established church and a hierarchical social order, began to preach and publish pamphlets. Republican and egalitarian groups such as the Levellers produced a political programme in 1647, the Agreement of the People, that pioneered the concept of a written constitution, based on inalienable natural rights. The Agreement urged religious toleration and equal rights for all adult males, including the right to vote in parliamentary elections without distinction due to parentage or possession of property. They found fault with the technicalities, fees and delays of the common law courts, which they viewed as weapons of the rich against the poor who could not afford legal counsel, and legal reform was an important part of the Levellers' programme. They succeeded in at least one change that improved ordinary persons' chances in lawsuits, securing the replacement of archaic Law French with English as the language of the courts in 1650.

The Levellers took little comfort from traditional interpretations of English history; instead, they formulated the doctrine of the 'Norman Yoke', a notion that the Norman conquerors had imposed alien landlords on the free Anglo-Saxons in 1066, seized their land and ground them down into serfdom. Although Magna Carta was cited in Leveller tracts, they exhibited ambivalence about its usefulness for their cause. Some shared Coke's regard for the Charter, seeing it as tempering to some degree the Normans' suppression of native English liberties. They found in it justification for their resistance to arbitrary rule and for their demands for equality under the law; one Leveller pamphlet denounced imprisonment for debt as against Magna Carta and the Petition of Right. Other Levellers, especially an extremist group known as the Diggers, denied the Charter's significance for working people; in their interpretation of medieval history, it was a document devised by the barons for their own benefit and irrelevant, if not injurious, to the peasantry.

In seventeenth-century England, the great fear was royal oppression, but the Levellers saw potential for parliamentary tyranny in the Long Parliament's rule. Their leader, John Lilburne (d. 1657), was ahead of his contemporaries in recognizing that sovereign parliaments could be as great a threat to popular liberties as despotic monarchs. A worker in the cloth trade, who rose to the rank of lieutenant-colonel in the parliamentary forces, Lilburne left the army to pursue his revolutionary agenda, arousing the ire first of the royal judiciary and later of the Long Parliament. Seeing a threat to liberty in Parliament's superiority over fundamental law, he turned to Magna Carta as a protector of the people's liberties beyond the reach of parliamentary enactments. When sent to the Tower in 1645 on orders of the House of Commons for slandering its speaker, he sought release by a writ of *habeas corpus* and he cited the Charter, announcing that 'I build upon the Grand Charter of England' and asserting that 'I have as true a right to all the privileges that do belong to a freeman, as the greatest man in England'. Eventually, he came to agree with other Levellers that the Charter was 'but a beggarly thing',[23] an insufficient protection for the poor against parliaments dominated by the prosperous, and he concluded that a written constitution was needed to prevent parliamentary oppression.

Lilburne's perception of the possibility for parliamentary tyranny was novel in the seventeenth century and made no impact at the time. Over a century later, in Britain's former North American colonies where numbers of religious radicals had settled, the newly independent states adopted written constitutions that raised fundamental law above and beyond statute law. The state constitutions contained bills of rights, unalterable by statute, that echoed Magna Carta's protection of individuals against the ruler's oppression. Before the federal constitution creating the United States could win adoption, it was necessary to promise to add amendments providing similar protections against the central government.

The Charter and the accomplishment of parliamentary supremacy

Two years after Oliver Cromwell's death in 1658, the Stuart claimant returned to England to take the throne as Charles II (1660–85), but royal rule restored in 1660 was not that of Elizabeth I or James I. Much of the revolution sweeping England in the two previous decades survived, for the new king could not repudiate all the constitutional changes made since the Long Parliament first met in 1640. All bills enacted before the outbreak of civil war in 1642 and some legislation of the Commonwealth and Protectorate remained in effect. Although the new king acknowledged limitations on royal sovereignty, the restored monarchy represented only an uneasy balance between king and Parliament, and the powers of the two branches of government remained ill-defined. While the Long Parliament's statutes somewhat circumscribed the king's freedom of action, he retained many old royal rights. The restoration settlement represented only an incomplete victory for the Charter's principle of the king's submission to the law or Coke's concept of the common law as a check on the royal prerogative. None the less, at the end of Charles II's first parliament, the speaker of the House of Commons thanked him 'for restoring us to our Magna Carta liberties'.[24]

Charles's first parliament in 1660 enacted legislation ratifying some of Magna Carta's principles. The necessity of Parliament's approval of new general taxes, long thought to flow from the Charter, was extended to other royal money-raising devices, stripping the customs duties from the royal prerogative. Also Parliament assumed the king's traditional right of regulating overseas trade, and the Navigation Acts enacted during the Interregnum to favour English shipping remained in effect. With the Tenures Abolition Act of 1660, Parliament confirmed Cromwellian legislation that had abolished knights' fees or military tenures as the basis of England's landholding, stripping the king of his feudal sources of funds, notably custody of minor nobles' lands. The disappearance of military tenures rendered large chunks of English land law irrelevant, including the clauses of Magna Carta concerned with the feudal obligations of the king's great men. Abandonment of lordship and vassalage as the basis for landholding gave the aristocracy full proprietary right over their estates, and they were free to exploit them efficiently by new methods that would lead to the eighteenth-century agricultural revolution.

The most important legal reform under the restored monarchy strengthening Magna Carta's principle of due process was the Habeas Corpus Amendment Act in 1679, providing protection from arbitrary arrest. This act sanctioned an old common law writ's new use to safeguard the king's subjects from imprisonment without stated cause, a writ wrongly thought to have grown out of chapter 29/39. Another advance for the rule of law was the abolition of the prerogative courts, although judges in the traditional royal tribunals remained the king's appointees, serving at his pleasure. The common law courts took jurisdiction over criminal cases formerly heard by the Court of Star Chamber and over some commercial disputes formerly heard in the Admiralty Court. The Court of High Commission, previously charged with enforcing conformity to the Anglican Church, ceased to exist. The traditional ecclesiastical courts limped along with shrunken jurisdiction, for the common law courts or the chancery took many cases formerly under their jurisdiction.

The royalist bias of judges aroused complaints, and the Commons took action against individual justices who failed to show proper respect for Magna Carta. In 1667, when a juror cited the Charter in protesting against a judge's reversal of the jury's verdict, the judge responded, 'Magna Farta, what ado with this have we?' Commons then accused the judge of having 'vilified' the Charter, endangering the people's liberties, and he was obliged to appear before the House to make a public apology. A few years later, another justice incurred the Commons' ire by mocking the Great Charter. When a member of the House declared that justices who had not read the Charter were unfit to hold their posts, he agreed, adding under his breath, 'And if they have, I had almost said, they deserve to lose their heads'. An incensed House of Commons initiated impeachment proceedings, charging the judge with seeking to 'subvert the fundamental laws and the established religion and government'.[25]

Common lawyers held in high respect the English tradition of trial by jury, which they assumed was guaranteed by Magna Carta. Until Charles II's reign, however, jurors lacked freedom to reach independent verdicts, for judges regularly tyrannized juries into returning the verdicts that they desired. Freedom for juries was won in 1670, following the Quaker William Penn's trial for unlawful and riotous assembly. When the jurors refused to render a guilty verdict, they were confined for two days in a cold room without food to force them to find Penn guilty. After this mistreatment failed to force them to convict the Quaker zealot, the court incarcerated them until they paid fines. Penn complained without success that the court's action contradicted chapters 14 and 29/39 of the Great Charter. When a member of the jury complained to the Court of King's Bench, the justices ruled in favour of independence for juries and denied judges' right to punish them, no matter how irrational or misguided their verdicts. They ruled that never before was a jury 'punished by fine or imprisonment by the judge for not finding according to their evidence', although they admitted that verdicts often were 'not according to the judge's opinion and liking'.[26]

In Charles II's last years, religious fears rose among the Anglican majority, more alarmed by resurgent Catholicism than by Puritanism, since repressive legislation, the so-called Clarendon Code, had cowed the Protestant 'dissenters' or 'non-conformists'. Despite continued official repression, the Roman Catholic threat seemed to grow more serious, since the king was suspected of papist sympathies and his younger brother and heir, James, duke of York, was openly Roman Catholic. The duke's ardent Catholicism provoked proposals in Parliament for legislation excluding him from the succession, and this split members into two factions or parties, the Whigs standing for limited monarchy and exclusion and the anti-exclusionist Tories standing for non-resistance to royal power. The Tories favoured the strict hereditary principle and advocated accepting the Catholic James's rule, confident that one of his two daughters married to Protestant princes would succeed him.

In the crisis over excluding Charles II's brother from the throne, propagandists on both sides turned to history, authoring pamphlets presenting conflicting versions of the origin of England's constitution. Tories supported their viewpoint by turning to royalist antiquaries' works written during the Interregnum on the 'feudal law' of dependent tenures. The recovery of the ties of lordship and vassalage brought to England by the Norman invaders caused a revolution in historical thinking that challenged Coke's myth of the ancient constitution. It showed the king's feudal lordship strengthening his hand, making even the greatest magnates royal dependants who held their estates of him. Anti-exclusionists made use of these findings, only published after the Restoration, to raise questions about Magna Carta's significance. They concluded that its liberties were due to Henry III's grace in granting the 1225 Charter; furthermore, its chief effect was to reduce the barons' financial burdens. By taking an approach foreshadowing that of modern scholars, positioning the Charter in a sounder historical context, royalist antiquaries limited its relevance as a liberty document and undermined the pseudo-history of Coke and his followers.

The propaganda war over exclusion also led to debates on the origin of England's representative assembly, with the royalist Tories arguing that Parliament was a royal invention and the exclusionist Whigs insisting on its existence from time immemorial. This was not a theoretical question, for the answer affected Parliament's right to intervene in the succession. Writings on parliamentary origins by Henry Spelman (d. 1641), based on his study of chapter 14 of John's Magna Carta and published posthumously in 1664, presented Parliament as a royal creation evolving out of councils of the Anglo-Norman kings' tenants-in-chief. Sir William Dugdale (d. 1686), another ardent royalist, authored propaganda pieces opposing the duke of York's exclusion, but also produced serious works continuing Spelman's linkage of Parliament's origin to lordship and vassalage. Dugdale connected the parliamentary principle of representation to the barons' authority to speak on behalf of their vassals in great councils.

Another scholar with strong royalist leanings was Robert Brady (d. 1700), the king's physician, who carried Spelman's findings about the feudal law to their logical conclusion. He concluded in his 1684 book, *Introduction to the Old English History*, that the Norman Conquest had totally transformed Anglo-Saxon laws and institutions, implanting arbitrary royal power. Brady refuted Whig claims of Parliament's antiquity by stressing the discontinuity between the Old English and Norman kingdoms, and he depicted Parliament as a post-Conquest creation, descended from councils of William I's tenants-in-chief. In his view, the liberties granted by the Great Charter were very limited, only freeing the Church from subjection to the king and easing the barons' obligations as the king's tenants. He wrote that the Charter was 'a relaxation of the feudal military law, and . . . contrived, and granted chiefly for the ease of military men', effective only because of King John's agreement to grant it.[27] By treating Magna Carta in its thirteenth-century context, Brady questioned its relevance for the political debates of his own day.

Most outspoken among royalist-leaning antiquarians was Sir Robert Filmer (d. 1653), author of *Patriarcha*, a work probably written during the civil war, but not published until 1680, in time for use by the anti-exclusionists. Filmer argued largely from biblical history or prehistory not from England's past. As the title *Patriarcha* suggests, he taught that the monarch is the divinely designated father of his people, possessing the same arbitrary power over his subjects that Old Testament patriarchs held over their wives, children and servants. Tracing the origin of kingship to Adam, ruler by God's will over the first family, Filmer found no place for popular sovereignty; kings succeeded Adam as sovereigns, the source of all laws, but themselves above the law. Because Magna Carta was extorted from King John, it was invalid; it 'first had an obscure birth by usurpation, and was secondly fostered and showed to the world by rebellion'.[28]

The royalists' feudal law called for a response from Whigs defending Coke's myth of a primeval law limiting royal authority, and to prove Parliament's right to exclude James from the succession they had to answer Tory arguments that the law derived from the monarch. The most prominent polemicist advocating parliamentary power over the succession was William Petyt (d. 1707), a lawyer familiar with historical documents. Like other believers in the 'ancient constitution', he traced Parliament to pre-Roman Britain and followed Coke in believing that William the Conqueror had confirmed his English subjects' ancient liberties, foreshadowing Magna Carta. Another defender of Parliament's antiquity was Petyt's friend William Atwood (d. 1705), who argued that the phrase 'common counsel/council [Latin *consilium*] of the realm' in the Great Charter was evidence for Commons' existence as part of Parliament by 1215.

Under Charles II, the question of sovereignty remained unanswered largely because he made certain that it was not asked. Unwilling to risk his father's fate, he took care to avoid provoking Parliament, and it proved unwilling to press him too hard; both parties thereby contented themselves with an uneasy balance of power. Charles's brother the duke of York, who followed him on the throne (1685–88), despite cries for his exclusion was impolitic enough to incite a crisis that demanded a definitive answer to the question of sovereignty. As King James II, he revived the Court of High Commission, transforming it from a prosecutor of papists and Puritans into an instrument for Catholic infiltration of the Anglican Church. He used the royal prerogative to champion his Catholic co-religionists, dispensing with laws or suspending them to appoint Catholics to government posts, issuing Declarations of Indulgence to free them from the Test Act's requirement that officeholders be Anglican communicants. Royalist propaganda labelled James's declarations a 'Magna Carta for liberty of conscience', since they covered Protestant dissenters. His opponents argued, however, against acceptance of religious freedom granted as a royal act of grace, for doing so admitted James's royal prerogative to make and unmake laws.

James II soon alienated powerful political groups who were the monarchy's natural allies, conservative Tory gentry and Anglican clerics. Both believed that passive obedience to a divinely ordained hereditary monarch was essential for the kingdom's stability, but James's actions against the Anglican Church forced them to choose between their commitment to non-resistance to the king and their devotion to the established Protestant religion. Furthermore, James's insistence on forcing Anglicans from posts that were considered forms of property, including Oxford University fellowships, and replacing them with Catholics posed a threat to private property rights. The patience of traditional royalists ended in the spring of 1688, when seven Anglican prelates, including the archbishop of Canterbury, were arrested and charged with seditious libel for refusing to read from their pulpits the king's most sweeping Declaration of Indulgence. The bishops won quick acquittal, for the justices of King's Bench found the king's demand unlawful because of Parliament's stand against his use of his dispensing power. The judgement against James II set off church bells ringing in celebration throughout the kingdom.

Following this outrage by James II, a greater cause for concern was the birth in June 1688 of a royal son and heir, certain to be brought up a Catholic. This child dashed hopes for a Protestant succession in the person of one of James's Protestant daughters and promised permanent Catholic rule. His birth pushed the Tories into abandoning their fidelity to the strict hereditary principle, and they joined the Whigs in offering the English crown to James II's elder daughter, Mary, and her husband, William of Orange, head of the Dutch Republic. Eager to extend his influence over England and gain an ally in his war against France, the Dutch prince declared his willingness to accept the crown in order to 'lay the foundation of a firm security for your religion, your laws and your liberties'. He condemned James's arbitrary acts as 'contrary to law, and to that express provision in Magna Carta, that no man shall lose life or goods but by the law of the land'.[29] In November 1688, William landed on the Channel coast, and James's support dissipated, forcing him to flee to France.

A commission of peers and members of previous parliaments meeting in December called elections for a so-called Convention Parliament that met in January 1689 to settle the kingdom's form of governance. The Convention Parliament agreed that William of Orange and Mary should rule as joint sovereigns, and should they die childless, the throne would pass to Mary's sister Anne, wife of Prince George of Denmark, and her progeny. By discarding ancient custom concerning hereditary succession, this assembly was in effect changing the constitution. It also demonstrated its power over the monarchy by applying to the king the Test Act; no Roman Catholic, nor the spouse of a Catholic, was to wear the English crown. The Convention Parliament faced the same dilemma of medieval usurpers: how to disguise the fact of the deposition of an anointed and crowned king? It adopted their face-saving formula, considering James II to have abdicated, with his flight from the kingdom in the face of William's forces designated as abandonment of the throne. This salved the consciences of Tories who rejected doctrines of popular sovereignty justifying the people's right to rid themselves of an unjust ruler. The Commons' resolution of January 1689 declared, 'That King James II, having endeavoured to subvert the Constitution of the Kingdom, by breaking the original contract between King and people, and . . . having violated the fundamental laws and withdrawn himself out of out of the kingdom, has abdicated the government and that the throne is thereby become vacant'.[30]

The Convention Parliament debated a new Magna Carta to define both the king's rights and his subjects' liberties, and it drafted the Bill of Rights, enacted in December 1689. Like the Great Charter, it is a pragmatic document responding to specific problems. The Bill first listed twelve unlawful acts that James II had committed repeatedly and followed with fifteen measures for remedying his wrongs. It denied the king's right to issue decrees with the force of law and also prohibited him from suspending or dispensing with the law or levying a tax without parliamentary approval. It deprived the king of control over the military, making it unlawful to maintain a standing army without parliamentary consent. The people were guaranteed their rights to jury trials and writs of *habeas corpus*. Another act reworded the coronation oath to reinforce the king's obligation to obey not only traditional law and custom, but also parliamentary statutes. No longer did a new monarch simply swear to 'grant and keep' the kingdom's laws and customs; instead, he was to swear to govern the kingdom 'according to the statutes in Parliament agreed on and the laws and customs of the same'.[31]

With the Glorious Revolution of 1688–89, Parliament made itself a branch of government superior to the monarch, ending any possibility of absolute monarchy in England. Over the years following James II's deposition, parliaments adopted a series of statutes forming the Revolution Settlement that along with the Declaration of Rights filled out details of the new constitutional arrangement. With the Act of Settlement enacted in 1701, Parliament decreed the rules of succession to the English throne; no longer would a monarch succeed according to divinely determined hereditary succession. The statute denied the Catholic Stuarts' claims and specified that after Queen Anne the throne should pass to descendants of James I's daughter, Elizabeth, and her German Protestant husband, and that no future English monarch could be a Roman Catholic. Additional legislation confirmed Parliament's superior position in the state, enacting portions of the Bill of Rights as statutes. The Triennial Act of 1694 ended any possibility of the king's governing without Parliament by requiring annual sessions and elections for the Commons at least every three years. The Mutiny Act strengthened parliamentary control over the armed forces; enacted for a limited duration, it required periodic parliamentary renewal of the king's power to enforce military discipline in courts martial. The Civil List Act prevented the monarch from regarding the kingdom as his private property, spending public funds as he pleased on himself, his family and friends, making him instead a salaried public servant dependent on annual parliamentary appropriations.

Thanks to the legacy of Magna Carta, the Revolution Settlement guaranteed the English people a high degree of individual liberty. William of Orange, on his acceptance of the English crown, had promised them an independent judiciary with lifetime appointments, secure salaries and dismissal only for proven misconduct; later, Parliament put his pledge into a statute as part of the Act of Settlement. Censorship of the press ended in 1695 with expiration of the Licensing Act, which had enabled the government to intimidate printers of unpopular or radical literature with the threat of losing their press licences. The Toleration Act rewarded

Protestant non-conformists for their support of the Glorious Revolution with freedom of conscience, rights to public worship and the vote, if they met property qualifications, although the Test Act continued to deny them the right to hold public office. The Act did not extend to Roman Catholics, who remained legally disfranchised and without the right to practise their religion, although they generally gathered for public worship without interference.

The English took pride in the events of 1688–89, inspiring the Whig interpretation of their history that reinforced Sir Edward Coke's myth of the ancient constitution. This triumphalist view of advancing liberty became an organizing principle for writers of English history, and Whig historians ranked the Glorious Revolution alongside King John's concessions at Runnymede, convinced that it represented another reconfirmation of an ancient compact between king and people, restoring the fundamental law and a limited monarchy. All educated persons in 1688–89 with any knowledge of English history would have seen parallels with the barons' rebellion of 1215, for Coke had made Magna Carta's principle of the rule of law and common law rights part of their intellectual inheritance. The revolution's supporters depicted the Great Charter as a renewal of earlier monarchs' promises to their subjects, not simply concessions coerced from a feudal lord by unruly vassals, as royalist historians portrayed it. Like Sir Edward Coke, they followed medieval political thinkers in describing government as a compact between the prince and his subjects, and they considered Magna Carta and its confirmations as renewals of such a compact. Late in the seventeenth century, these views would be elaborated into contract theory, a staple of modern political thought.

With John Locke's *Two Treatises on Government*, contract theory received a new twist to provide philosophical justification for the Glorious Revolution. Although written before James II's accession to justify Whig exclusionist policy, the *Two Treatises* were not published until 1690, after his deposition. Locke was a philosophical empiricist capable of supplying a rational justification for English resistance to a tyrannical ruler, a contract theory more complex than a simple bargain between ruler and subjects. His treatises do not mention Magna Carta, for he grounded his defence of the right of revolution on natural right, not on Coke's immemorial laws or English history. To explain government's origin, Locke turned instead to an imagined a state of nature without law or government that he assumed to have been much like the Dark Ages, without public officials enforcing justice and with private individuals – victims or their families – pursuing criminals themselves. In his state of nature, all people possessed natural rights to life, liberty and property, although they found it difficult to enforce them, particularly to safeguard their property, until they came together and created a political or civil society, surrendering their power of protecting their individual rights to the community or commonwealth.

Locke located the beginning of government in a compact that the people made to create a governing authority, an agreement taking the form of a trust, 'a fiduciary power to act for certain ends'. This agreement was not precisely a contractual arrangement because a contract gives rights to the two parties, people and ruler; Locke's trust gave the people alone rights, leaving the governing power only obligations. The people's commitment to this ruling authority, labelled by Locke the 'legislative', was conditional on its governing in accordance with the trust, protecting their rights. The people held a right to withdrew their consent and revolt, if the governing body destroyed their property or threatened their freedom, placing itself in 'a state of war' against them. Locke wrote that the people retained 'a right to resume their original liberty, and by the establishment of a new legislative . . . , provide for their own safety and security'; they retained 'a supreme power to remove or alter the Legislative [i.e. the government], when they find the Legislative act contrary to the trust reposed in them'.[32]

After the Glorious Revolution, Whigs considered England's constitution to be an implied contract, consisting of Magna Carta, supplemented by the Petition of Right of 1628, the 1679 Habeas Corpus Act, the 1689 Bill of Rights and the 1701 Act of Settlement. In the triumphant Whig version of English history, the 1688–89 revolution was one of a series of confirmations of the kingdom's fundamental law, a conservative revolution that marked the culmination of a long process of recovering liberties enjoyed by the ancient Britons and a moderate revolution, motivated by neither religious nor ideological fanaticism. The Whigs also depicted the Glorious Revolution as peaceful, overlooking fierce fighting in Ireland in the summer of 1690 that had repelled James II and his French allies and ensured its permanence. This interpretation instilled pride in the events of 1688–89, which would be contrasted later with the radical and bloody French Revolution, ignoring the earlier English civil war and the beheading of Charles I. The Whig account of English history as the recovery of ancient liberties through confrontations with tyrannical rulers proved popular in the American colonies, and the rebel colonists of the 1770s found parallels in England's past to their resistance to George III.

Although works by royalist historians opposing James II's exclusion fell into disfavour after the Glorious Revolution, their scepticism about a mythical ancient constitution would not be entirely forgotten. Their picture of the past, more accurate than Coke's portrayal, would win endorsement in the nineteenth century. A new scientific approach to history would confirm Robert Brady's version of medieval English history, crediting the Normans with installing unrestrained monarchical power and dismissing Magna Carta as a feudal document having little relevance beyond the thirteenth century. None the less, the Whigs' view would triumph in the eighteenth century. Symbolizing their victory over royalist historians was Brady's replacement as keeper of records at the Tower of London, guardian of sources for the kingdom's history, by William Petyt, a supporter of Coke's ancient constitution.

The eclipse and revival of Magna Carta in eighteenth-century England

Once the Glorious Revolution established Parliament's sovereignty and the Bill of Rights protected English liberties, Magna Carta lost its central place in political debates. The pattern of limited power for England's monarchs came into sharp focus under the first two Hanoverian kings, George I (1714–27), and George II (1727–60), who assumed less active roles in governance than their predecessors. Under the early Hanoverians, cabinet government evolved with direction of the state under a prime minister and his cabinet, who were members of Parliament responsible to a majority in the Commons. The principle of cabinet responsibility, in effect, reinforced Parliament's supremacy, placing government in the hands of a parliamentary committee. There was no 'separation of powers' between the legislative, judicial and executive branches, as under the United States constitution.

Although the implications of parliamentary supremacy did not become clear at once, it would make a powerful impact on Magna Carta's place in English political thought. While the myth of Magna Carta as a building block of the English constitution survived, Parliament's unlimited power of enacting and repealing laws ultimately would undermine long-held notions of the ancient constitution. The rule of law still stood as a cornerstone of the British constitution, yet an all-powerful Parliament, especially the House of Commons, was now expected to guard against tyrannical rulers, supplanting the Great Charter as a bulwark of liberty. Ideology played a lesser part in eighteenth-century politics than in the previous century, and shifts in political allegiances often owed more to personalities, pursuit of patronage and office, or local interests than to constitutional issues. During George III's reign (1760–1820), constitutional debates revived, however, with rebellion in the North American colonies and the French Revolution. Even earlier, some supporters of the balanced constitution of the 1689 Revolution Settlement could see

Parliament threatening individual liberty, and the Great Charter again appeared as a political weapon, this time against an all-powerful legislative branch.

Parliament was supreme in eighteenth-century Britain, but it hardly represented the mass of English or Scottish people. An oligarchy of great landed families dominated political life, commanding Parliament. These families were Whigs, whose strong support for the Revolution Settlement and the Protestant succession won them the Hanoverian monarchs' gratitude. The Tories' loyalty to the new dynasty was suspect, for many had sentimental feelings for the son and grandson of James I, the Jacobite pretenders, and the Tories would wander in the political wilderness for over half a century. Needless to state, the House of Lords, enlarged with sixteen Scottish peers since the 1707 Act of Union, represented the landed nobility, but the House of Commons made little pretence of speaking for the common people. The Commons had not been reapportioned for years, and many members represented 'pocket boroughs', so called because the borough was in the pocket of some powerful family that chose its member of Commons; and others represented 'rotten boroughs', abandoned town sites, whose owners still sent representatives to Parliament. Where elections actually took place, the vote was restricted to substantial freeholders, disfranchising the majority who owned no land. After an act of 1710, eligibility for election to the Commons was limited to a few thousand men possessing large private incomes. Despite members' wealth, corruption was rampant in eighteenth-century parliaments, and Robert Walpole, widely recognized as the first prime minister (1730–42), was a master at maintaining a pro-government majority through distribution of pensions and sinecures.

By the eighteenth century, English law was a centuries-old system closely guarded by a legal profession isolated from the latest intellectual currents and still revering the ancient constitution. The common law was a multi-layered repository of overlapping jurisdictions and procedural complexities expressed in archaic terminology incomprehensible to non-lawyers, created over many epochs. Furthermore, England had a parallel legal system alongside the common law courts, the Court of Chancery with equitable procedures, settling civil cases for which the common law's rigid forms of action supplied no remedy. English criminal law fell heavily on the needy, with vagrancy laws and poor laws subjecting them to a stern discipline, and hanging was the punishment for over 200 crimes, although transportation to overseas colonies was often substituted. With all the common law's drawbacks, the English political classes still looked to it as the guardian of their liberties. They depended on its procedures originally intended to protect property rights to safeguard their liberties, for example by bringing actions of trespass against government agents who searched their houses without proper authorization.

English law was drawn out of its disorganization and intellectual isolation by Sir William Blackstone (d. 1780), who was learned in both the common law and the civil law. His *Commentaries on the Laws of England*, published between 1765 and 1769, initiated a more scientific approach, setting forth basic rules and underlying principles of English law and comparing it with natural law and other nations' laws. Blackstone was an exponent of gradual evolution of the common law over centuries, adapting to changing conditions; he wrote: 'Our system of remedial laws resembles an old Gothic castle erected in the days of chivalry, but fitted up for modern habitation'.[33] The *Commentaries* explained substantive law without becoming bogged down in procedures, which had mired writers of earlier lawbooks, and it soon became a standard text for apprentice lawyers in both Britain and the North American colonies.

Blackstone believed that the British constitution steered a middle course between the extremes of absolutism and excessive liberty. His *Commentaries* impressed on readers the inviolable character of English subjects' rights, beyond royal or parliamentary authority. If an individual could not defend his rights against the king, then royal officials could be held accountable; for no monarch could 'misuse his power, without the advice of evil counsellors, and the assistance of wicked ministers'. Like seventeenth-century common lawyers, Blackstone celebrated the writ of *habeas corpus*, remarking that the 1679 Habeas Corpus Act was 'a second *magna carta*'. In his *Commentaries*, Blackstone traced three basic rights of individuals to Magna Carta: 'the free enjoyment of his life, his personal liberty and his property'. He applied his critical skills to the Charter in his edition published in 1759; he differentiated King John's 1215 Charter from subsequent issues, ending the confusion caused by conflation of various versions. Despite his critical approach, he did not break completely with the doctrine of the ancient constitution, for he followed Coke's assumption that Magna Carta 'was for the most part declaratory of the principal grounds of the fundamental laws of England'.[34]

Dominant political doctrines in eighteenth-century England were conservative and complacent, and the propertied classes looked with pride on a constitution that they imagined protected the people's freedom, while averting their eyes from its injustices. Despite the eighteenth century's reputation as an age of reason, religion still had a prominent place in political discourse, confirming political elites in their complacency. Most politicians and lawyers could see no danger to ancient liberties preserved in Magna Carta, yet a few feared possible threats to freedom by a powerful Parliament. As early as 1701, the House of Commons was assailed for its arbitrary actions threatening the rights of petitioners. A clamour arose over the Commons' imprisonment of five men from Kent who had presented a petition urging expenditures opposed by the government. The Commons' oppression inspired pamphlets, such as one by the novelist Daniel Defoe denouncing its 'illegal and unwarrantable practices'. Defoe warned of the potential for parliamentary oppression, writing that 'Englishmen are no more to be slaves to Parliament than to kings'. Another pamphleteer, enraged by the Kent petitioners' fate, complained that the Commons had 'invaded our rights contrary to Magna Carta'.[35]

The implications of parliamentary supremacy for doctrines of fundamental law became clear with repeal of the Triennial Act, enacted in 1694 as new fundamental law, binding 'for ever hereafter'. Requiring annual sessions of Parliament and elections for the Commons every three years, this statute ended any possibility of the king's dissolving Parliament and governing alone. By the second decade of the eighteenth century, Parliament was finding the Triennial Act too restrictive, and in 1716 it exercised its sovereign power to repeal the law and replace it with the Septennial Act, extending a parliament's life from three to seven years. Supporters of the new statute could not imagine that Parliament's changing the 1694 law diminished its moral commitment to the ancient constitution, yet critics insisted that such parliamentary tampering with fundamental law must be limited. Petitions protested against the bill, and an opponent in the Commons denounced it as 'a very dangerous step towards the undermining of that constitution which our ancestors have been so careful to preserve and thought no expense, either of blood or treasure, too much for that purpose'. He warned that a parliament free to repudiate the Triennial Act could also reject 'all the other privileges and immunities, which have been obtained to the people from the crown, from the date of Magna Carta to this very day'.[36]

The early-eighteenth-century Tories, languishing under the first two Hanoverian kings without possibility of power, depicted themselves as defenders of the ancient constitution and accused the Whig parliamentary majority of undermining historic English liberties. The prime minister, Robert Walpole, heightened Tory fears of an over-powerful executive by manipulating the legislative branch by marshalling votes of 'placemen' in the Commons bought by judicious awards of patronage. The satirist Jonathan Swift, writing in a Tory journal, warned that the government possessed 'a supreme, absolute, unlimited Power . . . of making Laws . . . without all Bounds; can repeal or enact at Pleasure whatever Laws it thinks fit'.[37] He pointed out that hereditary succession to the throne was subject to parliamentary statutes, and he warned that not even Magna Carta was safe from legislative alteration.

Another Tory, the Jacobite-leaning propagandist and historian Henry St John, Viscount Bolingbroke, campaigned tirelessly against Walpole. He twisted Coke's pseudo-history of England, turning it into a weapon against his rival. Bolingbroke echoed Whig praise for the Glorious Revolution, but complained that unscrupulous royal servants had corrupted it. He wrote that Magna Carta, that 'sacred Covenant', had secured justice and liberty for England until Walpole had 'rumpled it rudely up, and crammed it into his Pocket'. He accused the prime minister of reducing the English people to 'ignominious Slaves', who no longer possessed the qualities needed to defend the Charter. Bolingbroke insisted that Parliament was bound by fundamental law, 'that assemblage of laws, institutions, and customs derived from certain fixed principles of reason', and he wrote that Parliament 'cannot annul the constitution', but feared that it could erode the English people's freedom without formally repealing it.[38]

Tory support for the ancient constitution drove Whig defenders of Walpole to stress the superiority of the post-1688 'modern constitution' and even to question Magna Carta's relevance. One Whig journalist, repeating earlier royalist anti-exclusionist arguments, declared that the nobility alone had gained from the Charter, for it was 'only an exemption of a few great proprietors of land from some hardships they lay under on account of their conditional tenures'. In his view, it had afforded no relief to most of John's subjects, who were 'as much hewers of wood and drawers of water, as truly vassals and slaves after, as before this Great Charter'.[39] In fact, many eighteenth-century Whigs had less concern for principles of law and liberty than for economic, social and political privileges flowing to them from their domination of Parliament.

After George III ascended the throne in 1760, both American colonists and their English sympathizers began to question Parliament's supremacy, and a radical movement to broaden parliamentary representation challenged complacency about the glories of the English constitution. Opponents of the Whig oligarchy's monopoly on power, excluded from office, denounced its political machinations, graft and corruption. The reformers were a diverse group ranging from moderates seeking a more representative House of Commons through electoral reform to religious dissenters and political radicals, who looked back to the revolutionary era of Puritan parliaments and Cromwell's regime. Eventually, an extreme radical element, holding democratic and egalitarian views, turned to the Levellers' picture of England's past, longing for an egalitarian Anglo-Saxon society unburdened by the alien 'Norman Yoke' imposed after 1066. This amorphous group of reformers both inspired and was inspired by the thirteen North American colonies' fight for freedom in the 1770s. For a time after 1789, the French Revolution also was an inspiration to the reformers, but the beheading of Louis XVI and France's wars with Britain in the 1790s caused reaction and repression that set back reform for decades. Despite constant criticism of Parliament's unrepresentative character and corruption, no effective reform ensued in the late eighteenth century; instead, its oligarchical power grew as pressures of large-scale warfare promoted expansion of central authority.

With radical journalists stirring up public opinion against Parliament, freedom of the press came under attack, although the Licensing Act had expired before the end of the seventeenth century. The secretary of state sought to suppress anti-government publications by issuing general warrants for the arrest of persons suspected of writing seditious material, and his servants seized and searched suspects' papers, looking for evidence to support their prosecution. One radical writer arrested for seditious libel in 1762 showed an eye for publicity, arranging for his arrest to take place while he was teaching Magna Carta to his young son. After he sued for wrongful arrest and won damages, he became a hero, and a print picturing him pointing out chapter 29/39 to the boy was circulated widely (see Plate 11).

Another seditious libel case, brought in 1765, forced the government to abandon its issue of general warrants. When the defendant in this case brought an action of trespass against officials who had ransacked his house and carried off his books and papers, the chief justice interpreted the suit as turning on the common law's protection of private property, not on free speech. He stated in his decision, 'The great end for which men entered into society was to secure their property. That right is preserved sacred and incommunicable in all instances where it is not taken away or abridged by some public law for the good of the whole. . . . By the laws of England every invasion of private property is a trespass'.[40] Rejecting the government's argument of state necessity and failing to find that either the common law or statutes authorized search and seizure of a subject's papers, the justice arrived at Magna Carta's goal of due process by the circuitous path of protecting private property rights.

The fight for freedom of the press came to centre on John Wilkes (d. 1797), a rogue and a libertine, who used his position as a newspaper editor and member of the Commons for political agitation. Imprisoned in the Tower in 1763 for seditious libel because of scurrilous attacks on George III, Wilkes transformed his prosecution into a campaign for the English people's rights against oppression, invoking Magna Carta, 'that glorious inheritance, that distinguishing characteristic of the Englishmen'.[41] His parliamentary status won him quick release, for the Lords upheld his parliamentary privilege, finding that his prosecution by the Commons threatened 'the personal liberty of every common subject in these realms'.[42] After Wilkes countersued for wrongful arrest, won his suit and collected damages, crowds hailed him as a champion of liberty. The government's failure to silence him brought new charges, this time an accusation of blasphemy for publishing an obscene book, and the scandal caused his expulsion from the House of Commons and flight from the country in 1764.

John Wilkes eventually returned to England to win re-election to the Commons, which refused to seat him, raising the issue of its right to disqualify a duly elected candidate. Wilkes portrayed his expulsion from the Commons as oppression against the voters who had elected him, and he appealed again to the Charter, 'the great preserver of the lives, freedom, and property of Englishmen'. The Lords adjudged that the lower house had exceeded its authority, equating its denial of voters' right of free election with the Stuart kings' arbitrary exercise of 'a suspending and dispensing power . . . against the ancient and fundamental liberties of the kingdom'.[43] Shut out of Parliament, Wilkes won election to several offices in the City of London before the Commons finally readmitted him in 1774. He proved a master propagandist, who caught the public's attention, and printers did a good business selling portraits of him defending the Great Charter (see Plate 12).

Despite the tenuous link between Magna Carta and parliamentary elections, the Wilkes affair fuelled uneasiness about antiquated and corrupt electoral processes that made Parliament the preserve of an unrepresentative oligarchy. Some radicals simply used Magna Carta as convenient cover for demands for electoral changes under the cloak of restoring the ancient constitution, yet other reformers clung to doctrines of fundamental law, revering the Charter as a pillar of the constitution, beyond Parliament's power. Wilkes himself asked during a Commons debate, 'Can we . . . repeal Magna Carta?', and he answered, 'There are fundamental inalienable rights, landmarks of the constitution, which cannot be removed'.[44]

Cries of 'Wilkes and Liberty' raised in London resonated across the Atlantic. Restive colonists in North America found favour with reformers in England, and a London newspaper declared them to be struggling for 'an American Magna Carta'.[45] After the Seven Years War (or the French and Indian War, as Americans know it) ended in 1763, the colonists raised the constitutional issue of Parliament's power over them, protesting against what they considered its tyrannical rule. The relative powers of the British Parliament and the colonial legislative bodies were unclear, although earlier parliaments had legislated for the colonies, at least regulating their external trade, since the seventeenth-century passage of the

Navigation Acts. The American colonists' cry of 'no taxation without representation' found support from English radicals. One radical parliamentary reformer asked, 'If the people of Britain are not to be taxed, but by Parliament; . . . does it not directly follow, that the colonists cannot, according to Magna Carta, and the bill of rights, be taxed by Parliament, so long as they continue unrepresented?'[46]

American and British radical opposition to Parliament's power required discussion of its sovereignty, and defenders of the colonists' subordinate status expressed extreme statements. Such a prominent figure as Sir William Blackstone maintained in his *Commentaries* that 'there is and must be . . . a supreme, irresistible, absolute, uncontrolled authority, in which the . . . rights of sovereignty reside'. He acknowledged that in England this sovereign authority lay with Parliament, and as evidence enumerated parliamentary powers: 'It can regulate or new model the succession to the crown . . . It can alter the established religion . . . It can change and create afresh even the constitution of the kingdom and of Parliaments themselves.'[47] Despite Blackstone's views on parliamentary supremacy, he shared Sir Edward Coke's confidence that respect for the common law would never permit Parliament to transgress individual rights. Other believers in Parliament's sovereign power placed their faith in an independent judiciary to safeguard common law principles by hearing suits brought by persons harmed by statutes authorizing arbitrary acts.

The conservative political thinker Edmund Burke (d. 1797) also supported Parliament's authority to legislate for the colonies, writing of its 'unlimited and illimitable nature of supreme sovereignty'. None the less, Burke felt sympathy for the Americans and doubted the wisdom of some statutes affecting them; he advocated in the Commons extension of the privileges conferred by the Great Charter on British subjects at home to those across the Atlantic. He pointed out that 'your ancestors did not churlishly sit down alone to the feast of Magna Carta', but made it applicable to the Irish, whose status as the English king's subjects inhabiting a separate state with its own parliament he compared to the American colonists' situation.[48] Some supporters of the Americans' position continued to champion the fundamental law's limitations on Parliament, among them William Pitt the elder, earl of Chatham (d. 1788). He considered Magna Carta 'the Bible of the English Constitution', the standard for judging parliamentary acts. Chatham judged the government's actions against the Americans to be violations of the Charter, for they had 'an equitable claim to the full enjoyment of the fundamental rules of the English constitution'.[49]

Radical propagandists on both sides of the Atlantic worked to foster the illusion that King George III aimed at restoring Stuart absolutism.

Wilkes and his cronies, along with American revolutionaries, cultivated a caricature of the king subverting the constitution and crushing ancient English liberties. Even the traditionalist Edmund Burke felt that George III was acting against the spirit, if not the letter, of the Revolution Settlement. Although the king's opponents were correct in observing a contrast between his political activism and his Hanoverian predecessors' indolence, they were mistaken in crediting him with initiating his ministers' policies. Certainly the king was obstinate in his insistence that the unruly Americans must be brought to obedience, forcibly if necessary, but it was an opinion that both his cabinet and Parliament shared with him.

The Wilkes affair and the unsuccessful war against the American colonies undermined confidence in a government that pursued such disastrous policies, and the movement for reform of Parliament strengthened. Late in the century, the industrial revolution created a new urban working class in Midland and northern cities without parliamentary representation, and the need for reform became more and more apparent. As early as 1769, John Wilkes's followers founded a society devoted to parliamentary reform, the Supporters of the Bill of Rights. The radicals were without genuine political clout, however, and the movement proved short-lived. Like the seventeenth-century Levellers, the reformers' radicalism increased as their chances of success diminished, and some went as far as advocating universal manhood suffrage. Radical demands increased in the 1790s with deeper economic misery, and the French Revolution inspired a few to plot revolution. After the execution of Louis XVI, radicals' sympathy for the revolutionaries alienated moderate reformers, and the government took harsh counter-revolutionary measures. Reaction and repression became the rule in Britain by the last decade of the eighteenth century.

The Enlightenment spirit of rationalism and scepticism had previously spread to England, infecting attitudes toward history, and the Middle Ages fell out of fashion, disdained as a period of bigotry, ignorance and superstition. A more critical and analytical attitude brought a break in the late eighteenth century with both the common lawyers' traditional view that the Great Charter reaffirmed immemorial English law and intellectuals' theoretical constructs that ascribed English liberties to natural law. The new approach is seen in histories by Scottish writers reflecting a cosmopolitan outlook influenced by continental works of comparative history. A prime example is the Scottish philosopher David Hume's *History of England*, which displays eighteenth-century distaste for the Middle Ages. Hume denounced Whig notions that Magna Carta reaffirmed an ancient constitution, depicting instead a continuously changing English constitution, slowly evolving to meet new generations' needs. Yet in his account of the Charter he respected the thirteenth-century St Albans chroniclers' version, following them in giving credit to Stephen Langton, a churchman. Although Hume saw the Great Charter's chief consequence as merely shifting political power from a tyrannical king to a collective baronial despotism, he admitted its potential for expanding freedom by setting forth 'all the chief outlines of a legal government', especially 'the equal distribution of justice and the free enjoyment of property'.[50] Despite the popularity of Hume's history, his realistic approach did little to change the standard Whig version of England's past that stressed English exceptionalism, ranking Magna Carta and the Glorious Revolution as restorations of immemorial liberties.

Pride in the English constitution's uniqueness accorded more with the outlook of histories in the Romantic era than with the dominant rationalism of the eighteenth century. In Edmund Burke's 1790 book *Reflections on the Revolution in France*, his emotional appeal to the past, emphasis on the gradual growth of the English constitution and rejection of abstract ideas point toward the Romantic outlook. Although Burke's best-known work is his *Reflections*, an early work only published posthumously reveals Enlightenment influences. In his *Essay Towards an Abridgment of the English History*, written in about 1757, the medieval English constitution that he depicts is not the Whigs' perfect pattern passed down from prehistory, but only an outline of permanent principles. For the young Burke, English liberty's proper beginning was not Old English laws, but Magna Carta, which was a result of Norman and Angevin kings' exploitation of their lordship. Later, in the *Reflections on the Revolution in France*, Edmund Burke reverted to traditional views of the Great Charter, with the continuity of English history as his chief concern. He depicted the Charter as evidence of the people's 'powerful prepossession towards antiquity', and he followed the doctrine of the ancient constitution that reduced it to 'nothing more than a reaffirmation of the still more ancient standing law of the kingdom'. According to Burke's *Reflections*, Magna Carta was a confirmation of liberties that are 'an entailed inheritance derived to us from our forefathers, and to be transmitted to our posterity'.[51]

Despite Edmund Burke, natural law doctrines became widespread in late-eighteenth-century Britain, and Enlightenment thinkers defended the inviolability of human rights by appeals to abstract principles rather than to history. As an English writer stated in 1791, 'It is not because we *have* been free, but because we have a right to be free, that we ought to demand freedom'.[52] This repudiation of historical precedent as a basis for England's liberties led to denials of Magna Carta's significance.

Outspoken in rejecting the Charter as a cornerstone of English liberties was Thomas Paine (d. 1809), who considered 'superstitious reverence for ancient things' an obstacle to reform. He responded to Burke's reverence for the past and resistance to change in his best known work, *Rights of Man*. Paine depicted the Great Charter as only an incomplete restoration of rights belonging 'inherently in all inhabitants', and its effect was 'no more than compelling the Government to renounce a part of its assumptions'.[53] Other radicals, however, valued Magna Carta as an affirmation of natural right, 'a recognition of positive rights anteced-ently existing and inherent in the people'.[54]

With the guillotine working overtime in France, ideas suspected of springing from revolutionary French thinkers found little support among the English propertied classes. A French-supported uprising in Ireland in 1798 inflated fears, and English leaders rejected any thought of reform. With reactionary attitudes threatening free speech and the Habeas Corpus Act suspended, Paine fled England to escape charges of treason. Until Napoleon's exile in 1815, all reformers in the kingdom were tainted by charges of pro-French tendencies. The economic dislocation of the long wars and rapid industrialization created widespread discontent, height-ened by a postwar depression, and agitation for radical reform brought renewed repressive legislation with the Six Acts of 1816. A satirical article in a radical newspaper complained of the Habeas Corpus Act's 'bad family connexion', for *habeas corpus* was descended from 'two notorious traitors of old times, called Magna Carta and the Bill of Rights'. The article added that the Charter was 'so very old and infirm that he seldom stirs abroad, and when he does he is sure to be insulted, and is very glad to get back to his lodgings again'.[55]

Notes

1. Sir Benjamin Rudyerd, cited by Tanner (1961), 61.
2. Spelman, *Glossaria*, cited by Thompson (1948), 238, n. 14.
3. Hindley (1990), 187.
4. Burgess (1996), 176.
5. Thompson (1948), 242.
6. Meador (1965), 22, citing Coke, *Second Part of the Institutes of the Laws of England*.
7. Burgess (1996), 176.
8. Cited in Burgess (1996), 175.
9. Prynne, cited by Swindler (1965), 195–6.
10. Thompson (1948), 304.
11. Stephenson and Marcham (1937), 437–8.
12. Stephenson and Marcham (1937), 435–7.

13. Swindler (1965), 181.
14. Stephenson and Marcham (1937), 457–8.
15. Stephenson and Marcham (1937), 450–2.
16. Coke, cited by Goodhart (1966), 68. It is now alleged that Coke actually said that Magna Carta would have 'no saving', meaning no clause in the Petition of Right 'saving' the royal prerogative: Burgess (1996), 208.
17. Stephenson and Marcham (1937), 459.
18. Stephenson and Marcham (1937), 458–62.
19. Cited by Swindler (1965), 191.
20. Howell (1809–26), 4: 1009.
21. Swindler (1965), 198.
22. Pallister (1971), 24.
23. Ashley (1965), 39, 41.
24. Pallister (1971), 26.
25. Pallister (1971), 29–30, 31.
26. Stephenson and Marcham (1937), 579, Bushell's case.
27. Pallister (1971), 34.
28. Ashley (1965), 53–4.
29. Swindler (1965), 205; Pallister (1971), 39.
30. Prall (1972), 261.
31. Stephenson and Marcham (1937), 606.
32. Locke, *Two Treatises on Government*, excerpted in Ebenstein (1956), 387; Weston (1991), 636.
33. Simmons (1998), 72, quoting Blackstone's *Magna Carta*, xii.
34. *Commentaries*, bk i, ch. 7; bk iv, ch. 33; bk, i, ch. 1, in Jones (1973), 96, 233, 221, 61.
35. Pallister (1971), 49–50.
36. Pallister (1971), 44–5.
37. Pallister (1971), 51–2.
38. Pallister (1971), 52.
39. Pallister (1971), 53.
40. Stephenson and Marcham (1937), 707.
41. Pallister (1971), 59.
42. Stephenson and Marcham (1937), 681.
43. Horn and Ransome (1957), 173–5.
44. Pallister (1971), 64, n. 3.
45. Pallister (1971), 65.
46. Pallister (1971), 56–7.
47. Pallister (1971), 57.
48. Pallister (1971), 55.
49. Pallister (1971), 55–6.
50. Kenyon (1983), 49.
51. *Reflections*, excerpted in Ebenstein (1956), 452–3.
52. Pallister (1971), 76.
53. Pallister (1971), 77.
54. Epstein (1994), 21, citing *Sherwin's Political Register*, 12 September 1818.
55. Pallister (1971), 70–1.

chapter 7

MAGNA CARTA IN THE NINETEENTH AND TWENTIETH CENTURIES

The nineteenth century was an age of 'isms' when new ideologies influenced the English people's attitudes about Magna Carta. Among the movements were romanticism and nationalism, and by the century's end, a scientific and secular world-view contesting tradition-bound attitudes. In England, romanticism and nationalism fixed more firmly the Whig interpretation of history, giving Magna Carta a prominent place in the kingdom's progress toward liberty. Leaders of both movements saw nations and their institutions as living organisms, shaped by their historical evolution, not by human design. Historians seized on this organic concept of the state to stress England's unique qualities, looking to the Middle Ages for the source of its ancient constitution and common law heritage.

Among the new philosophies at odds with romantic reverence for England's medieval constitutional legacy was Utilitarianism, the brainchild of Jeremy Bentham. Nineteenth-century lawyers and judges abandoned long-held notions of fundamental law and adopted a Utilitarian outlook, refusing to revere the common law simply because of its antiquity and desiring to abrogate old law and update the common law. No significant legal reform was possible without parliamentary reform, however, and late-eighteenth-century radicals' agitation for a more representative Parliament, stifled by reactionary frenzy following the French Revolution, revived in the new century. Adding impetus to the renewed reform movement was fear that the growing industrial working class, pushed toward radicalism by economic distress, would reject the rule of law and seek relief from its misery through violence.

The Great Reform Bill of 1832 was a dramatic updating of Parliament's composition. As a result, towns transformed into cities during the eighteenth-century commercial and industrial revolutions gained representation, and leaders in trade and industry won places in political life alongside the landed aristocracy. With later reform bills further expanding the electorate, the people came to value parliamentary processes as stronger safeguards for English liberties than fundamental law in some medieval document. As a consequence, notions of the ancient constitution, losing ground throughout the eighteenth century, became irrelevant after 1832. Since Liberal political doctrine accepted parliamentary sovereignty, parliaments elected under new electoral laws applied Utilitarian concepts to modernize English law into a system befitting an advanced capitalistic society. By the mid-nineteenth century, legal reforms had erased most of Magna Carta's chapters from the statute books. Repeal of the Charter would not arouse fears of loss of freedom, for the Victorians were complacent about their liberties, holding their constitution as a model for the rest of the world. Not until the late twentieth century would some defenders of individual freedom sense a dangerous centralization of power.

As Magna Carta receded from the centre of political debate, history was changing from a preserve of learned amateurs into a profession, a distinct discipline imitating natural scientists' critical and sceptical methods. A relativistic streak in their thought would inspire historians to seek to understand the Middle Ages on the period's own terms, not as mere prelude to the perfection of Victorian Britain, and to question the quasi-official Whig interpretation. Scholars fastened onto the Great Charter as an object for 'scientific' investigation, some to demolish complacent Whig reverence for it and others to bolster it by nationalistic defence of England's precocious constitutionalism. Whatever the motivation, the Charter would occupy a central place in historians' debates until the late twentieth century.

The repeal of the Charter in the nineteenth century

The rationalism of the eighteenth-century Enlightenment inspired proposals for reform of English law, but the French Revolution kindled hostility toward all innovation, and no major legal reforms took place until the mid-nineteenth century. Since the late eighteenth century, it had become clear that without reforming the House of Commons – expanding the electorate and reapportioning seats – reform of the common law was impossible. Despite repression, agitation for wider parliamentary representation continued in the early nineteenth century, and students of social history today find many radicals active then, especially among the working class. The nineteenth-century movement for parliamentary reform would turn to Magna Carta for support, although reformed parliaments' legal legislation later would invalidate most of its chapters.

In 1809, the first advocate for radical reform elected to the Commons, Sir Francis Burdett, presented a 'Plan of Parliamentary Reform' to restore proper balance to the constitution. He regarded Magna Carta as a key component of England's constitution, threatened by unprincipled parliaments; in a Commons debate, he said of the Charter: 'Repealed it never can be until England herself shall have found her grave in the corruption of the House of Commons'.[1] Although Burdett's parliamentary reform proposal received no serious consideration, he attracted popular attention when he took up the cause of a radical imprisoned by order of the Commons for showing disrespect for the House. In a letter published in a radical journal, Burdett labelled the action contrary to the common law, the Great Charter, and the right of trial by jury, declaring that the House was acting as if 'an order of theirs is to be of more weight than Magna Carta and the laws of the land'. The Commons decried Burdett's speech as 'libellous and scandalous' and arrested him for breach of parliamentary privilege.[2] He followed an earlier radical's example, arranging to be arrested while teaching Magna Carta to his son; and as earlier, printers rushed to publish illustrations of the incident for sale (see Plate 13). Burdett's opponents responded to his attack on the Commons by claiming that its power to imprison for libel was part of the law of the land, and that his broad construction of the Charter would invalidate all law not contained in it.

Although radicalism was widespread in late-eighteenth-century Britain, the word itself did not appear in the English language until 1820, coined by an elite group calling itself Philosophical Radicals or Utilitarians. In a sense, they were successors to eighteenth-century Enlightenment thinkers in placing institutions and ideals on a rational basis. The Philosophical Radicals differed from Enlightenment philosophers, however, in rejecting universal principles, whether derived from divine revelation or from natural law; and they frowned on theories, instead deducing general precepts from their observation of human psychology. The most influential of the Philosophical Radicals was Jeremy Bentham, whose proposals for reforming almost all aspects of English law and government were implemented only after his death in 1832. In his 1789 work, *An Introduction to the Principles and Morals of Legislation*, his first sentences set forth the basis of his Utilitarian philosophy: 'Nature has placed mankind under the governance of two sovereign masters, pain and pleasure. It is for them alone to point out what we ought to do . . .'.[3] From this base of seeking pleasure and avoiding pain, he and his followers built up proposals for reform of Parliament, the common law and the courts, poor relief and punishment of prisoners. Above all, the Utilitarians were humanitarians, advocating drastic changes in almost everything that the governing classes considered most English, even attacking fox hunting. Applying the principle of utility, Bentham worked out a theoretical justification for parliamentary supremacy that depended on neither historical myths nor theoretical abstractions. Bentham asserted Parliament's sovereignty because of his strong desire for reform of English law, confident that a reformed legislature would enact a clear, rationally organized code. In his view, blind reverence for the common law and its antiquated procedures had produced legal chaos, interminable lawsuits and courtroom stratagems comprehensible only to legal professionals.

Social and economic dislocations caused by the industrial revolution and the Napoleonic wars had fuelled demands for reform that repression only temporarily silenced, and proposals for limited reforms surfaced in the 1820s. The Tories, who had gained power under George III, came round to the notion that modest reforms could dissuade radicals from revolutionary activity toppling the entire constitution. A younger generation of Tory party leaders supported reforms based on doctrines of classical liberalism, advocating free trade and free thought. The Whigs, now the minority party, supported parliamentary reform as a way to regain power, and by 1830 discussions centred on a bill to reform elections. Supporters of the *status quo*, echoing Burke's arguments against the French revolutionaries, maintained that they trusted their ancestors' wisdom more than modern theories, and they denounced the electoral reform bill for subverting hallowed constitutional principles. Advocates of the Great Reform Bill of 1832 pointed out that England's constitution underwent continual change and that Magna Carta itself had been 'a great innovation'; the Whig historian and politician Thomas Babington Macaulay called the proposed bill 'a greater charter of the liberties of England'.[4]

The 1832 Reform Bill proved a modest reform, for it extended the vote only to a few, property owners in the new industrial towns, and left the majority disappointed, enfranchising only an eighth of the kingdom's adult males. Out of widespread disillusionment arose the Chartist movement of the 1830s and 1840s, demanding a People's Charter, a new definition of English liberty. This new Charter had no conscious connection with Magna Carta, its six points treating chiefly further reforms for a democratic House of Commons. Yet the very word 'charter' reminded the English people, at least unconsciously, of their immemorial liberties, including Magna Carta. Like the Levellers, the Chartists turned to history to defend their demands, and their view of England's past was also more mythical than historical, imagining a romanticized pre-Conquest paradise of free peasants. Their leaders' remarks on the Great Charter were vague and unspecific, presenting it as more symbol than substance. At a rally in 1838, a speaker said, 'We stand upon our rights . . .

we say give us the good old laws of England unchanged.' When his audience shouted back 'Magna Carta', he replied, 'Aye, Magna Charta! The good old laws of English freedom – free meetings – freedom of speech – freedom of worship – freedom of homesteads – free and happy firesides, and no workhouses.'[5] The Great Charter, although a rallying cry against authority, had little to offer the new industrial working class for betterment of its abysmal condition. The Chartist movement failed, but its goals would be fulfilled as near-universal suffrage was achieved finally through the electoral reform bills in 1867, 1872, 1884–85, 1918 and 1928.

Once Parliament was reformed, Utilitarian followers of Jeremy Bentham could turn to reform of the common law, which seemed to them a severe stumbling block to progress. Although trained as a lawyer, Bentham imbibed little respect for the common law's hallowed traditions, and he became an important advocate of wholesale legal reform. He regarded Magna Carta with its protection of the 'law of the land' as an obstacle to replacing an antiquated common law with a modern law code. Even Bentham sometimes abandoned abstract principles in favour of appeals to history, however, and humanitarian concerns caused him to invoke the Charter. He condemned rule over Britain's colonial empire by royal prerogative as 'repugnant to Magna Carta', and he labelled the confinement of transported convicts after their sentences had expired a 'breach of Magna Carta'.[6] Rejecting historical precedent or natural law as a basis for the law, Bentham applied his pleasure versus pain principle to argue that people obey the law only when they determine it in their interest to do so. He wanted the law to be less a web of complexities comprehensible only to lawyers, and he set forth ideas for untangling it for ordinary people's understanding in his 1789 *Introduction to the Principles and Morals of Legislation*.

Bentham never realized his dream of a rational code of law for England, although reform legislation beginning in 1828 has simplified and clarified the United Kingdom's laws. A fully sovereign parliament had free rein to repeal old laws and consolidate them into a coherent system, and much of Magna Carta was abrogated, resulting in the repeal of all but four of the thirty-seven chapters of the 1225 Great Charter. As early as 1796, the Commons set up the first of a series of committees and commissions to study the problem of obscure, incongruous and obsolete laws still on the statute books. The committee compiled a list of about 1,000 obsolete laws and recommended an authoritative edition of the statutes as a first step toward law reform, resulting in publication of eleven oversized volumes of the *Statutes of the Realm* between 1810 and 1828. In 1816, the House of Lords proposed to simplify English law by consolidating statutes treating similar subjects. It called the vast quantity of statutes 'a perfect hotch-pot – a chaos of darkness, disorder and confusion' and contrasted their 'vile phraseology' with the 'clear, brief and intelligible' wording of the Great Charter.[7] A committee set to work in 1824, but legal reform would proceed piecemeal without sudden, sweeping overhaul of the law, and without codification, for English traditionalism stood in the way of total abolition of antiquated institutions. None the less, members of Parliament accepted the Utilitarian principle that the law was a practical product of legislation, not the wondrous work of centuries of history.

The issue of repealing parts of Magna Carta first arose between 1826 and 1832 with the Criminal Amendment Acts that consolidated much of the criminal law. Among the obsolete laws repealed by the 1828 Offences against the Person Act was chapter 26 of the Charter promising free writs for accused persons seeking juries of attaint, panels to determine whether an accusation was brought with malice. During the nineteenth century, statutes were enacted to afford additional protections for persons accused of crimes, expanding on Magna Carta's key provision, chapter 29/39. In 1836, accused persons gained the right to counsel; in 1898, they gained the right to testify on their own behalf; and in 1903, provision was made to pay for counsel for those unable to afford it. Not until the twentieth century were judicial appeals permitted in criminal cases, although a judge could reserve a point of law for consideration by a higher court. A 1907 statute established a Court of Criminal Appeal, and a 1960 act allowed appeals to the House of Lords in cases raising a point of law with wide public importance.

Both politicians and the legal profession favoured reorganization of the law by the mid-nineteenth century, and striking obsolete legislation from the statute books began in earnest with the first Statute Laws Revision Act in 1856. Two more acts revising the statutes soon followed; an 1861 act repealing almost 1,000 statutes enacted since 1770 was followed by an 1863 measure repealing earlier laws. Some in the Commons sought assurances that no statutes considered 'stones in the edifice of the constitution' would be abolished. One member offered an amendment that would have removed Magna Carta and other constitutional landmarks from the bill, but his amendment failed. The surprise is how easily abrogation of clauses of the Charter was accomplished, presenting a striking display of Parliament's sovereignty. During Commons debates, the solicitor-general dismissed the Great Charter's significance, reminding members that 'as signed by King John' it was not a statute;[8] and he added that if they wished to see it, they needed to consult ancient manuscripts.

Stricken from the statute books by the 1863 legislation were seventeen of the 1225 Charter's clauses, many of which had lost their practical effect two centuries earlier with the abolition of tenures by knight-service. Magna Carta's provisions concerning the king's rights of lordship had been out of date since 1660, among them chapters 2–6, 27 and 31 treating his custody of minor heirs and their estates, the part of chapter 37 limiting his demands for scutage from his tenants, and one on tenants' duty of castle-guard (20), although their formal repeal did not come until 1863. Also repealed were chapters 19 and 21 regulating the king's ancient right of purveyance or requisitions of goods for the royal house-hold's use, a right that became redundant once Parliament assumed responsibility for appropriating funds for the king's expenses. The 1863 statute also repealed the chapter limiting the writ *praecipe* (24), allegedly protecting the jurisdiction of lords' private courts from the common law courts.

The 1863 act repealed a number of other articles covering varied topics. It removed three clauses concerning spiritual property in the 1225 Charter, one treating the assize of darrein presentment or the right to nominate to a church's living (13), another protecting the right of patrons of religious houses to custody during vacancies (33), as well as one outlawing alienations of land disguised as gifts to religious houses (36), although Edward I's Statute of Mortmain had long ago replaced it. The statute removed from the lawbooks two archaic articles concerning criminal procedures, one dealing with the ancient oath of compurgation (28) and another denying a woman the right to bring charges of homicide against anyone but her husband's suspected killer (34). A statute of 1852 had already replaced old twelfth-century writs for possessory assizes, obsolete before the end of the Middle Ages, with a new uniform writ of summons. None the less, the chapter making the possessory assizes readily available to litigants (12) was not formally repealed until 1879. Surprisingly, Magna Carta's chapter prescribing standard weights and measures (25) did not receive significant revision until 1824, and its repeal did not take place until 1878 with the passage of a Weights and Measures Act.

By 1885, the repeal of so much obsolete or redundant legislation made it possible to publish a reduced and revised edition of the statutes, although it filled eighteen volumes. Many felt that further pruning of the laws was needed, and the result was repeal of still more chapters of Magna Carta. Some provisions fell following reforms restructuring the courts between 1873 and 1880. With the Judicature Act of 1873 and the Appellate Jurisdiction Act of 1876, Parliament merged the common law and chancery courts and created a supreme court of judicature, the

Law Lords headed by the lord chancellor. This consolidation of the courts rendered redundant the Charter's chapter ensuring that common pleas should meet in some fixed place (11), and it was repealed. The office of sheriff underwent scrutiny as well, and the Sheriffs Act of 1887 invalidated two chapters of Magna Carta treating sheriffs' judicial duties (17 and 35); in 1892, the Statute Law Revision Act completely repealed them. Formally repealed in 1887 was another long obsolete chapter (32 of the 1225 Charter) limiting tenants' alienations of land that reduced their ability to perform feudal services owed to their lords.

Some provisions of Magna Carta remained on the statute books until the twentieth century, a few until after the Second World War. Long after the seventeenth-century abolition of feudal tenures, English law retained the principle that all freeholds carried certain obligations, but modernization of property law in 1922 and 1925 negated any consequences of this doctrine. Yet the chapter limiting undue demands for services from a knight's tenure (10) was not repealed until the Statute Law Revision Act of 1948. This act also cancelled the Charter's promise that the king would hold convicted felons' lands no more than a year and a day (22). In 1925, a statute concerning the administration of estates repealed the article guaranteeing widows their marriage portions (7), although the Dower Act of 1833 had already made it partially obsolete. This statute also had superseded the chapter on clearing the debts of deceased crown debtors and protecting their heirs' shares (18), although it was not fully repealed until 1949.

In 1965, Parliament created the Law Commission to deal with statute revision, and the commissioners interpreted their task broadly, recommending repeal not only of obsolete legislation but also of laws that 'cannot be shown to perform a useful function'. They prepared a bill repealing over 200 laws, including eight clauses of the Great Charter (1, 7, 8, 15, 16, 23, 30, 37) that they found to be 'of no practical significance today, being either obsolete or superseded by the modern law on the subject'.[9] The only bits of the Charter left intact were chapter 29/39, curbing the crown's power to pursue individuals beyond the law, and chapter 9, the City of London's guarantee of its ancient liberties and free customs. A joint committee of the two Houses of Parliament decided to retain two more chapters. The first chapter promising freedom for the English Church remained, as did a general saving clause in chapter 37, important for proclaiming the perpetuity of the Charter's liberties and containing a key clause, 'and if anything contrary to this [charter] is procured from anyone, it shall avail nothing and be held for nought'. The amended Statute Law (Repeals) Bill took effect at the beginning of 1970, leaving four chapters of Magna Carta (1, 9, 29 and 37) intact.

In the nineteenth century, the British assumed that although they had no written constitution, the common law and its long-accepted principles guaranteed the rule of law, limiting the government and its agents to actions in accord with lawful authority. The assumption that the triumph of democracy secured popular liberty was unquestioned. The people expected Parliament to preserve Magna Carta's principle of personal liberty, that no one would be punished or suffer loss of property without appropriate legal process. They trusted that the judiciary would uphold the principle that no one was above the law, with individuals able to confront violators of their rights in the law courts. The repeal of nearly all the Great Charter's provisions by parliamentary enactments strongly indicates that majority opinion no longer saw a need for fundamental law, and not even chapter 29/39 of the Charter was immune from a sovereign parliament's tampering. As one justice said of the clause in a 1920 case, it 'is not condemned to that immunity from development or improvement which we attribute to the laws of the Medes and Persians'.[10] It is not surprising that less and less was heard of Magna Carta in the British courts, and from the eighteenth century on, fundamental rights were defended by tortured interpretations of common law protections of property rights that twisted them into guarantees of civil liberties. Yet it became clear that even a democratically elected Parliament exercising sovereign power could tend toward tyranny. A government with a secure majority in the Commons, subject to strong party discipline, need not always respect common law traditions, but may move to silence unpopular opinions and disperse dissident groups.

During the late eighteenth and early nineteenth centuries, fears of revolutionary conspiracies and working-class violence brought suspensions of the right of *habeas corpus*, and the rise of Marxism at the end of the nineteenth century reawakened fears of class warfare. Marxists rejected the very idea of the rule of law, for they considered the law a tool of the propertied classes for protecting their ill-gotten gain and permitting the oppression of propertyless workers. Nationalistic frenzy also threatened liberties long assumed to be secure in Britain. Strong tactics for suppressing troubles in Ireland, first the nineteenth-century movement for home rule and then the movement for unification of the entire island under the Republic, accustomed the British to periodic curtailments of liberties. Any challenge to the *status quo* alarmed many politicians and their supporters. They sanctioned violations of due process by government officials invoking national security, and they frequently overlooked unlawful police conduct. This situation continued during the desperate situation of two world wars and the Cold War, when the law courts acquiesced in an overzealous government's curbs on civil liberties and upheld wide discretionary powers for the executive.

Inflamed to fury during the First World War, the British people readily supported suspension of regular legal processes in the name of defence against subversives and spies. Under the Defence of the Realm Acts enacted at the outbreak of the conflict, government ministers obtained wide latitude in stifling political opposition to the war effort. When a German-born naturalized British subject was interned under the Defence of the Realm Acts as an enemy alien and a danger to national security, his case was appealed to the House of Lords in 1917. The lord chancellor declared that 'in a time of great public danger', Parliament could hand over great powers to the executive, 'feeling certain that such powers will be reasonably exercised'. The Lords accepted his view that 'supreme national danger' necessitated such a measure and rejected the appeal.[11] During the Second World War, the courts again endorsed the government's right to intern without trial aliens suspected of 'hostile origin or association'. When an appeal challenged a judge's refusal to question ministerial acts alleged to be in the national interest, the Law Lords sanctioned the government's power to intern persons merely on a minister's subjective judgement. A dissenting lord noted that the majority was granting the government 'an absolute power which . . . has never been given before to the executive', and he complained that arguments supporting the government's position 'might have been addressed acceptably to the court of King's Bench in the time of Charles I'.[12]

Between the two world wars, unchecked police violence in the name of national security against radical agitators and striking workers was not uncommon. The 1920 Emergency Powers Act gave the government authority to proclaim a state of emergency and issue regulations deemed essential for preserving the peace and providing public services whenever widespread disorder threatened. It could prosecute those violating the emergency regulations in extraordinary tribunals. Under this act, the government could hound and hinder labour union strikers or radical demonstrators, denying them freedom of assembly. The Incitement to Disaffection Act of 1934 was aimed at punishing propagandists who tried to dissuade soldiers from obeying their orders to disperse strikers, and the Public Order Act of 1936, intended to handicap fascist-style paramilitary organizations, had the effect of limiting other groups' right of public assembly. The Irish Republican Army's bombing campaigns led to passage of statutes in 1939 and 1974 that gave the police wide latitude in dealing with persons suspected of instigating or planning acts of violence.

Since the beginning of the twentieth century, both Parliament and the law courts, supposedly protectors of civil liberties, have often upheld the executive power's right to restrict individual liberties. Furthermore, growth of 'big government', triggered by the stresses of two world wars, interwar economic crises, the long Cold War and expansion of the welfare state gave greater power to the executive, creating a leviathan impossible for Parliament or the courts to master. A new threat to individual liberty surfaced after 1945 with the multitude of governmental or quasi-governmental agencies set up to supervise social and economic assistance to the aged, the poor and the weak. Parliament has not proven fully effective in safeguarding citizens from arbitrary handling by these new programmes. It lacked resources for supervising them once it had mandated their purpose in statutes, and it left the drafting of detailed rules and regulations to government ministers. As a result, these administrative bodies have a large sphere of administrative jurisdiction that blurs the boundary between judicial and administrative processes. Placed in a position of judging their own cases without procedures for protection of private rights, administrative agencies can seem startlingly similar to the old prerogative courts with their secrecy, arbitrary methods and capricious rulings. Their definition of the public interest sometimes seems to resemble the Stuarts' 'matters of state'.

The executive's growing power in relation to Parliament poses problems for individual liberties supposedly basic to the English legal tradition. At the beginning of the twenty-first century, some observers of the United Kingdom's politics question whether the two principles of parliamentary sovereignty and the rule of law, long assumed to underlie the modern British constitution, are compatible. They lament the increasing 'presidentialization' of the office of prime minister. Despite the principle of cabinet responsibility to a majority in Commons, strong party discipline enables the executive to win legislation and funding for its policies. Spurred by an Official Secrets Act enacted before the First World War, government officers become obsessed with secrecy. Ministers can turn to crown privilege, known to Americans as executive privilege, and invoke 'national security' concerns to avoid accountability and silence critics. Due to the shift of power to the executive, the odds often seem stacked against ordinary citizens seeking a sympathetic hearing for complaints against their arbitrary treatment, whether suffered at the hands of high-ranking officials or lesser civil servants.

If Parliament appears ineffective in curbing executive excesses, the law courts have proven no more effective. In the judiciary's own view, it cannot pass on the constitutionality of statutes enacted by a sovereign parliament, the ultimate protector of the people's liberties. The declaration of a law court in 1872 still holds true: 'There is no judicial body in the country by which the validity of an Act of Parliament can be questioned. An act of the Legislature is superior in authority to any court of law . . .'.[13] A recent book on the struggle for civil liberties from 1914 to 1945 fails to find a single significant instance of the higher levels of the judiciary acting to limit governmental actions restricting personal liberties. Between the two world wars, the judiciary was unwilling to protect unpopular groups from persecution by the police and the bureaucracy, except for occasional ostentatious interventions, such as confirming fascists' right to strut about in their uniforms. Judges' rulings often gave approval after the fact to previous unlawful conduct against unpopular groups by public authorities. Furthermore, the law courts recoiled from considering complaints against administrative agencies entrusted with substantial autonomy by parliamentary statute. In a complaint by coal-mine owners in 1943 against their colliery's seizure by the minister of fuel and power, the Court of Appeal upheld his statutory authority for taking it, deferring to Parliament. The judges stated: 'We cannot investigate the adequacy of [the minister's] reasons. . . . We cannot investigate any of those things because parliament in its wisdom has withdrawn these matters from the courts and entrusted them to the ministers concerned, the constitutional safeguard being . . . the supervision of the ministers exercised by parliament.'[14]

An erosion of protections for the individual against the government, long assumed to have been secured by chapter 29/39 of Magna Carta, became noticeable during the later twentieth century. The public's panic over escalating crime rates generated strong support for law and order legislation changing the criminal law to limit rights of suspects. Under popular pressure, Parliament could readily revoke suspects' legal safeguards, protected only by statutes or case law. In 1967, the Criminal Law Act was passed with little or no comment from members of Parliament or the media, although it seemed to undermine defendants' rights thought for centuries to be protected by Magna Carta. Among its provisions was the abandonment of the principle, stated in chapter 14, that punishment must be in accordance with the seriousness of the crime. The act also made convictions easier by ending the requirement for unanimous jury verdicts, allowing conviction with two jurors dissenting. The Police and Criminal Evidence Act of 1984, an attempt to codify procedures for detention and interrogation of suspects, aimed at strengthening the hand of the police in securing confessions. Although the public's desire for law and order often outweighs its concern for criminal suspects' rights, proposals to limit the traditional right of the accused to remain silent under police questioning set off loud objections in 1994, as have recent proposals for restricting the right to a jury trial.

In response to terrorist outrages in Northern Ireland by the Irish Republican Army (IRA) and Protestant militants since the late 1960s, the British government has employed emergency measures, suspending protections for suspected terrorists, engaging in random searches, interning them without charges and suspending jury trials. When the IRA carried its bombing campaign to England, similar measures were applied to the rest of the United Kingdom under the 1974 Prevention of Terrorism Act. When doubts arose about police and prosecution methods of obtaining confessions from alleged terrorists operating outside Northern Ireland, the judiciary asserted its independence, overturning convictions. One justice in 1970 ringingly reaffirmed a 1765 judgement against unlawful search, writing: 'The common law does not permit police officers . . . to ransack anyone's house, or to search for papers or articles therein, or to search his person simply to see if they have committed some crime or another'.[15] Lengthy detention of suspects without bringing charges in violation of the revered right of *habeas corpus* also aroused complaints.

It is ironic that under Margaret Thatcher, a champion of Whiggish historical myths, some Britons felt compelled to clamour for a new bill of rights; and in the absence of such a safeguard, others who failed to find justice within the kingdom's boundaries turned to continental supranational courts. The United Kingdom ratified in 1953 the European Convention on Human Rights, giving British subjects access to an equivalent of a bill of rights. Article 5 restates in somewhat stilted language Magna Carta's principle that governments must follow the law in proceeding against their subjects: 'Everyone has the right to liberty and security of person. No one shall be deprived of his liberty save in the following cases [lawful arrest or detention for specified reasons] and in accordance with a procedure prescribed by law.'[16] The Convention created the European Commission of Human Rights to receive complaints from both member-states and individuals. If the Commission cannot resolve a complaint through negotiations, the case then moves to the European Court of Human Rights at Strasbourg. Once individual Britons gained the right to petition the Strasbourg tribunal in 1966, it frequently found that British government actions violated a complainant's rights, although the prospect for enforcement of these decisions was dim. Even before appealing to Strasbourg, a complainant had to exhaust all legal remedies in the courts of the United Kingdom, a process that could take years.

Although British jurists contributed to the drafting of the European Convention, the government of the United Kingdom failed for half a century to take steps to bring its laws into conformity with its treaty obligations. This situation inspired talk of a new bill of rights to protect the people's inalienable liberties, or what a leading jurist termed in 1970 'a new Magna Carta for the little man'.[17] Finally, Parliament in 1998 enacted the Human Rights Act, incorporating the European Convention into British law and enabling Britons to seek enforcement of their rights under the Convention in the United Kingdom's courts. They can bring suits against individuals and also against any 'public authority' denying them their rights. The principle of parliamentary sovereignty is preserved, for judges cannot strike down statutes in conflict with the European Convention; they can only make a 'declaration of incompatibility', leaving it to the government to amend the offending legislation. None the less, the Human Rights Act signals a noteworthy shift of power from Parliament to the judiciary.

The European Convention and the Human Rights Act mark the impact that Magna Carta's central principle of the rule of law has made throughout western Europe. At the dawn of the twenty-first century, the guarantees in the Great Charter and the 1689 Bill of Rights are again relevant in Britain's political debates. In the eyes of concerned citizens, the central idea that government and its officials must act within the law in dealings with individuals first expressed in Magna Carta still needs defending. Fears remain that Britons' liberties can be jeopardized under the present constitutionally sanctioned parliamentary sovereignty just as they were earlier under a despotic monarchy with a subordinate Parliament.

Impact of the new scientific history on views of the Charter

The nineteenth century was a crucial period for the emergence of history as a distinct discipline, as it left its traditional place among the liberal arts as a branch of literature or philosophy and passed from the hands of learned amateurs into those of trained professionals. While this process was under way, several powerful intellectual movements were influencing historians, first romanticism and nationalism early in the century and later a scientific and materialist world-view. The romantic and nationalist movements sparked popular enthusiasm for medieval history, and illustrations of this infatuation are Sir Walter Scott's novels, which reinforced the notion of 'Bad King John' and his Norman officials inflicting their autocratic rule on the downtrodden Saxons. Yet these two trends also had serious consequences for English historians' views of Magna Carta.

Rejecting eighteenth-century Enlightenment attitudes toward the past scornful of medieval society and glorifying Greco-Roman civilization, the romantics extolled the Middle Ages. They gloried in tribal villagers' sense of community, the spirituality of the saints, the mystery of medieval epics and romances, knights' code of personal honour and pursuit of fame. They contrasted medieval villagers' happy and harmonious lives with the misery of workers in the new industrial towns. For some writers, William Cobbett (d. 1835) for example, this nostalgia for lost English rural life made them advocates of radical political change. Other romantics' preference for gradual evolution over revolutionary change in history encouraged an organic view of nations, societies, laws and institutions. This view led them to reject the rationalists' pragmatic study of primitive cultures as results of trial and error, adopted for practical results; instead, they admired earlier societies as unplanned living and growing things, evolving gradually toward a predetermined end or purpose.

Paradoxically perhaps, the romantics' organic outlook encouraged the idea of evolution spreading among natural scientists. In Victorian England, the doctrine of evolution combined with romantic attachment to the Middle Ages to encourage appreciation for institutions that had evolved from medieval origins, among them Parliament and the common law. An outgrowth of this was the Victorians' 'idea of progress', a view of history as modernization, slowly but steadily advancing toward higher levels of civilization. Evolutionary and organic views melded with nation-alism and nation-building to incite historians to stress the uniqueness – even the superiority – of their own country's history, traditions and institutions. In much of Europe, this reverence for history fostered a conservative or reactionary outlook that discouraged reform or revolution. In England, however, the Whig interpretation defined liberty as the 'goal' of England's history, sprouting from a native instinct for freedom and self-government, budding with Magna Carta and flowering fully in the Glorious Revolution of 1688–89.

With the increasing prestige of science in the nineteenth century, historians strived for a scientific attitude and method, aspiring to reshape history as a social science. Most influential for advocating a new objectivity for historians was the German scholar Leopold von Ranke (d. 1886), who advocated basing history on scientific analysis of archival documents. He was confident that his new methodology made it possible to write history 'as it actually happened'. Such auxiliary disciplines as diplomatics or paleography developed to enable historians to decipher, date and authenticate medieval documents. Stress on scientific method made history a distinct discipline, requiring specialized training that drew a line between professional historians and amateurs, and it tended to detach history from political debates, diminishing its relevance.

Yet professional historians never achieved the objectivity they craved, and contemporary ideologies, especially nationalism, often biased their investigations of their own nation's past. Many nineteenth-century nationalist historians were eager to arouse readers' pride in their country's past and provoke them to struggle for its unification or expansion. Nationalism inspired historians in Britain and France to concentrate on the evolution of the medieval English and French kingdoms into strong nation-states. In England, unified as early as Alfred the Great's time, historians could be more complacent than their German, Italian or Slavic colleagues who were struggling for liberation from reactionary, multinational empires. The Whig interpretation gave English historians confidence in their country's destiny to be a model for other nations seeking freedom as well as giving a justification for British rule over a colonial empire. A growing reading public purchased books that confirmed their pride in Britain's pattern of government and asserted their superiority over lesser peoples.

Historians in Victorian Britain took pride in their pragmatic approach and shied away from metaphysical speculations about the meaning of history. They found theory uncongenial to the English character, distrusted sweeping generalizations and avoided over-arching schemes or structures, unlike the Germans who were enticed by philosophical idealism into painting an over-arching 'spirit of the age' that overshadowed individual actors on the historical stage. Not even the English escaped entirely efforts to divine a lofty end or purpose giving meaning to their nation's history, and in the nineteenth century a teleological element crept into their work perpetuating the Whig interpretation of progress toward liberty as the key to England's past. Confidence in progress toward nineteenth-century liberal democracy caused historians to look on Magna Carta with enormous pride as a symbol of English exceptionalism. Victorian glorying in Magna Carta is illustrated by the popular 1874 book *A Short History of the English People*, authored by John Richard Green. Presenting England's history as the successful achievement of liberty, Green wrote: 'It is impossible to gaze without reverence on the earliest monument of English freedom . . . the great Charter to which from age to age patriots have looked back on as the basis of English liberty'.[18]

The origins of the Whig approach to England's history lie in seventeenth-century constitutional conflicts that culminated in the Glorious Revolution. According to Whig history, the great events of 1688–89 perpetuated an English constitution that had taken shape by the fourteenth century: a monarchy under the law, with parliamentary scrutiny of the king enforcing his submission to the law. Thomas Babington Macaulay was unashamedly Whiggish in his influential account of the seventeenth century in his five-volume *History of England*

(1848–55). In the twentieth century, his grand-nephew, George Macaulay Trevelyan (d. 1962), also a widely read popular historian, upheld the Whig interpretation in his one-volume *History of England*, first published in 1926 and reprinted as late as 1973. In Trevelyan's view, 'the common sense and good nature of the English people' had made possible the evolution of a constitution that combined 'executive efficiency, popular control, and personal freedom'.[19]

The Whig interpretation won a pioneer professional historian's stamp of approval in the three-volume *Constitutional History of England* (1874–78) by William Stubbs. For generations of students down to the mid-twentieth century, the *Constitutional History* was a standard text, presenting 'the history of liberty . . . , treated with a sense of providential destiny' as the over-arching theme of English history.[20] To scholars and students today, Stubbs's depiction of England's past is distorted by his unthinking acceptance of nineteenth-century preconceptions, notably his belief in the organic nature of English constitutional and legal institutions and their positive role in expanding liberty. None the less, as late as 1960, the author of an American textbook on medieval England could write of Stubbs that 'his insights into constitutional history will never be superseded'.[21]

An obvious failing of Stubbs in the view of today's scholars is his 'Germanist' bias in the great historical debate of his day over ancient Roman or Germanic barbarian sources for medieval laws and political principles. The division between 'Romanist' and 'Germanist' partisans lay along national lines, with the French tracing all positive elements in medieval civilization to classical survivals. 'Germanist' adherents – English, German, and a handful of Americans – found the origins of democracy in what they thought were the barbarian tribes' self-governing communities. Stubbs found Germanist theories appealing because they elevated supposed popular elements in Anglo-Saxon governance at the expense of the Normans, whom he blamed for bringing Roman-style absolutist rule to England from France. Stubbs's discussion of Magna Carta's guarantee of lawful judgement by peers illustrates his Germanist bias; he wrote that this was 'no novelty', for it 'lay at the foundation of all German law'.[22]

Stubbs had no doubt of the organic nature of England's political and legal institutions, and his work traces the gradual evolution of the constitution from Anglo-Saxon origins. He explained the growing political consciousness of various communities or classes within the kingdom, and he presented Magna Carta as a giant step toward the shaping of the English people into a united politically conscious 'nation'. It marked a union of the oppressed native English with their Norman conquerors' descendants and of isolated local communities into a single national one. For Stubbs, the party negotiating with King John in 1215 was not the rebel baronage alone, but 'the collective people' or 'the three estates of the realm . . . combined in one national purpose'. He states without hesitation: 'The Great Charter is the first great public act of the nation after it has realised its own identity'.[23]

Britain lagged behind France and Germany in adopting the apparatus of modern academic and professional historical study, but by Stubbs's time at Oxford, history in the United Kingdom was becoming a profession practised by specialists. Early in the nineteenth century, wider interest in history had generated support for historical studies and inspired the founding of historical societies, building of libraries and archives, and publishing of medieval records. As early as 1800, the British government showed concern for its scattered and neglected records by creating the Record Commission, charged with ensuring official documents' preservation and publication. Although the Record Commission lasted only until 1837 and demonstrated dubious ability, producing poorly edited publications, it implanted the idea of a central collection of the nation's historical materials. In 1857, publication of another series of medieval sources began under the sponsorship of the master of the rolls. Eleven volumes of *The Chronicles and Memorials of Great Britain and Ireland during the Middle Ages*, known to students as the *Rolls Series*, appeared the next year, and by the time the final volume was completed in 1911, over 200 volumes had been published. Stubbs edited medieval chronicles for the *Rolls Series*, making them available to researchers without access to original manuscripts.

A fire at the Palace of Westminster in 1834 that destroyed all the Commons records gave impetus for a central collection of official documents. In 1838, Parliament passed the Public Record Office Act, mandating more effective control over England's medieval royal records; documents scattered in fifty-six separate repositories came under the supervision of the master of the rolls, who was also keeper of the public records. The efforts of the mid-nineteenth-century civil servants who organized these records to make them accessible gave a powerful boost to the study of medieval English history. Generations of scholars pored over medieval materials at the Public Record Office in Chancery Lane until the records were removed to new quarters at Kew in 1997. Surprisingly, the Public Record Office never housed a copy of King John's Magna Carta, since royal clerks had not enrolled the 1215 Charter on the chancery rolls. It did acquire a copy of Henry III's 1225 Charter, part of the archives of the duchy of Lancaster that had passed to the crown, and a copy of Edward I's 1297 confirmation, enrolled on the

Parliament Rolls (class C 65). Also facilitating research in medieval history was the library constructed within the British Museum that housed great manuscript collections, including two original 1215 Charters as part of the Cottonian collection.

A landmark for the professionalization of history in the United Kingdom was the appearance in 1886 of the first issue of the *English Historical Review*, 'the house journal of the new university-based and professional historians'.[24] Stubbs himself played an important part in the process of turning history over to specialists. As Regius Professor of Modern History at Oxford (1866–84), he helped to break the long tyranny of the classics over the university's history curriculum and to add 'modern' history, that is, history since the fall of the Roman Empire. A similar expanded curriculum spread to other British universities, creating career opportunities for professional historians as lecturers. Stubbs's editing of volumes for the *Rolls Series* made medieval chronicles available in print, and his collection of documents, *Select Charters and Other Illustrations of English Constitutional History*, contains the Latin text of King John's Magna Carta along with the three versions of Henry III's early years. *Select Charters* became a standard text for undergraduates in British universities from its publication in 1870 until the 1960s, published in nine editions and last reprinted in 1948.

Important for making the history of English law an academic subject was Frederic William Maitland (d. 1906), a barrister who became Cambridge University's first reader in English law in 1884. While Stubbs had concentrated on narrative sources, Maitland centred his attention on record materials, but his crowning achievement was a broad survey, *The History of English Law before the Time of Edward I* (1895), still readable and relevant for students today. He wished to see the early common law 'as though we ourselves lived under it', to grasp how its seeming complexities had responded to actual twelfth- and thirteenth-century needs. Maitland once wrote: 'If history is to do its liberating work, it must be as true to fact as it can possibly make itself; and true to fact it will not be if it begins to think what lessons it can teach', and his studies filtered out of many of Stubbs's Whiggish assumptions. He did not envisage English common law as the product of a dialectical struggle between despotism and liberty, but a result of 'the choices, ambitions, and decisions of many people, each suiting his own interest'.[25] Rejecting the Whigs' depiction of England's past as a quest for liberty, he acknowledged the common law to be a largely royal creation, the work of Henry II, his servants and their successors in the judiciary. While recognizing Magna Carta's importance for placing the king under the law, Maitland admitted that some of the clauses most acclaimed by his contemporaries were 'immature', and as a lawyer he found that 'the very definite promises about smaller matters . . . are perhaps of greater value'.[26]

By the first decade of the twentieth century, scholars were taking a supposedly scientific approach that rejected traditional interpretations and inspired combats about Magna Carta's true character. Since Maitland showed the way, professional historians had turned to administrative records, convinced that they give a truer picture of the past than chronicles burdened with their authors' presuppositions and prejudices. Such materials, often financial accounts or inventories of property, demanded quantitative or statistical studies that hardly resulted in gripping reading. As a result, historians turned away from their predecessors' grand narratives to write narrowly focused works on short periods or technical analyses of specific topics for their colleagues to read in learned journals, not for a larger reading public. As medieval scholarship became more technical and less accessible to the public, debates among academics over the meaning of Magna Carta struck general readers of history as hairsplitting reminiscent of the late medieval Scholastic theologians. Despite their incomprehensibility for the public, specialized studies of the Charter made an impact on popular perceptions, as their findings trickled down to undergraduate lectures and popular histories for pleasure readers.

Another characteristic of professional historians' writing that lost a wider reading public was a desire to shock, to 'debunk' traditional ideas and interpretations and discredit hallowed heroes and institutions. Magna Carta did not escape the debunkers' attention, and some took pleasure in undermining its image, maligning it as a reactionary 'feudal' document. They regarded the Charter as an obstacle to construction of a powerful state, imposed by selfish and greedy barons looking back to an earlier age when weak rulers had presented no barrier to baronial exploitation of the peasantry. Typical of this approach is a 1902 paper by Edward Jenks, a professor of law at Liverpool and London, who set out to refute Stubbs's views. Jenks considered the Charter 'a positive nuisance and stumbling block to the generation which came after it'; in his view, its impetus was 'jealousy of the growing power of the monarchy' by reactionary barons aiming at preservation of the feudal organization of society. Jenks concluded that 'the real author of the Myth of Magna Carta' was Sir Edward Coke, who employed his 'unsound historical doctrines' to defend his political ideas.[27] A 1920 book on the English Parliament by A.F. Pollard also questioned the Charter's fame as a liberty document. For Pollard, it was 'the great charter of liberties, but not of liberty', a grant of 'definite concrete privileges, which some people enjoyed, but most did not', not an abstract right possessed by all free men. He explained that in the Middle Ages, 'Liberty was an adjunct, almost a form of property; and it was prized for its material and financial attributes'.[28]

With the beginnings of the welfare state, historians came to esteem central government and to appreciate bureaucrats for their delivery of services to the people. Growth of big government in the first half of the century under the pressures of two world wars and a great depression sparked further interest in study of the medieval royal administration. American and British historians, living under regimes that had mobilized their nations to win two world wars, held a benign view of bureaucracy and a hostile opinion of the barons who perpetuated 'feudal anarchy'. They admired medieval civil servants in offices at Westminster, whom they pictured following established procedures, curbing the king's will and strengthening the rule of law.

At the same time, the disasters of the twentieth century – deficient military leadership in the First World War and politicians' failure to make a lasting peace or prevent the Second World War – led many historians to disavow heroes in history. Marxism, which saw historical change as resulting from class conflict generated by impersonal socio-economic forces, drew other scholars away from 'great man' theories of history. Between the two world wars, Marxist doctrines also contributed to academics' rejection of political history as grand narrative, and even those who doubted that class conflict was the key to historical change emphasized economic conditions and the material environment. A French journal founded in 1929, *Annales: économies, sociétés, civilisations*, illustrates historians' shift toward economics, sociology and anthropology. Since the Second World War, *Annales* has exercised a powerful influence on historians across the English Channel and across the Atlantic, and the British historical journal *Past and Present*, founded in 1952, also advocates interdisciplinary and quantitative studies typical of the social sciences.

Scholars' preoccupation with such topics as peasant societies or family history in place of law and politics diverted them from Magna Carta; even those still studying it felt pressure to abandon a purely political or legal approach. J.C. Holt's 1961 book *The Northerners*, exposing multiple ties of kinship, vassalage, patronage, geography, debt, and shared resentments that bound the northern rebels into a political community, illustrates the impact of the *Annales* group. He is unlikely to claim membership in a French methodological school, and he sees his group-study of the barons from northern England who rebelled against King John as primarily a study in politics. No doubt the most direct influence on Holt was a British school of social politics pioneered by Lewis B.

Namier (d. 1960), who studied eighteenth-century parliaments through collective biographies and explained their members' political activity through ties of family and patronage, not party or ideological affiliation.

Through most of the twentieth century, American medieval historians' research focused on royal government in England and France. As the title of a 1970 book has it, they were seeking 'the medieval origins of the modern state'.[29] Leaders of this school, Sidney Painter (d. 1960) and Joseph R. Strayer (d. 1987), held a benign view of twelfth- and thirteenth-century monarchs who were expanding royal power. Their appreciation for English and French kings' rationalizing, centralizing and bureaucratizing programmes likely grew out of their admiration for activist US presidents in the pre-First World War Progressive era and the 1930s New Deal. Their students dominated medieval studies in the United States until the Cold War consensus dissipated in the late 1960s, when both New Left opponents of the Vietnam War and conservative haters of the welfare state grew disenchanted with strong federal government.

Magna Carta posed a problem for both Painter and Strayer because they hardly wished to present such a hallowed symbol of liberty as an obstacle to effective central government. Painter, in his 1949 book *The Reign of King John*, questioned John's reputation as a bad king, explaining his arbitrary acts as necessitated by 'a political system that had lost all touch with economic reality'. Painter admitted that John engaged in autocratic actions 'more enthusiastically than his predecessors', but dismissed them as 'a question of degree not of nature' and concluded that he 'simply wanted to develop his power as king and feudal suzerain to the greatest extent possible'. Painter described the Charter's detailed articles as 'for the most part obsolete when they were written' and scorned the rebel barons' views as 'essentially conservative if not reactionary', although he admits that their feudal outlook instilled in them certain lasting concepts that pointed toward limited monarchy.[30] Strayer had a higher opinion of the barons, crediting them with realistic moderation in securing 'the maximum concessions which were possible without doing serious damage to the central government'. For him, the Charter's imposition of 'reasonable restraints on the central government without making it impossible for the central government to operate' made it exceptional.[31] In both Britain and America, some historians are still committed to the approach of Painter and Strayer and continue to pore over medieval records in the archives. They hail King John as a premature practitioner of 'administrative kingship', a phrase not meaning a monarch who is himself an administrator, but one no longer governing through household servants, relying instead on specialized agencies following a fixed routine and functioning without his personal oversight.

At the beginning of the twenty-first century, most historians disavow Stubbsian interpretations that find in the Middle Ages progress toward representative democracy or the modern nation-state. Instead, they stress the 'otherness' of the Middle Ages as an epoch alien to modern modes of thought and hostile to modern relativist morality, and they refuse to see the period as the 'birthplace' or 'childhood' of modern European civilization. Influenced by mid-twentieth-century socialist scholars, many medievalists embrace a 'new social history' that rates popular culture higher than official high culture and deprecates historians' traditional concentration on critical analysis of documents. Instead of studying princes, politicians or political institutions, the new generation of scholars searches for victims, casualties of persecution by dominant elites of their own era and later by historians' condescension or indifference. Their research focuses on the poor and the powerless, minorities and the marginalized, groups that escaped earlier scholars' attention. Because of sparse source material, those studying such groups sometimes abandon a historical method stressing the scientist's approach in their readings of sources; seeking new meanings in old texts, they borrow methods from their colleagues in literature departments. Like literary critics, they hold that the reconstruction of 'reality' by any reader of a document is merely a product of language, no more valid than another's.

A document such as Magna Carta, concerned with liberties of free English males and a bulwark of Whiggish history as progress toward liberal democracy, has little appeal to historians today except as a stick with which to beat an earlier generation. In Britain, one result is a shift away from the growth of the nation-state as a central theme and an emphasis on the non-English regions of the British Isles and the immigrants settled in today's United Kingdom. An example is Norman Davies's 1999 book reacting against the English bias that he finds in histories of the British Isles. He finds the Charter significant only because it forms 'the centrepiece of a very particular historical myth' of English constitutionalism that conflates English history with British history.[32] To note the new social history's impact, a comparison of Robert Bartlett's volume in the *New Oxford History of England*, *England under the Norman and Angevin Kings 1075–1225* (2000), with its predecessor, A.L. Poole's *From Domesday Book to Magna Carta* (1951), is revealing. Poole's book, heavy with political narrative, concludes with a lengthy chapter on King John and Magna Carta, while Bartlett's treatment of the Charter covers only four pages. A reviewer of Bartlett's book remarked that it contains 'far more on twelfth-century attitudes to animals, wild or domestic, than there is on the constitutional significance of Magna Carta'.[33]

Not all historians of the Middle Ages embrace current fads, and a number still find politics worthy of study; none the less, the temper of the times affects their approach to royal government, perhaps unconsciously. Whatever their methodology, most students of medieval monarchies today reject mid-twentieth-century historians' chastened faith in progress. Many take a tough-minded tone, finding medieval rulers less beneficent and more predatory, preying on rather than protecting their subjects and striving to expand their territory. They stress administrative kingship's exploitative character, its oppression of the peasantry for the benefit of the royal family, courtiers and aristocracy. They attach less relevance to the growth of administrative agencies, for they picture royal servants primarily concerned with patronage for themselves and their relatives.

A hard-headed view of political change characterizes much medieval history written today, identifying tangible matters of royal fiances, court factions or patronage as more significant factors than acknowledged by optimistic Whig historians. They are influenced by scholars of the late Roman Republic or eighteenth-century parliaments whose collective biographical studies portray social relations within ruling elites, and they see medieval English political factions revolving around noble families' rivalries for royal favour, not ideological convictions. They find the royal household significant not as a nursery for specialized governmental agencies, but as a stage on which parvenu courtiers and aristocrats of ancient lineage acted out their competition for patronage. When they turn to the Great Charter, they find it less interesting as a leap forward for English liberties than as a detailing of the Angevin kings' oppressive acts. Indeed, the author of a 1987 book titled his section on the Charter, 'Magna Carta as a critique of Angevin government'.[34]

Notes

1. Smith (1987), 139.
2. Pallister (1971), 68.
3. Bentham excerpted in Ebenstein (1956), 484.
4. Pallister (1971), 73.
5. Pallister (1971), 74.
6. Pallister (1971), 85.
7. Pallister (1971), 94.
8. Smith (1987), 194.
9. Pallister (1971), 99, 100.
10. Pallister (1971), 103.
11. *King* v. *Halliday* in Stephenson and Marcham (1937), 867–71.
12. Ewing and Gearty (2000), 396–8.

13. *Ex Parte Selwyn*, Swindler (1965), 233.
14. Law report cited by Marcham (1960), 441.
15. Ewing and Gearty (2000), 233.
16. *Aspects of Human Rights* (1995), 145.
17. Pallister (1971), 106.
18. Green (1990), 123.
19. Cannadine (1992), 111, citing Trevelyan, *History of England*.
20. Quotation from Campbell (1995), 78.
21. Lyon (1960), xviii.
22. Stubbs (1874–78), quotations from Cantor (1966), 18, 121.
23. Stubbs (1874–78), quotations from Cantor (1966), 114–16.
24. Levine (1986), 165.
25. Cantor (1991), 51, 60.
26. Pollock and Maitland (1898), 1: 172.
27. Holt (1972), 25–37, reprinting Jenks, 'The myth of Magna Carta', *Independent Review*, 4 (1902).
28. Pollard (1926), excerpted in Holt (1972), 149–58.
29. Strayer (1970).
30. Painter (1949), 223, 226–7; 'Magna Carta', in Painter (1961), 244–53.
31. Strayer (1955), 170–1.
32. Davies (1999), 384.
33. Vincent (2001), 410.
34. Warren (1987), 164–9.

chapter 8

MAGNA CARTA IN
THE NEW WORLD

With the expansion of the British Empire in the modern era, English common law and liberties spread over much of the globe, although Magna Carta's lessons would not be learned by all subject peoples of the Empire. Centuries were required before the sense of 'law-abidingness' essential for effective governance under the law took root in England, and English political customs could hardly be expected to flower in faraway lands among unwilling subjects with their own heritage and history. English patterns of law and government became deeply rooted chiefly in countries with large numbers of settlers from the British Isles, including Canada, Australia, New Zealand and the United States. Nowhere was Magna Carta's principle of the rule of law held in more reverence than in the thirteen British colonies established along North America's eastern seaboard.

As the Great Charter's relevance receded in eighteenth-century England, it remained fundamental for the American colonists, who held themselves to be fully English, the king's free subjects possessing all rights of their compatriots at home. John Adams wrote that no people were 'more strongly attached to their natural and constitutional rights and liberties than the British Colonists of the American Continent'.[1] They regarded earlier struggles of the English against arbitrary rulers as part of their own history; in one scholar's words, 'The ghost of Sir Edward Coke, pursuing his crusade against early-seventeenth century Stuart monarchs, still walked in England's [thirteen] colonies'.[2] As a result, Magna Carta would take on new life in the new world, shaping the law and politics of a new nation, the United States of America.

The Charter in colonial North America

Just as provincials on the periphery of earlier empires had held tightly to the civilization of the centre, English colonists across the Atlantic prided themselves on being authentically English. They were confident that historical documents starting with Magna Carta remained valid for them across the ocean, guarding against arbitrary government. The Great Charter known by Americans was Sir Edward Coke's version. Following Coke's anachronistic interpretation, they held it to be the guarantor of ancient English liberties, including rights to trial by jury and the writ of *habeas corpus*. Features of the society they created in the new world strengthened this tradition of liberty. A plurality of settlers were religious dissenters, motivated to migrate by a search for religious freedom, and patterns of congregational governance in their independent churches gave training in democracy. All thirteen colonies had elected representative assemblies, and although the right to vote was restricted, they were the most democratically elected legislative bodies in the western world. There was never a titled nobility in the North American colonies, and a lesser degree of inequality prevailed than elsewhere. The poor were less poor and the rich less rich than in the old world, although a large slave population set apart by race was a stark exception to this prevalent equality.

American colonists did not derive their claims to fundamental rights solely from English experience, for they knew the writings of eighteenth-century political thinkers expounding natural rights doctrines of liberty. Indeed, some consider the American Revolution 'a revolution of natural law against common law'.[3] Natural rights theories depicting men living in a state of nature and coming together to create institutions for governing themselves seemed to describe the colonists' own experience in drafting documents devising basic arrangements for governing their several colonies. When the Pilgrims found themselves far north of the Virginia Company's bounds, they had constituted themselves 'into a civil body politic, for our better ordering and preservation'.[4] The colonists considered charters setting forth fundamental principles for governance to be solemn contracts with the English king, spelling out rights and responsibilities of the two contracting parties.

English common law tradition exerted an enormous influence on the founders of the thirteen colonies, and their charters, beginning with the one granted by King James I to the Virginia Company in 1606, included guarantees of settlers' rights as free English subjects. The first Virginia charter, largely drafted by Coke, stated that the colonists 'shall have and enjoy all liberties, franchises and immunities . . . as if they had been abiding and born within this our realm of England'. The 1629 Charter of the Massachusetts Bay Colony contained a similar promise of 'all liberties and immunities of free and natural subjects . . . as if they and every of them were born within the realm of England'.[5] Both the 1765

Stamp Act Congress and the first Continental Congress in 1774 would reaffirm the colonists' conviction that their immigrant ancestors had brought with them 'all the inherent rights and liberties of [the king's] natural-born subjects within the realm of Great Britain' and that they were entitled to the common law, especially jury trial, as 'the inherent and invaluable right of every British subject in these colonies'.[6]

The charters of several colonies contained clauses borrowed directly from chapter 29/39 of Magna Carta and from the 1689 Bill of Rights. When the Massachusetts colonists saw a need for a basic law, they agreed 'that some men should be appointed to frame a body of grounds of law, in resemblance to Magna Carta, which . . . should be received for fundamental laws'.[7] The similarity of the Massachusetts Body of Liberties, adopted in 1641, to chapter 29/39 is striking in its promise that 'no man's life shall be taken away . . . no man's person shall be arrested, restrained, banished, dismembered, nor any ways punished . . . no man's goods or estate shall be taken away from nor any way damaged . . . unless it be by virtue or equity of some express law of the country warranting the same'.[8] Similar wording appeared in the charters of later colonies; indeed, the 1732 charter of Georgia, last of the thirteen colonies, mirrors almost exactly the Massachusetts Bay Charter's wording over a century earlier.

Because colonial charters contained provisions requiring that laws enacted by the legislative body be in harmony with the laws of England, books of English law were in great demand. Chief among books circulating throughout the colonies were Coke's works. As early as 1647, the leaders of the Massachusetts colony ordered two copies of his work on Magna Carta and other lawbooks to assist them in preparing a second version of their Body of Liberties. Virginia's legislative assembly in 1666, sensing a need for 'the better conformity of the proceedings of the courts of this country to the laws of England', ordered a number of lawbooks from England.[9] The 1225 version of the Great Charter was published in Philadelphia in 1687, part of a tract authored by William Penn, founder of the Quaker colony. In *The Excellent Privilege of Liberty & Property; Being the Birth-right of the Free-Born Subjects of England*, he wished to acquaint 'such who may not have leisure from their plantations to read large volumes' with their rights and liberties. In addition to Magna Carta, it included Edward I's Confirmation of the Charters of 1297 and an early-fourteenth-century document, the so-called statute *De Tallagio non concedendo*. Penn's comments on the Great Charter show his uncritical acceptance of Sir Edward Coke's views, approving the assertion that it 'is for the most part only Declaratory of the principal ground of the Fundamental Laws and Liberties of England', not 'mere emanations of Royal Favour, or new Bounties granted'.[10]

The practice of law was a route to profit and status in the American colonies, and numbers of young men, especially from the southern colonies, read law at the inns of court. Many of the founding fathers of the United States were lawyers: twenty-five of the fifty-six signers of the Declaration of Independence and thirty-one of the fifty-five delegates to the constitutional convention. Thomas Jefferson, a lawyer as well as a planter and politician, had the finest private library in the colonies; among his books were major English legal texts from the medieval treatises *Glanville* and *Bracton* to Coke's *Institutes* and Sir William Blackstone's *Commentaries on the Laws of England*. Colonial youths trained for the law by studying Coke's *Institutes* and Blackstone's *Commentaries* published in American editions by the late eighteenth century. Such lawbooks inculcated in American lawyers anachronistic interpretations of Magna Carta, finding in chapter 29/39 guarantees of rights to jury trial and the writ of *habeas corpus*.

During the first hundred years of North American colonization, the British government had little time for the thirteen colonies that seemed much less valuable than the sugar islands of the West Indies. The resulting 'salutary neglect' enabled the colonists to evade close supervision and escape effective taxation. Although the Americans became accustomed to considerable autonomy, neither the king nor Parliament shared their broad view of their liberties. The king's North American possessions were regarded as part of the royal prerogative, and the crown claimed the power to disallow acts adopted by the colonial legislatures. The constitutional relationship of the thirteen colonies' legislative assemblies with the British Parliament was unclear, however. The Navigation Acts of 1660 and 1696 and the 1733 Molasses Act seemed to prove Parliament's right to enact legislation for the colonies, at least regulation of their external trade, although some authorities disagreed about the authority of parliamentary acts treating purely internal matters. Such an authority as William Blackstone, writing on the eve of the American Revolution, held that neither the common law nor parliamentary statutes applied to English overseas territories. He concluded that since they were acquired either by conquest of native peoples or by treaties with them, 'The common law of England, as such, has no allowance or authority there; they being no part of the mother country, but distinct (though dependent) dominions. They are subject however to the control of the parliament, though ... not bound by any acts of parliament, unless particularly named.'[11] Blackstone had some justification for his view, for the tribunal hearing appeals from the colonial courts was not one of the common law courts at Westminster, but a committee of the Privy Council, a body that placed Britain's military and commercial interests ahead of legal concerns. Furthermore, cases involving the colonies' trade and taxation were prosecuted in branches of the admiralty court, where such common law procedures as trial by jury were unavailable.

After the defeat of the French in 1763 in the Seven Years War or French and Indian War, the thirteen colonies' dissatisfaction swelled. The British Parliament claimed direct authority over the colonies, enacting legislation that applied mercantilist economic doctrines that colonies exist for the mother-country's benefit. Closer supervision by the central government was part of an eighteenth-century trend toward bureaucratic centralization in most European monarchies, but the British also hoped to increase their revenues from the colonies. After fighting a costly war to rid the Americans of a threat from France, Parliament expected them to finance their own defence and imposed new taxes, no longer limited to import and export duties alone. Especially enraging to the colonists was the Stamp Act of 1765, an internal levy mandating purchase of stamps for printed matter ranging from legal documents to playing cards. Westminster's assertion of direct control over the thirteen colonies led the Americans to rebellious acts and to British reprisals that spiralled toward war in the 1770s.

In the decade before the outbreak of fighting, colonial lawyers and pamphleteers turned to Magna Carta for support against the government across the ocean. Like parliamentary critics of Charles I, Americans interpreted the 1215 Charter's clauses on scutage and aids anachronistically, and their cries of 'no taxation without representation' claimed a basis in the Charter. The Stamp Act awakened the colonists to a threat to their autonomy in expanding parliamentary claims to authority over them that rejected their rights as Englishmen. Colonial assemblies adopted resolutions opposing the Stamp Act that complained of its violations of Magna Carta's liberties, namely imposing taxes without the consent of the taxed and trial of violators of the act without juries in the admiralty courts. John Adams, drafting his Massachusetts community's protest against the stamp tax, wrote that it violated the British constitutional principle that 'no freeman would be subject to any tax to which he had not given his own consent, in person or by proxy'. He added that British reprisals were 'directly repugnant to the Great Charter itself'. In Virginia, Patrick Henry presented a resolution to the colonial legislature declaring that Virginia's earliest settlers had brought with them 'all the liberties, franchises, privileges and immunities, that have at any time been held, enjoyed and possessed, by the people of Great Britain'.[12]

New taxes on other goods in everyday use followed in 1767, and Parliament in 1773 granted the East India Company a monopoly on the sale of tea in the colonies. This new mercantilist measure provoked a boycott of the company's tea and the Boston Tea Party, a protest by Bostonians who boarded company ships disguised as Indians to jettison the cargo of tea chests. Violent resistance to these financial innovations pushed Westminster to punitive measures, culminating in the 'intolerable acts' of 1774 that closed the port of Boston and suspended the Massachusetts Bay Colony's charter, its punishment an example to the other colonies. Clearly, the North American settlers and Britons at home had different interpretations of the constitutional relationship between the two territories. Americans viewed their various colonies' founding charters in the light of seventeenth-century lawyers' notions of the Great Charter. Just as they imagined a contract between lord and vassals or king and subjects justifying the deposition of James II, so they viewed their relationship with George III as a contractual one. The first Continental Congress in October 1774 adopted a resolution claiming that the colonists were doing 'as Englishmen their ancestors in like cases have usually done, for asserting and vindicating their rights and liberties'.[13]

Not surprisingly, Parliament rejected the colonies' constitutional claim that its power was limited to regulating their external commerce. To Americans' complaint that Parliament had no authority to tax them because they were not represented, the British replied with an argument of 'virtual representation', responding that members of the Commons represented the interests of the kingdom as a whole and the entire British Empire, not simply their local constituencies. In rebuttal, the colonists cited writings of English reformers protesting the injustice of the Commons' antiquated system of representation, denying many localities their own spokesmen. After the colonists' protests led to repeal of the Stamp Act, Parliament passed the Declaratory Act, a statement of authority over the thirteen colonies, asserting that the king in Parliament 'had, hath, and of right ought to have, full power and authority to make laws and statutes of sufficient force and validity to bind the colonies and people of America, subjects of the crown of Great Britain, in all cases whatsoever'.[14]

Colonial leaders began to question openly Britain's right to rule over them. Benjamin Franklin, speaking before a parliamentary committee about the Stamp Act on behalf of the American colonies, stated that the colonial assemblies held exclusive control over internal taxation. Citing the Petition of Right's statement that taxes are to be levied by 'common consent in Parliament', he told the committee that 'the people of America have no representatives in Parliament, to make a part of that common consent'.[15] By 1775, American political tracts were refuting parliamentary power over the colonies. James Wilson confronted Blackstone's opinion that the colonies were subject to a legislative body in which they were unrepresented; in his pamphlet *Considerations on the Nature and Extent of the Legislative Authority of the British Parliament*, he applied Locke's doctrine that a government's legitimacy rests on the consent of the governed. Wilson maintained that Parliament had 'no dominion over their equals and fellow-subjects in America', and he asked, 'What act of ours has rendered us subject to those, to whom we were formerly equal? . . . Do those, who embark, freemen, in Great-Britain, disembark, slaves in America?'[16] Anticipating the twentieth-century British Commonwealth, he stated that the proper object of the colonists' devotion was the crown; however, he argued that when the king failed to defend the colonists' interests, they no longer owed him allegiance.

The Americans found a model for their armed rebellion in the barons' extortion of Magna Carta from King John, and they reinterpreted the baronial rebels as champions of popular liberty. Indeed, the design selected by the commonwealth of Massachusetts for its seal at the beginning of the Revolutionary War depicted a militiaman with a sword in one hand and a copy of Magna Carta in the other. Magna Carta was perhaps more important for strengthening the colonists' commitment to a constitution or body of fundamental law standing above both king and Parliament and unalterable by statute, inclining them toward the concept of a written constitution. A 1768 circular letter drafted by the Massachusetts firebrand Samuel Adams asserted that 'in all free states the Constitution is fixed; and as the supreme legislative derives its power and authority from the Constitution, it cannot overleap the bounds of it, without destroying its own foundation'.[17] Americans' dedication to fundamental law was growing in the years since 1688, an age when British political thinkers were discarding it in favour of parliamentary sovereignty.

In the course of the eighteenth century, the North American settlers began to buttress their arguments from history questioning their rule from Westminster with Enlightenment doctrines of universal natural rights espoused by thinkers such as John Locke. His *Two Treatises on Government* supplied a purely philosophical justification for revolution that was as influential as historical precedent, if not more so. Samuel Adams mixed newer natural law arguments with traditional appeals to the Great Charter in his protests against the Stamp Act. Adams wrote that 'the essential rights of the British Constitution' were founded on 'the law and God and nature . . . the common rights of mankind', but he also declared that 'an act of parliament made against Magna Carta in violation of its essential parts, is void'.[18] Christian teaching, always a major source for American political thought, mingled with natural law doctrines. Four Presbyterian pastors wrote in 1775 that 'to take any man's money, without his consent, is unjust and contrary to reason and the law of God, and the Gospel of Christ', as well as contrary to Magna Carta and the English constitution.[19]

Concrete evidence for the impact of natural law teaching is the Declaration of Independence, signed on 4 July 1776. It paraphrases Locke's teaching that all people possess basic natural rights – 'life, liberty, and the pursuit of happiness', in Jefferson's words – and that when a government threatens them, 'it is the right of the people to alter or to abolish it, and to institute new government'. The Declaration proclaims that George III's fundamental contract with his American subjects was broken because he aimed at 'the establishment of an absolute tyranny over these states'. It charges the king with waging war on his subjects and 'taking away our Charters, abolishing our most valuable laws, and altering fundamentally the forms of our government', an accusation similar to earlier ones against John and Charles I.[20] The Americans mistakenly blamed King George III instead of Parliament and, however unjustly, made him their symbol for Britain's tyranny. It was easier for the colonists to depict their war with the mother-country as another episode in English history's series of rebellions against tyrannical monarchs than as a repudiation of Parliament's authority.

After the Declaration of Independence, the American colonies considered themselves free and independent states, and eleven of them drafted new state constitutions to replace their old colonial charters. In them, the colonists put into practice popular eighteenth-century social contract theories; indeed, the 1780 Massachusetts Bill of Rights defines the body politic as 'a social compact by which the whole people covenants with each citizen and each citizen with the whole people'. Having rejected their old governments and reverted to a state of nature, their representatives met in special assemblies or constitutional conventions to frame their new patterns for governing themselves. Nine former colonies inserted into their constitutions bills of rights with statements much like chapter 29/39 of Magna Carta. The Virginia Bill of Rights of 1776, significant for supplying a model for the later federal Bill of Rights, protects against loss of liberty 'except by the law of the land or the judgment of [one's] peers'.[21]

A thorough grounding in the common law continued to be a necessity for American lawyers after the Revolutionary War, since most states enacted legislation 'receiving' the common law as it stood at the time of their establishment. For example, New York's state constitution received 'such parts of the common law of England, and of the statute law of England and Great Britain' as were in force at the time that it won independence.[22] As new states to the west were admitted into the Union, they too would receive the common law as the basis for their own legal systems. This reception of English law reinforced lawyers' need for compilations of British statutes, and several were published in the early nineteenth century. Among them was William Schley's *Digest of the English Statutes*, commissioned by the Georgia legislature in 1826. It included the complete text of the 1225 Charter, which Schley hailed as 'undoubtedly the foundation, and great corner stone of that system of civil and political liberty, which the English people enjoy in a greater degree, than in any other nation, except the citizens of the United States'.[23]

The American Revolution represented a rejection of a central sovereign authority, and after the war ended in 1783, the thirteen newly independent states were united only loosely under the Articles of Confederation. It soon became clear that a stronger central government was essential, and an assembly meeting at Philadelphia in 1787 devised the Constitution of the United States. The founding fathers' task was to create a central government that was not contrary to the spirit of 1776, incapable of tyrannizing the thirteen states, yet powerful enough to protect them; and the federal Constitution adopted in 1789 was a compromise between a confederation of sovereign states and a single, unitary state. The United States Constitution limited the central government's power in two ways. First, it put into practice Magna Carta's fundamental lesson of limitations on a government's power over the people's liberties. The drafters saw that the legislature could pose as serious a threat to liberty as the executive, and the first three articles enumerate three separate branches of the federal government, legislative, executive and judicial, each acting as a restraint on the other's power. Second, the Constitution divides responsibilities between the federal government and the states, cataloguing the powers belonging to the central government and leaving others to the several states. The resulting tension between federal and state sovereignty would generate conflicts that continue today.

As the states considered ratifying the federal Constitution, anti-federalists pointed out the absence of an enumeration of citizens' rights, such as Magna Carta or the 1689 Bill of Rights. They objected to the absence of protections against arbitrary acts by a powerful central government, but supporters of a federal union responded that earlier grants of liberties were concessions from sovereign rulers and unnecessary for a government 'professedly founded upon the power of the people, and executed by their immediate representatives and servants'.[24] The Charter featured prominently in this debate, and in 1791 the first ten amendments to the federal Constitution, America's Bill of Rights, were ratified. The first amendment goes further than Magna Carta in circumscribing government by barring specific actions infringing on the people's liberties: no establishment of an official religion, no abridgement of freedom of speech or the press, no prohibition of peaceable assembly or petitions for redress of grievances. The ninth amendment added protection of any rights not specified in the previous amendments, declaring that 'The enumeration in the Constitution of certain rights, shall not be construed to deny or discharge others retained by the people'.[25]

Americans in their constitutional documents carried guarantees of rights against government oppression a step farther than had England. There oppression by the monarch had aroused the greatest alarm since King John's tyrannical reign. Only a few radicals during the seventeenth century had worried that an all-powerful parliament could prove to be as tyrannical as the king. By the eighteenth century, with Parliament's superior place secure and ideas of fundamental law fading, the British constitution stood as a series of statutes that parliamentary acts could abolish or alter, so long as supported by public opinion. The founding fathers of the United States remained faithful to earlier doctrine that placed the Great Charter above statute law, and they accorded the Constitution a similar lofty position as fundamental law. 'Due process of law' is mandated by the Constitution, fundamental law that can be overcome only by a Supreme Court ruling or a constitutional amendment, invulnerable to acts of Congress, unlike in the United Kingdom where the people's liberties depend on statutes or case law. An 1884 Supreme Court decision sets forth the justices' understanding of the difference between the United States constitutional system and the British parliamentary system: 'In English history . . . the omnipotence of Parliament over the common law was absolute, even against common right and reason. In this country written constitutions were deemed essential to protect the rights and liberties of the people against the encroachments of power delegated to their governments, and the provisions of Magna Carta were incorporated into the Bill of Rights.'[26]

Among the ten amendments to the Constitution forming the American Bill of Rights, the fifth amendment's promise in that no person shall be 'deprived of life, liberty, or property without due process of law' echoes Magna Carta. The sixth amendment spells out precisely the phrases 'lawful judgement of peers' and 'law of the land' in chapter 29/39, reflecting the identification of those terms with trial by jury and *habeas corpus*, rights that had won acceptance over the centuries. The sixth amendment also promises those accused of crimes 'the right to a speedy and public trial, by an impartial jury of the State and district wherein the crime shall have been committed', and it grants them means for defending themselves. The accused has the right 'to be informed of the nature and cause of the accusation', and also the right 'to be confronted with the witnesses against him; to have compulsory process for obtaining witnesses in his favor, and to have the assistance of counsel for his defense'.[27]

The Charter in the courts of the United States

Once the United States became an independent nation with federal and state constitutions and the Bill of Rights as its own fundamental law, Magna Carta's principles came into the courts second-hand, not directly as in colonial days. None the less, the new federal judiciary continued to hold the Charter in high regard, having learned its chief lesson, the guarantee of due process. A Supreme Court justice wrote as early as 1819: 'As to the words from Magna Carta . . ., the good sense of mankind has at length settled down to this: that they were intended to secure the individual from the arbitrary exercise of the powers of government, unrestrained by the established principles of private right and distributive justice'.[28]

Sometimes American judges engaged in rhetorical flights of fancy that echoed Coke's doctrine of the ancient constitution and mythologized histories of nineteenth-century Whigs. In 1855, a justice wrote that Magna Carta was 'an affirmance of the ancient standing laws of the land, as they had existed among the Saxons ere the power of Norman chivalry, combined with the subtlety of Norman lawyers, had deprived the Saxons . . . of their ancient civil and political institutions'.[29] Courts continued to trace the right to jury trial to the Charter until New York state judges questioned the tradition in 1899, and in a 1968 opinion the US Supreme Court noted that 'historians no longer accept this pedigree'.[30] Over a hundred citations of the Great Charter appear in US Supreme Court decisions, and American jurists today still cannot resist citing it in proceedings and taking it as a subject for speeches and papers. In Paula Jones's infamous sexual harassment suit in 1994 against the sitting president, Bill Clinton, a federal district judge ruled against delaying the suit during the president's term of office, stating that 'It is contrary to our form of government, which asserts as did the English in the Magna Carta and the Petition of Right, that even the sovereign is subject to God and the law'.[31] Whatever their hyperbole and distortions of history, jurists' references to the Charter indicate its lasting place as a symbol of limited government in American legal and political thought.

Under John Marshall, chief justice of the United States (1801–35), the Supreme Court secured its position as arbiter of the Constitution, claiming the right of judicial review, judging the constitutionality of federal statutes as well as scrutinizing state courts' judgements on matters touching the federal Constitution. Some maintain that Coke's citation of medieval English statutes declaring that legislation contrary to Magna Carta should be 'holden for none' pointed the authors of the Constitution toward a concept of fundamental law standing above statute law, although they included no specific provision for the judiciary's assessment of congressional enactments. In *Marbury v. Madison* in 1803, the Supreme Court asserted its power to decide that statutes enacted by Congress were in violation of the Constitution; Chief Justice Marshall proclaimed that it is 'emphatically the province and duty of the judicial department to say what the law is'.[32] America's acceptance of the federal judiciary's right to measure both executive actions and legislative enactments against the Constitution ensures that its provisions would be a paramount law superior to legislative acts. With the cementing of that precept, Magna Carta's principles are implemented most often by the opinions of federal judges, especially the Supreme Court's rulings. In 1855, a Supreme Court justice reiterated the right of review, interpreting the fifth amendment's due process clause as binding on congressional legislation. He wrote: 'The article is a restraint on the legislative as well as on the executive and judicial powers of the government, and cannot be so construed as to leave congress free to make any process "due process of law", by its mere will'.[33]

One of the first enactments by Congress empowered the federal courts to issue writs of *habeas corpus* to persons detained by federal authority, calling for an inquiry into the cause for their detention. Since the seventeenth century, students of English law had assumed that this limitation on arbitrary arrest had originated in Magna Carta. Although guaranteed by the fifth amendment, the writ did not provide adequate armament against the executive branch, and it has not always had success in affording relief from extra-legal detention by federal officials. The president, taking advantage of his power as commander-in-chief of the armed forces, can defy federal judges when he chooses, and US history offers numerous examples of presidents suspending *habeas corpus* during wartime. Among them is Abraham Lincoln, who authorized Union Army commanders to arrest and imprison suspects without a warrant or civil process at the beginning of the Civil War in 1861. When a Maryland citizen was taken prisoner by army officers, he filed a *habeas corpus* petition with the federal court. Chief Justice Roger B. Taney held that the chief executive's suspension of the writ was unconstitutional, for the power to suspend it lay with Congress alone; but Taney acknowledged that he was powerless to enforce his decision, since he was 'resisted by a force too strong for me to overcome'. He directed that a copy of his opinion be sent to the president, concluding that 'It will then remain for that high officer, in fulfillment of his constitutional obligation to "take care that the laws be faithfully executed" to determine what measures he will take to cause the civil process of the United States to be respected and enforced'.[34] Lincoln refused to respect or enforce the chief justice's judgement, and in 1863 Congress passed a statute legalizing his earlier suspension of the writ.

Steps toward preserving and expanding the Great Charter's principles, cementing the connection between *habeas corpus* and the fifth amendment's due process clause, were taken in the Reconstruction era following the Civil War (1865–76). To extend full citizenship to the newly freed slaves, Congress adopted three amendments to the United States Constitution. The thirteenth amendment, ratified by the states in 1865, barred slavery in the United States, and the fifteenth amendment in 1870 protected the new black citizens' right to vote, declaring that no citizen should be disfranchised 'on account of race, color, or previous condition of servitude'. The fourteenth amendment, ratified in 1868, proclaimed that the former slaves were citizens of the United States and of the state in which they resided, and it forbade state governments from depriving 'any person of life, liberty, or property without due process of law; nor deny to any person within its jurisdiction the equal protection of the laws'.[35] The amendment's 'due process of law' phrase gave the federal courts wide latitude to intervene in the states to protect the newly freed slaves, making federal *habeas corpus* writs available to those detained by the states in violation of federal law. The fourteenth constitutional amendment had unanticipated consequences, for the federal judiciary would construe it in unexpected ways in the later nineteenth and early twentieth centuries, interpreting corporations as 'persons' deserving of its protection. This shifted the amendment from a protector of personal liberties to a guardian of private property, only returning many years later to its original purpose of defending civil rights.

Congress had foreshadowed the Reconstruction amendments with the Civil Rights Acts of 1866 and 1875, safeguarding former slaves' right to vote and equal access to public accommodations. These statutes gave the federal courts 'power to grant writs of habeas corpus in all cases where any person may be restrained of his or her liberty in violation of the constitution, or of any treaty or law of the United States'.[36] Despite the post-Civil War constitutional amendments and statutes, the United States failed to live up to its promises of equality under the law for black citizens. This failure marks perhaps the greatest stain on Americans' fidelity to Magna Carta's principles. The white southern population remained convinced that their former slaves were innately inferior and incapable of the responsibilities of full citizenship, and faced with federal military occupation during Reconstruction, they turned to secret societies and terrorist tactics to intimidate blacks. Not only southerners feared the consequences of the fourteenth amendment, for some northerners saw it creating a United States citizenship that would override the states' authority. After the Civil War, the federal courts reverted to their earlier fear of an all-powerful central government threatening property rights, and their decisions blocked effective enforcement of the amendments. The Reconstruction enactments made little impact on the states' prosecution of suspected criminals until the mid-twentieth century, despite injustices inflicted on poor and uneducated persons – both black and white – in state courts.

By 1876, northerners had lost interest in the former slaves' plight, and they lacked the will to continue confronting southern whites' fierce resistance to black claims to citizenship. Once federal troops were withdrawn, the southern states enacted legislation known as 'Jim Crow laws' to establish a racially segregated society and to disfranchise their black inhabitants. In a series of decisions, the Supreme Court sanctioned the southern states' policies of official racial discrimination denying full citizenship to blacks. The first Supreme Court review of the fourteenth amendment came in 1873 with the Slaughterhouse Cases, in which a slim majority found that the amendment prohibited barring blacks from voting solely on the basis of race, but sanctioned barring them with such subterfuges as literacy tests or property qualifications. In the Civil Rights Cases of 1883, the court heard five cases brought by blacks denied equal public accommodations in violation of the 1875 Civil Rights Act, and it declared the act invalid on grounds that it protected social rather than political rights. Furthermore, it ruled that the fourteenth amendment only protected a person's civil rights from a state's action, not from individuals acting without the aid of state authority. This ruling ended federal efforts at prohibiting discrimination against blacks by private individuals and businesses. The Supreme Court gave its sanction to state segregation laws in the 1896 case *Plessy v. Ferguson*. Upholding a Louisiana law mandating racially segregated facilities for railway passengers, it decreed that so long as non-whites were provided 'separate but equal' accommodations the fourteenth amendment's requirement of equal protection of the laws was not violated.

From the Gilded Age of the late nineteenth century until the twentieth century, American jurists assumed that government power constituted the greatest threat to individual liberty, and they found statutes unconstitutional on grounds that they deprived individuals of rights accorded to them by universal principles of law, namely, their rights to liberty and property. In practice, the Supreme Court narrowly focused on protection of private property rights, and its interpretations of statutes severely limited the ability of both federal and state governments to protect the poor and the powerless from a new plutocracy. In this pro-business atmosphere, both federal and state judges overturned numerous statutes aimed at regulating businesses on grounds that they violated companies' right to due process, and they readily issued injunctions against labour union activities. The Supreme Court's 1886 ruling that the term 'persons' in the fourteenth amendment extended to legal persons or corporations as well as to living and breathing citizens converted the ancient principle of personal rights against an oppressive government into a screen behind which private companies were free to exploit their workers, defraud competitors and fleece the buying public. The tribunal's constant overturning of state regulations to improve employees' working conditions brought a retort from Justice Oliver Wendell Holmes, who wrote in a 1905 dissent that the fourteenth amendment had not enacted 'Mr. Herbert Spencer's Social Statics' and that the Constitution 'is not intended to embody a particular economic theory, whether of paternalism . . . or of *laissez-faire*'.[37] Support for unrestrained capitalism reached such a peak that William D. Guthrie, a lawyer and litigant for corporate interests, gave an address on Magna Carta's seven-hundredth anniversary in 1915 reinterpreting it as a guardian of property rights against state agencies.

Only in the 1930s with New Deal legislation aimed at overcoming the Great Depression did the Supreme Court turn aside from dogmas that had reshaped the fourteenth amendment into a barrier to government regulation of businesses. By the mid-twentieth century, the amendment's 'due process of law' and 'equal protection of the laws' clauses were no longer limited to preserving property rights. Federal courts revived the original purpose of protecting civil liberties, guaranteeing blacks' rights against racially discriminatory state laws, and they also reinvigorated the first amendment's protection for freedom of expression. The result was a vast extension of Magna Carta's protection of personal liberties far beyond the imagination of the barons at Runnymede or Coke and the common lawyers.

Beginning with 1938 and 1948 decisions ruling that blacks must be admitted to state-supported law schools for whites if the state maintained no separate institution for their education, the Supreme Court began to deconstruct the 'separate but equal' doctrine. In 1946, it outlawed state statutes that segregated passengers travelling on interstate railways, although the southern states continued to require the separation of blacks from whites on intrastate public transport. The court's boldest step toward full equality for black citizens came in 1954 with the *Brown v. Board of Education of Topeka, Kansas*, a unanimous ruling that racial segregation in state-supported schools was unconstitutional because it denied the equal protection of the law. This revitalized the struggle for blacks' civil rights dormant since their disfranchisement in the 1890s, resulting in non-violent protests against segregated facilities across the South. Massive resistance by elected state officials and violence by scattered groups of whites in the southern states forced federal authorities to intervene in what came to be called a second Reconstruction. Federal troops were sent into the South for the first time since the end of the first Reconstruction era, first to Little Rock, Arkansas, in 1957 to enforce court-ordered integration of Central High School and then to Oxford, Mississippi, in 1962 to protect the first black student admitted to the University of Mississippi.

Eventually, a combination of black protests, northerners' moral indignation and the federal judiciary's rulings forced Congress to adopt laws safeguarding blacks' civil rights, finally implementing promises made during the first Reconstruction. A high point for blacks' rights was the Civil Rights Act of 1964 that revived Reconstruction era legislation, opening public accommodations to all regardless of race or colour. The 1965 Voting Rights Act abolished literacy tests and similar subterfuges used by southern voter registrars to prevent blacks from voting, and it authorized federal agents to register voters in localities with a pattern of discrimination. Despite some dampening of enthusiasm in Congress and among the majority population for federal protection of minority rights since the 1960s, implementation of the principles of due process and equality under the law continues. With the 2003 *Lawrence v. Texas* decision overturning a Texas sodomy law, the Supreme Court rejected earlier precedent to extend equal protection of the law to homosexuals. It applied the fourteenth amendment's due process clause to prevent the majority from applying state power through the criminal law to enforce its definition of morality, and it carried out 'a realm of personal liberty which the government may not enter'.[38]

In the mid-twentieth century, the federal courts cast a sceptical eye on America's criminal justice system and strengthened protections for defendants, even after their conviction. A new look at the fourteenth amendment made possible novel applications of the writ of *habeas corpus*, previously regarded solely as a remedy for detention without charges or trial. Earlier, the *habeas corpus* writ had afforded no protection to a complainant already incarcerated after conviction by a competent court's judgement. By the 1930s, however, the federal courts began to allow *habeas corpus* writs to persons convicted before state tribunals if they alleged violations of their constitutional right of 'due process' or 'equal protection of the law' in the course of their trials. In a 1940 finding, the Supreme Court found support in Magna Carta's central concept of the rule of law for its reversal of the death sentences of four Florida black men, and in rejecting confessions coerced from them after five days of continuous police interrogation, it paraphrased chapter 29/39. The so-called Warren Court of the 1960s, headed by Chief Justice Earl Warren, moved ahead of public opinion in protecting unpopular minorities, including criminal defendants. A number of Supreme Court rulings shored up defendants' rights, allowing them court-appointed counsel and racially representative juries, reinforcing their right to remain silent under police interrogation, and restricting the prosecution's use of unlawfully obtained evidence or coerced confessions.

Magna Carta's principle that the English monarch must deal with his subjects by the 'law of the land' proved a flexible concept, capable of limitless expansion. Defined in the fifth and fourteenth amendments to the US Constitution as 'due process of law', chapter 29/39 of the Charter has brought freedom, dignity and equality to people living in a republic on a continent across the sea unknown to King John and his barons. Yet Americans need to remain vigilant in protecting the hard-won principle of the rule of law. The two world wars of the twentieth century brought threats to civil liberties as a public hostile toward dissenters tolerated restrictions on free speech and roundups of radicals or persons of 'enemy' descent for detention or deportation. In the panic of world war and during the Cold War (1945–89), American leaders often used the excuse of foreign threats to the country's freedom to suppress personal liberties, and many Americans, opting for safety, proved willing to surrender their rights.

At the beginning of the twenty-first century, Magna Carta's great message of limits on government's pursuit of individuals is again unheeded by a power-hungry executive, just as in thirteenth-century and seventeenth-century England, and in the thirteen colonies in the late eighteenth century. In both the United Kingdom and the United States, fears of war, internal subversion and terrorist attack threaten to tip the balance of power within the country, enabling the executive power to place itself beyond the law's reach. An American president, following unmindfully in the footsteps of King John and Charles I, takes advantage of the people's fears in the face of threats of terrorist attacks to invade their privacy and curtail their liberties, detaining persons indefinitely without specific charges and denying them their right of *habeas corpus.* Today, at least a few journalists and jurists still stand ready to challenge individuals' subjection to arbitrary state power in the name of a war on terrorism, and the Great Charter still affords them a rallying point.

Notes

1. Cited in Swindler (1965), 217.
2. Clark (1994), 12.
3. Clark (1994), 4.
4. Commager (1968), the Mayflower Compact, 1: 16.
5. Commager (1968), 1: 10, 17.
6. Commager (1968), 1: 58, Stamp Act Congress Resolutions; slightly different wording in Resolves of the First Continental Congress, 1: 83.
7. Hindley (1990), 194, citing John Winthrop's journal.
8. Swindler (1965), 214–15.
9. Howard (1968), 30.
10. Swindler (1965), 213, citing Penn's work.
11. Blackstone, *Commentaries*, bk i, 107–8, cited in Jones (1973), xlix–l.
12. Adams, 'Instructions of Town of Braintree', in Commager (1968), 1: 57; Virginia Resolutions, Commager, 1: 56.
13. Commager (1968), 1: 83.
14. Commager (1968), 1: 60–1.
15. Franklin's testimony, Swindler (1965), 218.
16. Wilson, cited by Swindler (1965), 222–3.
17. Commager (1968), 1: 66.
18. Howard (1968), 166.
19. Clark (1994), 360, citing 'An Address to the Ministers and Presbyterian Congregations of North Carolina'.
20. Declaration of Independence, Commager (1968), 1: 100–3.
21. Massachusetts Bill of Rights, Commager (1968), 1: 107; Virginia, Commager, 1: 103–4.
22. New York Constitution, Swindler (1965), 224.
23. Howard (1968), 250, citing Schley.
24. The Federalist Papers, excerpted in Pole (1987), 315.
25. Bill of Rights, Commager (1968), 1: 146.
26. *Hurtado* v. *California*, Hindley (1990), 199.
27. Bill of Rights, Commager (1968), 1: 146.
28. Swindler (1965), 231.
29. Hindley (1990), 200, quoting Justice William Johnson.
30. Howard (1968), 344, n. 37.
31. Web site: http://laws.findlaw.com/us/000/95-1853.
32. Commager (1968), 1: 293–4.
33. Thorne et al. (1965), 62, citing Benjamin R. Curtis.
34. *Ex parte* Merryman, Commager (1968), 1: 401.
35. Amendments in Commager (1968), 1: 147–8.
36. Fourteenth Amendment, Commager (1968), 1: 501; Civil Rights Act cited in Meador (1965), 56.
37. Commager (1968), 2: 41.
38. *New York Times*, 27 June 2003.

MAGNA CARTA, 1215
TEXT IN TRANSLATION[1]

John, by the grace of God, king of England, lord of Ireland, duke of Normandy and Aquitaine, and count of Anjou, to the archbishops, bishops, abbots, earls, barons, justiciars, foresters, sheriffs, stewards, servants, and to all his bailiffs and faithful subjects, greeting. Know that we, out of reverence for God and for the salvation of our soul and those of all our ancestors and heirs, for the honour of God and the exaltation of holy church, and for the reform of our realm, on the advice of our venerable fathers, Stephen, archbishop of Canterbury, primate of all England and cardinal of the holy Roman church, Henry archbishop of Dublin, William of London, Peter of Winchester, Jocelyn of Bath and Glastonbury, Hugh of Lincoln, Walter of Worcester, William of Coventry and Benedict of Rochester, bishops, of master Pandulf, subdeacon and member of the household of the lord pope, of brother Aymeric, master of the order of Knights Templar in England, and of the noble men William Marshal earl of Pembroke, William earl of Salisbury, William earl of Warenne, William earl of Arundel, Alan of Galloway constable of Scotland, Warin fitz Georld, Peter fitz Herbert, Hubert de Burgh seneschal of Poitou, Hugh de Neville, Matthew fitz Herbert, Thomas Basset, Alan Basset, Philip de Aubeney, Robert of Ropsley, John Marshal, John fitz Hugh, and others, our faithful subjects:

1. In the first place have granted to God, and by this our present charter confirmed for us and our heirs for ever that the English church shall be free, and shall have its rights undiminished and its liberties unimpaired; and it is our will that it be thus observed; which is evident from the fact that, before the quarrel between us and our barons began, we willingly and spontaneously granted and by our charter confirmed the freedom of elections which is reckoned most important and very essential to the English church, and obtained confirmation of it from the lord pope Innocent III; the which we will observe and we wish our

heirs to observe it in good faith for ever. We have also granted to all free men of our kingdom, for ourselves and our heirs for ever, all the liberties written below, to be had and held by them and their heirs of us and our heirs. [also 1225 Charter[2]]

2.   If any of our earls or barons or others holding of us in chief by knight service dies, and at his death his heir be of full age and owe relief he shall have his inheritance on payment of the old relief, namely the heir or heirs of an earl £100 for a whole earl's barony, the heir or heirs of a baron £100 for a whole barony, the heir or heirs of a knight 100s, for a whole knight's fee; and he who owes less shall give less according to the ancient usage of fiefs. [also 1225]

3.   If, however, the heir of any such be under age and a ward, he shall have his inheritance when he comes of age without paying relief and without making fine. [also 1225]

4.   The guardian of the land of such an heir who is under age shall take from the land of the heir no more than reasonable revenues, reasonable customary dues and reasonable services, and that without destruction and waste of men or goods; and if we commit the wardship of the land of any such to a sheriff, or to any other who is answerable to us for its revenues, and he destroys or wastes what he has wardship of, we will take compensation from him and the land shall be committed to two lawful and discreet men of that fief, who shall be answerable for the revenues to us or to him to whom we have assigned them; and if we give or sell to anyone the wardship of any such land and he causes destruction or waste therein, he shall lose that wardship, and it shall be transferred to two lawful and discreet men of that fief, who shall similarly be answerable to us as is aforesaid. [also 1225]

5.   Moreover, so long as he has the wardship of the land, the guardian shall keep in repair the houses, parks, preserves, ponds, mills and other things pertaining to the land out of the revenues from it; and he shall restore to the heir when he comes of age his land fully stocked with ploughs and the means of husbandry according to what the season of husbandry requires and the revenues of the land can reasonably bear. [also 1225]

6.   Heirs shall be married without disparagement, yet so that before the marriage is contracted those nearest in blood to the heir shall have notice. [also 1225]

7.   A widow shall have her marriage portion and inheritance forth-with and without difficulty after the death of her husband; nor shall she pay anything to have her dower or her marriage portion or the inheritance which she and her husband held on the day of her husband's death; and she may remain in her husband's house for forty days after

his death, within which time her dower shall be assigned to her. [also 1225]

8. No widow shall be forced to marry so long as she wishes to live without a husband, provided that she gives security not to marry without our consent if she holds of us, or without the consent of her lord of whom she holds, if she holds of another. [combined with ch. 7, 1225]

9. Neither we nor our bailiffs will seize for any debt any land or rent, so long as the chattels of the debtor are sufficient to repay the debt; nor will those who have gone surety for the debtor be distrained so long as the principal debtor is himself able to pay the debt; and if the principal debtor fails to pay the debt, having nothing wherewith to pay it, then shall the sureties answer for the debt; and they shall, if they wish, have the lands and rents of the debtor until they are reimbursed for the debt which they have paid for him, unless the principal debtor can show that he has discharged his obligation in the matter to the said sureties. [1225, ch. 8]

10. If anyone who has borrowed from the Jews any sum, great or small, dies before it is repaid, the debt shall not bear interest as long as the heir is under age, of whomsoever he holds; and if the debt falls into our hands, we will not take anything except the principal mentioned in the bond. [omitted from all reissues]

11. And if anyone dies indebted to the Jews, his wife shall have her dower and pay nothing of that debt; and if the dead man leaves children who are under age, they shall be provided with necessaries befitting the holding of the deceased; and the debt shall be paid out of the residue, reserving, however, service due to lords of the land; debts owing to others than Jews shall be dealt with in like manner. [omitted from all reissues]

12. No scutage or aid shall be imposed in our kingdom unless by common counsel of our kingdom, except for ransoming our person, for making our eldest son a knight, and for once marrying our eldest daughter; and for these only a reasonable aid shall be levied. Be it done in like manner concerning aids from the city of London. [omitted from all reissues]

13. And the city of London shall have all its ancient liberties and free customs as well by land as by water. Furthermore, we will grant that all other cities, boroughs, towns, and ports shall have all their liberties and free customs. [1225, ch. 9]

14. And to obtain the common counsel of the kingdom about the assessing of an aid (except in the three cases aforesaid) or of a scutage, we will cause to be summoned the archbishops, bishops, abbots, earls and greater barons, individually by our letters – and, in addition we will

cause to be summoned generally through our sheriffs and bailiffs all those holding of us in chief – for a fixed date, namely, after the expiry of at least forty days, and to a fixed place; and in all letters of such summons we will specify the reason for the summons. And when the summons has thus been made, the business shall proceed on the day appointed, according to the counsel of those present, though not all have come who were summoned. [omitted from all reissues]

15.   We will not in future grant any one the right to take an aid from his free men, except for ransoming his person, for making his eldest son a knight and for once marrying his eldest daughter, and for these only a reasonable aid shall be levied. [omitted from all reissues]

16.   No one shall be compelled to do greater service for a knight's fee or for any other free holding than is due from it. [1225, ch. 10]

17.   Common pleas shall not follow our court, but shall be held in some fixed place. [1225, ch. 11]

18.   Recognitions of *novel disseisin*, of *mort d'ancestor*, and of *darrein presentment* shall not be held elsewhere than in the counties to which they relate, and in this manner – we, or, if we should be out of the realm, our chief justiciar, will send two justices through each county four times a year, who, with four knights of each county chosen by the county, shall hold the said assizes in the county and on the day and in the place of meeting of the county court. [1225, ch. 12]

19.   And if the said assizes cannot all be held on the day of the county court, there shall stay behind as many of the knights and freeholders who were present at the county court on that day as are necessary for the sufficient making of judgments, according to the amount of business to be done. [included in 1216 and 1217 reissues, but omitted from the 1225 Charter]

20.   A free man shall not be amerced for a trivial offence except in accordance with the degree of the offence, and for a grave offence he shall be amerced in accordance with its gravity, yet saving his way of living; and a merchant in the same way, saving his stock-in-trade; and a villein shall be amerced in the same way, saving his means of livelihood – if they have fallen into our mercy: and none of the aforesaid amercements shall be imposed except by the oath of good men of the neighbourhood. [1225, ch. 14]

21.   Earls and barons shall not be amerced except by their peers, and only in accordance with the degree of the offence. [1225, combined with ch. 14]

22.   No clerk shall be amerced in respect of his lay holding except after the manner of the others aforesaid and not according to the amount of his ecclesiastical benefice. [1225, combined with ch. 14]

23. No vill or individual shall be compelled to make bridges at river banks, except those who from old are legally bound to do so. [1225, ch. 15]

24. No sheriff, constable, coroners, or others of our bailiffs, shall hold pleas of our crown. [1225, ch. 17]

25. All counties, hundreds, wapentakes and trithings [i.e. ridings] shall be at the old rents without any additional payment, except our demesne manors. [omitted from all reissues]

26. If anyone holding a lay fief of us dies and our sheriff or bailiff shows our letters patent of summons for a debt that the deceased owed us, it shall be lawful for our sheriff or bailiff to attach and make a list of chattels of the deceased found upon the lay fief to the value of that debt under the supervision of law-worthy men, provided that none of the chattels shall be removed until the debt which is manifest has been paid to us in full; and the residue shall be left to the executors for carrying out the will of the deceased. And if nothing is owing to us from him, all the chattels shall accrue to the deceased, saving to his wife and children their reasonable shares. [1215, ch. 18]

27. If any free man dies without leaving a will, his chattels shall be distributed by his nearest kinsfolk and friends under the supervision of the church, saving to every one the debts which the deceased owed him. [omitted from all reissues]

28. No constable or other bailiff of ours shall take anyone's corn or other chattels unless he pays on the spot in cash for them or can delay payment by arrangement with the seller. [1225, ch. 19]

29. No constable shall compel any knight to give money instead of castle-guard if he is willing to do the guard himself or through another good man, if for some good reason he cannot do it himself; and if we lead or send him on military service, he shall be excused guard in proportion to the time that because of us he has been on service. [1225, ch. 20]

30. No sheriff, or bailiff of ours, or anyone else shall take the horses or carts of any free man for transport work save with the agreement of that freeman. [1225, ch. 21]

31. Neither we nor our bailiffs will take, for castles or other works of ours, timber which is not ours, except with the agreement of him whose timber it is. [1225, combined with ch. 21]

32. We will not hold for more than a year and a day the lands of those convicted of felony, and then the lands shall be handed over to the lords of the fiefs. [1225, ch. 22]

33. Henceforth all fish-weirs shall be cleared completely from the Thames and the Medway and throughout all England, except along the sea coast. [1225, ch. 23]

34.   The writ called *Praecipe* shall not in future be issued to anyone in respect of any holding whereby a free man may lose his court. [1225, ch. 24]

35.   Let there be one measure for wine throughout our kingdom, and one measure for ale, and one measure for corn, namely 'the London quarter'; and one width for cloths whether dyed, russet or halberget, namely two ells within the selvedges. Let it be the same with weights as with measures. [1225, ch. 25]

36.   Nothing shall be given or taken in future for the writ of inquisition of life or limbs [jury of attaint]; instead it shall be granted free of charge and not refused. [1225, ch. 26]

37.   If anyone holds of us by fee-farm, by socage, or by burgage, and holds land of another by knight service, we will not, by reason of that fee-farm, socage, or burgage, have the wardship of his heir or of land of his that is of the fief of the other; nor will we have custody of the fee-farm, socage, or burgage, unless such fee-farm owes knight service. We will not have custody of anyone's heir or land which he holds of another by knight service by reason of any petty serjeanty which he holds of us by the service of rendering to us knives or arrows or the like. [1225, ch. 27]

38.   No bailiff shall in future put anyone to trial upon his own bare word, without reliable witnesses produced for this purpose. [1225, ch. 28]

39.   No free man shall be arrested or imprisoned, or disseised or outlawed or exiled or in any way victimised, neither will we attack him or send anyone to attack him, except by the lawful judgment of his peers or by the law of the land. [1225, ch. 29]

40.   To no one will we sell, to no one will we refuse or delay right or justice. [1225, combined with ch. 29]

41.   All merchants shall be able to go out of and come into England safely and securely and stay and travel throughout England, as well by land as by water, for buying and selling by the ancient and right customs free from all evil tolls, except in time of war and if they are of the land that is at war with us. And if such are found in our land at the beginning of a war, they shall be attached, without injury to their persons or goods, until we, or our chief justiciar, know how merchants of our land are treated who were found in the land at war with us when war broke out; and if ours are safe there, the others shall be safe in our land. [1225, ch. 30]

42.   It shall be lawful in future for anyone, without prejudicing the allegiance due to us, to leave our kingdom and return safely and securely by land and water, save, in the public interest, for a short period in time

of war – except for those imprisoned or outlawed in accordance with the law of the kingdom and natives of a land that is at war with us and merchants (who shall be treated as aforesaid). [omitted from all reissues]

43. If anyone who holds of some escheat such as the honour of Wallingford, Nottingham, Boulogne, Lancaster, or of other escheats which are in our hands and are baronies dies, his heir shall give no other relief and do no other service to us than he would have done to the baron if that barony had been in the baron's hands; and we will hold it in the same manner in which the baron held it. [1225, ch. 31]

44. Men who live outside the forest need not henceforth come before our justices of the forest upon a general summons, unless they are impleaded or are sureties for any person or persons who are attached for forest offences. [1216, ch. 36; omitted from other reissues]

45. We will not make justices, constables, sheriffs or bailiffs save of such as know the law of the kingdom and mean to observe it well. [omitted from all reissues]

46. All barons who have founded abbeys for which they have charters of the kings of England or ancient tenure shall have the custody of them during vacancies, as they ought to have. [1225, ch. 33]

47. All forests that have been made forest in our time shall be immediately disafforested; and so be it done with river-banks that have been made preserves by us in our time. [1225, ch. 16]

48. All evil customs connected with forests and warrens, foresters and warreners, sheriffs and their officials, river-banks and their wardens shall immediately be inquired into in each county by twelve sworn knights of the same county who are to be chosen by good men of the same county, and within forty days of the completion of the inquiry shall be utterly abolished by them so as never to be restored, provided that we, or our justiciar if we are not in England, know of it first. [omitted from all reissues]

49. We will immediately return all hostages and charters given to us by Englishmen, as security for peace or faithful service. [omitted from all reissues]

50. We will remove completely from office the relations of Gerard de Athée so that in future they shall have no office in England, namely Engelard de Cigogné, Peter and Guy and Andrew de Chanceaux, Guy de Cigogné, Geoffrey de Martigny and his brothers, Philip Marc and his brothers and his nephew Geoffrey, and all their following. [omitted from all reissues]

51. As soon as peace is restored, we will remove from the kingdom all foreign knights, cross-bowmen, serjeants, and mercenaries, who have

come with horses and arms to the detriment of the kingdom. [omitted from all reissues]

52.   If anyone has been disseised of or kept out of his lands, castles, franchises or his right by us without the legal judgment of his peers, we will immediately restore them to him: and if a dispute arises over this, then let it be decided by the judgment of the twenty-five barons who are mentioned below in the clause for securing the peace [ch. 61]: for all the things, however, which anyone has been disseised or kept out of without the lawful judgment of his peers by king Henry, our father, or by king Richard, our brother, which we have in our hand or are held by others, to whom we are bound to warrant them, we will have the usual period of respite of crusaders, excepting those things about which a plea was started or an inquest made by our command before we took the cross; when however we return from our pilgrimage, or if by any chance we do not go on it, we will at once do full justice therein. [omitted from all reissues]

53.   We will have the same respite, and in the same manner, in the doing of justice in the matter of the disafforesting or retaining of the forests which Henry our father or Richard our brother afforested, and in the matter of the wardship of lands which are of the fief of another, wardships of which sort we have hitherto had by reason of a fief which anyone held of us by knight service, and in the matter of abbeys founded on the fief of another, not on a fief of our own, in which the lord of the fief claims he has a right, and when we have returned, or if we do not set out on our pilgrimage, we will at once do full justice to those who complain of these things. [omitted from all reissues]

54.   No one shall be arrested or imprisoned upon the appeal of a woman for the death of anyone except her husband. [1225, ch. 34]

55.   All fines made with us unjustly and against the law of the land, and all amercements imposed unjustly and against the law of the land, shall be entirely remitted, or else let them be settled by the judgment of the twenty-five barons who are mentioned below in the clause for securing the peace [ch. 61], or by the judgment of the majority of the same, along with the aforesaid Stephen, archbishop of Canterbury, if he can be present, and such others as he may wish to associate with himself for this purpose, and if he cannot be present the business shall nevertheless proceed without him, provided that if any one or more of the aforesaid twenty-five barons are in a like suit, they shall be removed from the judgment of the case in question, and others chosen, sworn and put in their place by the rest of the same twenty-five for this case only. [omitted from all reissues]

56.   If we have disseised or kept out Welshmen from lands or liberties or other things without the legal judgment of their peers in England or in Wales, they shall be immediately restored to them; and if a dispute arises over this, then let it be decided in the March by the judgment of their peers – for holdings in England according to the law of England, for holdings in Wales according to the law of Wales, and for holdings in the March according to the law of the March. Welshmen shall do the same to us and ours. [1216, ch. 40; omitted from other reissues]

57.   For all the things, however, which any Welshman was disseised of or kept out of without the lawful judgment of his peers by king Henry, our father, or king Richard, our brother, which we have in our hand or which are held by others, to whom we are bound to warrant them, we will have the usual period of respite of crusaders, excepting those things about which a plea was started or an inquest made by our command before we took the cross; when however we return, or if by any chance we do not set out on our pilgrimage, we will at once do full justice to them in accordance with the laws of the Welsh and the foresaid regions. [omitted from all reissues]

58.   We will give back at once the son of Llywelyn and all the hostages from Wales and the charters that were handed over to us as security for peace. [omitted from all reissues]

59.   We will act toward Alexander, king of the Scots, concerning the return of his sisters and hostages and concerning his franchises and his right in the same manner in which we act towards our other barons of England, unless it ought to be otherwise by the charters which we have from William his father, formerly king of the Scots, and this shall be determined by the judgment of his peers in our court. [omitted from all reissues]

60.   All these aforesaid customs and liberties which we have granted to be observed in our kingdom as far as it pertains to us towards our men, all of our kingdom, clerks as well as laymen, shall observe as far as it pertains to them towards their men. [1225, contained within ch. 37]

61.   Since, moreover, for God and the betterment of our kingdom and for the better allaying of the discord that has arisen between us and our barons we have granted all these things aforesaid, wishing them to enjoy the use of them unimpaired and unshaken for ever, we give and grant them the under-written security, namely, that the barons shall choose any twenty-five barons of the kingdom they wish, who must with all their might observe, hold and cause to be observed, the peace and liberties which we have granted and confirmed to them by this present charter of ours, so that if we, or our justiciar, or our bailiffs or any one of our servants offend in any way against anyone or transgress any of the

articles of the peace or the security and the offence be notified to four of the aforesaid twenty-five barons, those four barons shall come to us, or to our justiciar if we are out of the kingdom, and, laying the transgression before us, shall petition us to have that transgression corrected without delay. And if we do not correct the transgression, or if we are out of the kingdom, if our justiciar does not correct it, within forty days, reckoning from the time it was brought to our notice or to that of our justiciar if we were out of the kingdom, the aforesaid four barons shall refer that case to the rest of the twenty-five barons and those twenty-five barons together with the community of the whole land shall distrain and distress us in every way they can, namely, by seizing castles, lands, possessions, and in such other ways as they can, saving our person and the persons of our queen and our children, until, in their opinion, amends have been made; and when amends have been made, they shall obey us as they did before. And let anyone in the land who wishes take an oath to obey the orders of the said twenty-five barons for the execution of all the aforesaid matters, and with them to distress us as much as he can, and we publicly and freely give anyone leave to take the oath who wishes to take it and we will never prohibit anyone from taking it. Indeed, all those in the land who are unwilling of themselves and of their own accord to take an oath to the twenty-five barons to help them to distrain and distress us, we will make them take the oath as aforesaid at our command. And if any of the twenty-five barons dies or leaves the country or is in any other way prevented from carrying out the things aforesaid, the rest of the aforesaid twenty-five barons shall choose as they think fit another one in his place, and he shall take the oath like the rest. In all matters the execution of which is committed to these twenty-five barons, if it should happen that these twenty-five are present yet disagree among themselves about anything, or if some of those summoned will not or cannot be present, that shall be held as fixed and established which the majority of those present ordained or commanded, exactly as if all the twenty-five had consented to it; and the said twenty-five shall swear that they will faithfully observe all the things aforesaid and will do all they can to get them observed. And we will procure nothing from anyone, either personally or through anyone else, whereby any of these concessions and liberties might be revoked or diminished; and if any such thing is procured, let it be void and null, and we will never use it either personally or through another. [omitted from all reissues]

62.   And we have fully remitted and pardoned to everyone all the ill-will, indignation and rancour that have arisen between us and our men, clergy and laity, from the time of the quarrel. Furthermore, we have

fully remitted to all, clergy and laity, and as far as pertains to us have completely forgiven, all trespasses occasioned by the same quarrel between Easter in the sixteenth year of our reign and the restoration of peace. And besides, we have caused to be made for them letters testimonial patent of the lord Stephen archbishop of Canterbury, and of the lord Henry archbishop of Dublin and of the aforementioned bishops and of master Pandulf about this security and the aforementioned concessions. [omitted from all reissues]

63.   Wherefore we wish and firmly enjoin that the English church shall be free, and that the men in our kingdom shall have and hold all the aforesaid liberties, rights and concessions well and peacefully, freely and quietly, fully and completely, for themselves and their heirs from us and our heirs, in all matters and in all places for ever, as is aforesaid. An oath, moreover, has been taken, as well on our part as on the part of the barons, that all these things aforesaid shall be observed in good faith and without evil disposition. Witness the above-mentioned and many others. Given by our hand in the meadow which is called Runnymede between Windsor and Staines on the fifteenth day of June, in the seventeenth year of our reign. [omitted from all reissues]

Notes

1. Rothwell (1975), 316–24.
2. I indicate in square brackets where each chapter appeared in the 1225 Charter. Chapters 13, 32, 35 and 36 of the 1225 Charter were not taken from the 1215 Charter. Chapter 13 was taken from the 1217 Forest Charter, and chapters 32, 35 and 36 were taken from the 1217 Magna Carta.

BIBLIOGRAPHY

Works cited in notes

Original sources

Aspects of human rights (1995), London: Her Majesty's Stationery Office.

Cheney, C.R. and Semple, W.H. (eds) (1953), *Selected letters of Pope Innocent III concerning England*, London: Thomas Nelson.

Commager, Henry Steele (ed.) (1968), *Documents of American history*, 8th edn, 2 vols in 1, New York: Appleton-Century-Crofts.

Ebenstein, William (1956), *Great political thinkers*, 2nd edn, New York: Rinehart.

Elton, Geoffrey R. (1982), *The Tudor constitution: documents and commentary*, 2nd edn, Cambridge: Cambridge University Press.

Hall, G.D.G. (ed. and trans.) (1965), *Tractatus de legibus et consuetudinibus regni Anglie qui Glanvilla vocatur*, London: Thomas Nelson.

Hardy, T.D. (ed.) (1833–34), *Rotuli litterarum clausarum*, 2 vols, London: Record Commission.

Hardy, T.D. (ed.) (1835), *Rotuli litterarum patentium 1201–1216*, London: Record Commission.

Hardy, T.D. (ed.) (1837), *Rotuli chartarum, 1199–1216*, London: Record Commission.

Horn, D.B. and Ransome, Mary (eds) (1957), *English historical documents*, vol. 10: *1714–1783*, gen. ed. David C. Douglas, London: Eyre & Spottiswoode.

Howell, Thomas B. (ed.) (1809–26), *A complete collection of state trials*, 34 vols, London: C.T. Hansard.

Johnson, Charles (ed. and trans.) (1950), *Dialogus de scaccario*, London: Thomas Nelson.

Jones, Gareth (ed.) (1973), *The sovereignty of the law: selections from Blackstone's Commentaries on the Laws of England*, Toronto: University of Toronto Press.

Luard, H.R. (ed.) (1864–69), *Annales monastici*, 5 vols, London: Rolls Series.

Luard, H.R. (ed.) (1872–84), *Matthaei Parisiensis chronica majora*, 7 vols, London: Rolls Series.

Maitland, F.W. (ed.) (1887), *Bracton's note book*, 3 vols, London: C.J. Clay.

Myers, A.R. (ed.) (1969), *English historical documents*, vol. 4: *1327–1485*, gen. ed. David C. Douglas, London: Eyre & Spottiswoode.

Plucknett, T.F.T. and Barton, J.L. (eds) (1974), *St German's doctor and student*, London: Selden Society, vol. 91.

Pole, J.R. (ed.) (1987), *The American Constitution: for and against*, New York: Hill & Wang.

Rothwell, Harry (ed.) (1975), *English historical documents*, vol. 3: *1189–1327*, gen. ed. David C. Douglas, London: Eyre & Spottiswoode.

Stephenson, Carl and Marcham, Frederick George (eds and trans.) (1937), *Sources of English constitutional history: a selection of documents from A.D. 600 to the present*, New York: Harper & Row.

Stevenson, J. (ed.) (1875), *Radulphi de Coggeshall chronicon anglicanum*, London: Rolls Series.

Stubbs William (ed.) (1872–73), *Memoriale Walteri de Coventria*, 2 vols, London: Rolls Series.

Stubbs, William (ed.) (1913), *Select charters and other illustrations of English constitutional history*, 9th edn rev. by H.W.C. Davis, Oxford: Oxford University Press.

Thorne, S.E. (trans. and rev.) and Woodbine, G.E. (ed.) (1968–77), *Bracton de legibus et consuetudinibus Angliae*, 4 vols, Cambridge MA: Harvard University Press.

Treharne, R.F. and Sanders, I.J. (eds) (1973), *Documents of the baronial movement of reform and rebellion, 1258–1267*, Oxford: Oxford University Press.

Whittaker, W.J. (ed.) (1893), *The mirror of justices*, London: Selden Society, vol. 7.

Secondary works

Ashley, Maurice (1965), *Magna Carta in the seventeenth century*, Charlottesville: University of Virginia Press.

Baldwin, John W. and Hollister, C. Warren (1978), 'The rise of administrative kingship: Henry I and Philip Augustus', *American Historical Review*, 83; reprinted in Hollister (1986), *Monarchy, magnates and institutions in the Anglo-Norman world*, London: Hambledon.

Bartlett, Robert (2000), *England under the Norman and Angevin kings 1075–1225*, New Oxford History of England, Oxford: Oxford University Press.

Brooks, Christopher W. (1993), 'The place of Magna Carta and the ancient constitution in sixteenth-century English legal thought', in Ellis Sandoz (ed.), *The roots of liberty: Magna Carta, ancient constitution and the Anglo-American tradition of rule of law*, Columbia: University of Missouri Press.

Burgess, Glenn (1996), *Absolute monarchy and the Stuart constitution*, New Haven CT: Yale University Press.

Cam, Helen (1965), *Magna Carta: Event or Document?*, London: Selden Society Lecture.

Campbell, James (1995), 'William Stubbs (1825–1901)', in H. Damico and J.B. Zavadil (eds), *Medieval scholarship: biographical studies on the formation of a discipline, vol. 1: History*, New York: Garland.

Cannadine, David (1992), *G.M. Trevelyan: a life in history*, New York and London: W.W. Norton.

Cantor, Norman F. (1966), *William Stubbs on the English constitution*, New York: Thomas Y. Crowell.

Cantor, Norman F. (1991), *Inventing the middle ages*, New York: William Morrow.

Carpenter, David A. (1990), *The minority of Henry III*, Berkeley and Los Angeles: University of California Press.

Carpenter, David A. (1999), 'The Plantagenet kings', in David Abullafia (ed.), *New Cambridge medieval history, vol. 5: c. 1198–c. 1300*, Cambridge: Cambridge University Press.

Cheney, C.R. (1979), *Innocent III and England*, Stuttgart: Hiersemann.

Clark, J.C.D. (1994), *The language of liberty 1660–1832: political discourse and social dynamics in the Anglo-American World*, Cambridge: Cambridge University Press.

Coss, Peter (1989), 'Bastard feudalism revised', *Past and Present*, 125.

Davies, Norman (1999), *The Isles: a history*, Oxford: Oxford University Press.

Doe, Norman (1990), *Fundamental authority in late medieval English law*, Cambridge: Cambridge University Press.

Epstein, James A. (1994), *Radical expression: political language, ritual and symbol in England, 1790–1850*, Oxford: Oxford University Press.

Ewing, K.D. and Gearty, C.A. (2000), *The struggle for civil liberties: political freedom and the rule of law in Britain 1914–1945*, Oxford: Oxford University Press.

Galbraith, V.H. (1945), 'Good kings and bad kings in English history', *History*, 30; reprinted in Galbraith (1982), *Kings and chronicles: essays in English medieval history*, London: Hambledon.

Goodhart, Arthur L. (1966), *Law of the land*, Charlottesville: University of Virginia Press.

Gransden, Antonia (1974), *Historical writing in England c. 550–1307*, Ithaca NY: Cornell University Press.

Green, J.R. (1990), *A short history of the English people*, revised edn, New York: Colonial Press.

Harding, Alan (1993), *England in the thirteenth century*, Cambridge: Cambridge University Press.

Hindley, Geoffrey (1990), *The book of Magna Carta*, London: Constable.

Holt, J.C. (1961), *The Northerners: a study in the reign of King John*; 1992 reprint with corrections, Oxford: Oxford University Press.

Holt, J.C. (1972), *Magna Carta and the idea of liberty*, New York: John Wiley.

Holt, J.C. (1992), *Magna Carta*, 2nd edn, Cambridge: Cambridge University Press.

Howard, A.E. Dick (1968), *The road from Runnymede: Magna Carta and constitutionalism in America*, Charlottesville: University of Virginia Press.

Kenyon, John P. (1983), *The history men: the historical profession in England since the Renaissance*, London: Weidenfeld and Nicolson.

Levine, Philippa (1986), *The amateur and the professional: antiquaries, historians, and archaeologists in Victorian Britain, 1838–1886*, Cambridge: Cambridge University Press.

Lyon, Bryce (1960), *A constitutional and legal history of medieval England*, New York: Harper & Row.

McKisack, May (1971), *Medieval history in the Tudor Age*, Oxford: Oxford University Press.

Maddicott, J.R. (1984), 'Magna Carta and the local community', *Past and Present*, 102.

Maddicott, J.R. (1994), *Simon de Montfort*, Oxford: Oxford University Press.

Marcham, Frederick George (1960), *A constitutional history of modern England, 1485 to the present*, New York: Harper & Row.

Meador, Daniel John (1965), *Habeas Corpus and Magna Carta: dualism of power and liberty*, Charlottesville: University of Virginia Press.

Musson, Anthony (2001), *Medieval law in context: the growth of legal consciousness from Magna Carta to the Peasants' Revolt*, Manchester: Manchester University Press.

O'Brien, Bruce R. (1999), *God's peace and King's peace: the laws of Edward the Confessor*, Philadelphia: University of Pennsylvania Press.

Painter, Sidney (1949), *The reign of King John*, Baltimore: Johns Hopkins University Press.

Painter, Sidney (1961), 'Magna Carta', in F. Cazel (ed.), *Feudalism and liberty, articles and addresses of Sidney Painter*, Baltimore: Johns Hopkins University Press.

Pallister, Anne (1971), *Magna Carta, the heritage of liberty*, Oxford: Oxford University Press.

Pollard, A.F. (1926), *The evolution of Parliament*, 2nd edn, London: Longmans Green.

Pollock, Frederick and Maitland, F.W. (1898), *The history of English law before the time of Edward I*, 2 vols, 2nd edn, Cambridge: Cambridge University Press.

Prall, Stuart E. (1972), *The bloodless revolution: England, 1688*, Garden City NY: Doubleday.

Prestwich, Michael (1980), *The three Edwards: war and state in England, 1272–1377*, London: Weidenfeld and Nicolson.

Prestwich, Michael (1988), *Edward I*, Berkeley and Los Angeles: University of California Press.

Simmons, Clare A. (1998), 'Absent presence: the romantic-era Magna Carta and the English constitution', in R. Utz and T. Shippey (eds), *Medievalism in the modern world: essays in honour of Leslie J. Workman*, Turnhout: Brepols.

Smith, R.J. (1987), *The Gothic bequest: medieval institutions in British thought, 1688–1863*, Cambridge: Cambridge University Press.

Stenton, Doris M. (1965), *After Runnymede: Magna Carta in the later middle ages*, Charlottesville: University of Virginia Press.

Strayer, Joseph R. (1955), *Western Europe in the middle ages*, New York: Appleton-Century-Crofts.

Strayer, Joseph R. (1970), *On the medieval origins of the modern state*, Princeton NJ: Princeton University Press.

Stubbs, William (1874–78), *Constitutional history of England*, 3 vols, 1st edn, Oxford: Oxford University Press; 6th edn (1897), as excerpted in N. Cantor

(1966), *William Stubbs on the English constitution*, New York: Thomas Y. Crowell.

Swindler, William F. (1965), *Magna Carta, legend and legacy*, Indianapolis: Bobbs Merrill.

Tanner, J.R. (1961), *English constitutional conflicts of the seventeenth century 1603–1689*, Cambridge: Cambridge University Press.

Thompson, Faith (1925), *The first century of Magna Carta: why it persisted as a document*, Minneapolis: University of Minnesota Press.

Thompson, Faith (1948), *Magna Carta: its role in the making of the English constitution, 1300–1629*, Minneapolis: University of Minnesota Press.

Thorne, Samuel E. et al. (1965), *The Great Charter: four essays on Magna Carta and the history of our liberty*, American Council of Learned Societies, New York: Pantheon.

Treharne, R.F. (1970), 'The nature of Parliament in the reign of Henry III', in E.B. Fryde and E. Miller (eds), *Historical studies of the English Parliament*, vol. 1: *Origins to 1399*, Cambridge: Cambridge University Press.

Vincent, Nicholas (2001), review of Bartlett, *England under the Norman and Angevin kings 1075–1225*, in *English Historical Review*, 116: 410.

Warren, W.L. (1978), *King John*, 2nd edn, Berkeley and Los Angeles: University of California Press.

Warren, W.L. (1987), *The governance of Norman and Angevin England 1086–1272*, London: Edward Arnold.

Weston, Corinne C. (1991), 'England: ancient constitution and common law', in J.H. Burns and M. Goldie (eds), *The Cambridge history of political thought: 1450–1700*, Cambridge: Cambridge University Press.

Wood, Charles T. (1988), *Joan of Arc and Richard III: sex, saints, and government in the middle ages*, Oxford: Oxford University Press.

Other useful works

Collections of original sources

Aspinall, A. and Smith, E.A. (eds) (1959), *English historical documents*, vol. 11: *1783–1832*, gen. ed. David C. Douglas, London: Eyre & Spottiswoode.

Browning, A. (ed.) (1953), *English historical documents*, vol. 8: *1660–1714*, gen. ed. David C. Douglas, London: Eyre & Spottiswoode.

Urofsky, Melvin I. (ed.) (1989), *Documents of American constitutional and legal history*, 2 vols, Philadelphia: Temple University Press.

Williams, C.H. (ed.) (1967), *English historical documents*, vol. 5: *1485–1558*, gen. ed. David C. Douglas, London: Eyre & Spottiswoode.

Secondary works: medieval

Carpenter, David A. (1996), *The reign of Henry III*, London: Hambledon, collected articles.

Cheney, C.R. (1982), *The papacy and England in the 12th–14th centuries*, Aldershot: Variorum, collected articles.

Chrimes, S.B. (1936), *English constitutional ideas of the fifteenth century*, Cambridge: Cambridge University Press.

Church, Stephen D. (ed.) (1999), *King John: new interpretations*, Woodbridge: Boydell.

Clanchy, Michael T. (1998), *England and its rulers 1066–1272*, 2nd edn, Oxford: Blackwell.

Collins, A.J. (1948), 'The documents of the Great Charter', *Proceedings of the British Academy*, 34.

Davis, G.R.C. (1985), *Magna Carta*, revised edn, London: British Library.

Dunbabin, Jean (1988), 'Government', in J.H. Burns (ed.), *The Cambridge history of medieval political thought c. 350–1450*, Cambridge: Cambridge University Press.

Edwards, R. Dudley (1940), 'Magna Carta Hiberniae', in J. Ryan (ed.), *Essays and studies presented to Professor Eoin MacNeill on the occasion of his seventieth birthday*, Dublin: The Sign of the Three Candles.

Fox, J.C. (1924), 'The originals of the Great Charter of 1215', *English Historical Review*, 39.

Fryde, Natalie (2001), *Why Magna Carta? Angevin England revisited*, Neue Aspekte der europäischen Mittelalteforschung 1, Münster: LIT Verlag.

Galbraith, V.H. (1966), 'Runnymede revisited', *Proceedings of the American Philosophical Society*, 110.

Gransden, Antonia (1982), *Historical writing in England*, vol. 2: *c. 1307 to the early sixteenth century*, Ithaca, NY: Cornell University Press.

Holt, J.C. (1985), *Magna Carta and medieval government*, London: Hambledon, collected articles.

Hudson, John (1996), *The formation of the English common law: law and society in England from the Norman Conquest to Magna Carta*, London: Longman.

Jolliffe, J.E.A. (1963), *Angevin kingship*, 2nd edn, London: A. & C. Black.

Jones, J.A.P. (1971), *King John and Magna Carta*, London: Longman.

Lander, J.R. (1989), *The limitations of English monarchy in the later middle ages*, Toronto: University of Toronto Press.

Langmuir, Gavin (1972), '*Per commune consilium regni* in Magna Carta', *Studia Gratiana*, 15.

McKechnie, W.S. (1914), *Magna Carta: a commentary on the Great Charter of King John*, 2nd edn, Glasgow: J. Maclehose.

Malden, H.E. (ed.) (1917), *Magna Carta commemoration essays*, London: Royal Historical Society.

Powicke, F.M. (1947), *Henry III and the Lord Edward*, Oxford: Oxford University Press.

Reynolds, Susan (1997), *Kingdoms and communities in Western Europe, 900–1300*, 2nd edn, Oxford: Oxford University Press.

Rigby, S.H. (ed.) (2003), *A companion to Britain in the later middle ages*, Oxford: Blackwell.

Turner, Ralph V. (1994), *King John*, London: Longman.

Turner, Ralph V. (1994), *Judges, administrators and the common law in Angevin England*, London: Hambledon, collected articles.

Turner, Ralph V. (1996), 'King John's concept of royal authority', *History of Political Thought*, 17.

Turner, Ralph V. (1999), 'John and justice', in Stephen D. Church (ed.), *King John: new interpretations*, Woodbridge: Boydell.

Secondary works: post-medieval

Bailyn, Bernard (1967), *The ideological origins of the American Revolution*, Cambridge MA: Harvard University Press.

Brentano, Robert (1995), 'Frederic William Maitland (1850–1906)', in H. Damico and J.B. Zavadil (eds), *Medieval scholarship: biographical studies on the formation of a discipline*, vol. 1: *History*, New York: Garland.

Brundage, Anthony (1994), *The people's historian: John Richard Green and the writing of history in Victorian England*, Westport CT: Greenwood.

Burgess, Glenn (1992), *The politics of the ancient constitution: an introduction to English political thought, 1603–1642*, London and University Park PA: Penn State Press.

Butterfield, Herbert (1931), *The Whig interpretation of history*, reprinted 1965, New York: W.W. Norton.

Butterfield, Herbert (1969), *Magna Carta in the historiography of the sixteenth and seventeenth centuries*, Reading University: Stenton Lecture.

Clark, J.C.D. (2000), *English society 1660–1832: religion, ideology and politics during the ancien regime*, Cambridge: Cambridge University Press.

Colley, Linda (1992), *Britons: forging the nation, 1707–1837*, New Haven CT: Yale University Press.

Ewing, Keith (1990), *Freedom under Thatcher: civil liberties in modern Britain*, Oxford: Oxford University Press.

Friedman, Lawrence (1984), *American law*, New York: W.W. Norton.

Friedman, Lawrence (2002), *American law in the twentieth century*, New Haven CT: Yale University Press.

Hill, Christopher (1997), *The intellectual origins of the English Revolution revisited*, Oxford: Oxford University Press.

Jennings, Ivor (1965), *Magna Carta: its influence on the world today*: London: Her Majesty's Stationery Office.

Jones, Gareth Stedman (1983), 'Re-thinking Chartism', in his *Languages of class: studies in English working-class history, 1832–1982*, Cambridge: Cambridge University Press.

Lottes, Günther (1991), 'Radicalism, revolution and political culture: an Anglo-French comparison', in Mark Philip (ed.), *The French Revolution and British popular politics*, Cambridge: Cambridge University Press.

McWilliam, Rohan (1998), *Popular politics in nineteenth-century England*, London: Routledge.

Pocock, J.G.A. (1987), *The ancient constitution and the feudal law*, Cambridge: Cambridge University Press.

Stivison, David E. (ed.) (1993), *Magna Carta in America*, Baltimore: Gateway Press.

Thorne, Samuel E. (1957), *Sir Edward Coke, 1552–1952*, London: Selden Society Lecture.

Wood, Gordon S. (1969), *The creation of the American Republic 1776–1787*, Chapel Hill: University of North Carolina Press.

Some web-sites

Avalon Project, Yale Law School, Magna Carta with explanations: www.yale.edu/lawweb/avalon/medieval/magframe

British Library, for its copies of Magna Carta: www.bl.uk.collections/treasures/magna

Internet Medieval Sourcebook, texts of historic English documents, including Magna Carta: http://www.fordham.edu/halsall/source

Findlaw for Legal Professionals, US federal court decisions: http://laws.findlaw.com/US

Magna Carta Plus, for historic declarations of rights and current civil liberties issues in the United Kingdom: www.magnacartaplus.org

US National Archives and Record Administration, for the significance of the Charter for Americans: www.archives.gov/exhibit_hall

Public Record Office, Kew, for its copies of the Charter: www.pro.gov.uk/virtualmuseum

US Supreme Court, for representations of King John and Magna Carta in its building: www.supremecourtus.gov

INDEX

Adams, John, 208, 212
Adams, Samuel, 214
Agard, John, 140
Agreement of the People, 160
aliens, foreigners, 46, 49–50, 70, 81, 85, 86, 88, 90, 94, 95, 110, 125, 155
  enemy, internment of, 192, 224
American Bar Association, 5
American Revolution, Revolutionary War, 171, 175, 209, 212–15, 216
'ancient constitution' doctrine, 3, 5, 110, 134, 141, 145, 147–8, 153, 164, 165, 169, 170–1, 173, 174, 175, 179, 180, 183, 184, 218
Anglo-Saxon England, 10, 12, 15, 23, 38, 45, 134, 137, 140, 149, 160, 175, 199, 218
Angoumois, 35
Anjou, Greater (including Maine & Touraine), 14, 34, 35, 44, 50
Annales, Annales school, 203
antiquaries, antiquarians, 3, 104, 137, 138–41, 145–6, 164
Aquitaine, duchy of, 14, 34, 35, 36, 44, 94, *see also* Gascony, Poitou
arbitration, 60, 99
archives, public records, 140, 150, 171, 197, 200
  French, 61
  Lambeth Palace, 62
  National Archives, Washington DC, 105
  Public Record Office, 86, 200–1
aristocracy, *see* barons, baronage, peerage
army, standing, 128, 135, 168
Arthur, legendary king, 110, 149
Arthur of Brittany, 33, 34, 36
Articles of Confederation, 216
Articles of the Barons, 62, 63, 68
Articles upon the Chtrs., 1300, 105–7, 155, 157
attorney-general, 147, 154, 156
Atwood, Wm., 165
Australia, 6, 8, 206
  National Library, Canberra, 105

Bacon, Sir Francis, 153
Bale, John, 138–9
barons, baronage, 1, 8, 12–13, 17–22, 24–5, 31, 33, 36, 39, 40, 41, 43–5, 45–51, 52, 56, 64, 82, 88, 90, 91, 92, 101, 103, 105, 107, 109, 112, 114, 117, 121, 126, 164
  overseas military service, 36, 44, 46–7, 54, 62, 103
  political outlook under John, 22, 33, 41, 45, 48, 49, 51, 52, 54, 56–62, 66–7, 71, 75–7
  under Hen. III, 77, 80, 84–5, 91–7, 114
baronial rebellions, 21–2, 118–21, 126, 128
  under John, 1215–16, 2, 12, 21, 23, 30, 37, 43, 45, 46–7, 49, 50, 52–63, 76–8, 129, 137, 138, 139, 146, 147, 151, 169, 214, 224
  leadership, 18, 49, 54–5, 56–7, 84
  historians' view of, 56, 200, 202, 203, 204
  under Hen. III, 21, 31, 80, 81–2, 88, 95–9, 129, 139, 147, 151
Bartlett, Robert, 205
bastard feudalism, 25
Bates, John, 155
Beale, Robert, 142
Bentham, Jeremy, 183, 185–6, 187
bills of attainder, 131, 134
Bill of Rights, English, 1689, 167–8, 170, 171, 181, 196, 210, 216
  US, 161, 215, 216–18, *see also* US constitution, amendments
bishops & abbots as barons, 18–19, 37–8
black citizens, US, 220–21, 222–24
Black Death, 127
Blackstone, Sir Wm., 4, 65, 68, 173, 178, 211, 213–14
Bodleian Library, Oxford Univ., 83
Bolingbroke, Henry; *see* Henry I
Bolingbroke, Viscount; Henry St. John, 175
Boroughbridge, battle of, 120
boroughs, royal, 15, 27, 45, 107, 172